To dear MJ,

~~best~~ friend ever.

Big love,

K xx

Christmas 2008

'And be you ~~blithe~~ & ~~bonny;~~

Converting all your sounds of woe

Into Hey nonny, nonny.'

Much Ado...

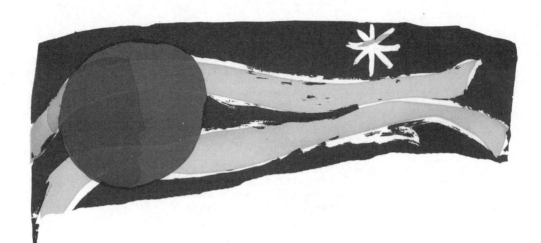

The Hey Nonny Handbook

By Julia Jeffries and Janice Warman

HARRIMAN HOUSE LTD

3A Penns Road
Petersfield
Hampshire
GU32 2EW
GREAT BRITAIN

Tel: +44 (0)1730 233870
Fax: +44 (0)1730 233880
Email: enquiries@harriman-house.com
Website: www.harriman-house.com

First published in Great Britain in 2007
Copyright © Harriman House Ltd

The right of Julia Jeffries and and Janice Warman to be identified as Authors has been
asserted in accordance with the Copyright, Design and Patents Act 1988.

ISBN: 1-905641-20-6
ISBN 13: 978-1905641-20-8

British Library Cataloguing in Publication Data
A CIP catalogue record for this book can be obtained from the British Library.

Printed and bound by Cambridge Printing, University Printing House, Cambridge

Illustrations and text therein on pp, 11, 21, 29, 44, 49, 52, 63, 67, 75, 80, 84, 96, 103, 109, 114, 124,
140, 148, 156, 161, 180, 191, 194, 205, 208, 223, 228, 229, 230, 231, 232, 233, 234, 235, 236, 237,
240, 250, 255, 266 © Sally Ann Lasson

Biography

Julia Jeffries is a designer, teacher and writer. She follows in the illustrious footsteps of other art school trained authors such as Beryl Bainbridge and Alice Thomas Ellis.

Janice Warman is a South African born writer and journalist whose career spans the BBC, the *Financial Times*, *The Guardian*, *The Observer* and the *Daily Mail*. She lives in Sussex with one husband, two children and several animals.

Acknowledgements

We would like to thank all the authors and publishers who have been so helpful in allowing us to reproduce material. We have done our utmost to contact all the necessary copyright holders prior to publication. In order for the book to flow, we have compiled a detailed reference section at the back.

Dedication

To the memory of Morag Mactaggart, who gave the original warning

Julia Jeffries

For my parents, George and Lynne, with love

Janice Warman

Contents

General Review of the Sex Situation

Woman wants monogamy;
Man delights in novelty.
Love is woman's moon and sun;
Man has other forms of fun.
Woman lives but in her lord;
Count to ten, and man is bored.
With this the gist and sum of it,
What earthly good can come of it?

Dorothy Parker

Prologue

Hey Nonny has been part of our lives for such a long time that it is hard to recall its exact genesis. The original Hey Nonny Club was a loose collection of women, (not a collection of loose women!) who had troubles in their life and these troubles were often to do with the 'one foot in sea and one on shore' kind of men. As C.S. Lewis has written, 'Friendship is born at that moment when one person says to another, "What! You too? I thought I was the only one".'

We were also becoming conscious of what Elizabeth Jane Howard said in her novel *Something in Disguise*: 'Most of the ordinary bad things happen to women.'[1] In fact, wherever we looked, there were abandoned wives and discarded mistresses. That said, we have tried not to be too high-minded about it. Falling in love is one of life's great adventures and is seldom timely or appropriate; there can be few of us who can say hand on heart that we have not betrayed or let someone else down badly. As G.K. Chesterton has said, 'There is the road from the eye to the heart that does not go through the intellect'.

Certainly it is women who bear the brunt of the fallout. Apart from nursing themselves through disaster and picking up the emotional pieces, women are invariably the ones keeping the family together and are often left to shoulder the responsibilities. Fathers not welcome in their children's home often have difficulty accepting financial responsibility... witness the disasters of the Child Support Agency. As Fay Weldon's mother told her: 'Of course this Charlie of yours is not going to support you. Men only support women if they're in front of their noses, filling the bed and cooking the food.'[2] Financially, women can be particularly vulnerable after separation. Even middle-class women of a certain age can be thrust into poverty when they are too old to retrain.

There should be a special branch of the Hey Nonny Club for MPs' wives and abandoned mistresses, perhaps with offices at *The Spectator*. While we laugh at the antics of Boris Johnson, behind all these stories there must be a great deal of private grief. Nicholas Fairburn, Cecil Parkinson, David Mellor, Robin Cook, David Blunkett, John Prescott: the list of these miscreants is long. By the time this book is published, they will have been replaced in the headlines, although the memories of humiliated partners and their children are rather longer.

We saw that what was happening in Parliament was happening in every town, in every community, here on our own doorsteps. We discovered women at our stage of life were not just troubled by the misdeeds of men; we also had illnesses of our own, teenage children, elderly parents and financial problems to contend with. Some of us had layer upon layer of difficulties that were seriously affecting our psychological health. In short, husbands were needy, tyrannical or both, parents cranky, children capricious, teenagers obstructive and bosses despotic. Nothing abnormal you might say, but together these things were impacting on our very being.

For complex reasons of family loyalty, financial constraints or sheer lack of energy, it is often not easy for women to escape. Responsibilities can be overwhelming, sapping energy and draining vitality. This book has been written in the context of this struggle and we have tried to collate as much shared experience as possible.

As the Hey Nonny Club, we began helping each other in every way we could. Being literary and bookish, we shared jokes, cartoons, short stories, poems, novels, and biographies; in fact anything that would shed light on our situation. We were constantly alert for material that would offer support, or explain or illuminate our difficulties. This became the backbone of the book and is hard to quantify; it's part debate, part information, part humour. Women, after all, major in self-doubt and self-parody and we have made a point of sending ourselves up before others try.

Sally Ann Lasson's *As If* cartoons (published in *The Independent*) inspired our writing as well as illustrating the book. She treats the sexes with an even hand and does not hold back on the unpleasant subject of female hypocrisy, which is why we've dedicated a chapter to her: *Plus ca change, plus c'est la même chose*. Women have always banded together for reasons of safety and mutual support, but often because of their powerlessness, have resorted to deviousness and sexual manipulation to get their way.

Although several years in the making, 'long awaited, long despaired of' by our friends (one so-called friend said, 'Your book has had the gestation of an elephant'), it has been in a sense a book that wrote itself. We were never short of ideas or material, we tried to avoid evangelising on topics we were not sure of and every book mentioned has been read from cover to cover. All experiences are our own or from sources in which we have absolute trust.

As Beryl Bainbridge said in *The Week*: 'I myself have never really written fiction; what would be the point? What is more peculiar, more riveting, devious and horrific than real life?' And in any case we agree with the words of Richard Eyre: 'Reality will always mock the way that fiction seeks to tidy up chaos and provide a passage through the fog.' We began to feel like Alan Bennett: 'For a writer, nothing is ever quite as bad as it is for other people, because, however dreadful, it may be of use.'

Our main problem became finding the time to write it in the face of our own personal difficulties. As Virginia Woolf observed, 'The devilish thing about writing is that it calls upon every nerve to keep itself taut'. How could we isolate ourselves to achieve this with everything that was going on around us?

What we have written is unashamedly feminist, but we have always attempted to see the male point of view (though we have not always succeeded). It is an irony that many of our most perceptive quotations have been from men whose behaviour has not always matched their insight.

Women have always tried to express themselves in whatever limited ways were available to them. Even in Isabella Beeton's day, readers of ladies' magazines were encouraged to send in their own pieces. As Kathryn Hughes says in her biography: 'Fiction, biography, translations and what we now call 'think pieces' were all supplied at a furious rate by eager reader-writers. The work was not paid, which suggests that what drove the contributors was the need to speak beyond the drawing room.' Women wrote cookery books 'because writing such allowed you to make a modest income without having to leave the kitchen, or at least the house'.[3]

Feminism is not popular at the moment (the immediate past seldom is) and is often regarded as outmoded, outdated and unnecessary. One of the purposes of this book is not to say 'all men are bastards' but to point out that women's rights still have a long way to go. In a Britain where four women die each week at the hands of their men, where arranged marriages, honour killings, slavery and prostitution still thrive, where rape convictions have fallen, it would surely be premature to say 'we're all post-feminists now'.

We should never underestimate the importance of the Women's Movement, which meant so much to so many. Mildred Levius, a lifelong feminist who died recently, said: 'I have begun to reclaim parts of me that have been cut off, repressed, denigrated and devalued because of women's status in family and wider society. I have gained a new 'pair of spectacles' to understand myself and my position in society.'[4]

Hilary Mantel said in her memoir, *Giving up the Ghost*, which recalls her time at Sheffield University: 'It is important to remember why women rose up in the seventies, 'burnt their bras' and rebelled...one of my tutors was a bored local solicitor who made it plain that he didn't think women had any place in his classroom. They were just a waste of space; they'd only go and have babies wouldn't they? Some people have forgotten, or never known, why we needed the feminist movement so badly. This was why: so some talent-less prat in a nylon shirt couldn't patronise you.'[5(i)]

Julia found this book sustained her during a time of serious doubt: 'Why was I writing my first book in my fifties? Why did I think I could do it?' The answer lay in Hilary's story: 'Just because you have an idea doesn't mean you are ready to write it. You may have to creep towards it, dwell with it, and grow up with it: perhaps for half your lifetime.'[5(ii)]

W.B. Yeats has said, 'It is many years before one can believe enough in what one feels even to know what the feeling is' while Virginia Woolf was once quoted in *The Independent* as saying: 'I am going to hold myself from writing till I have it impending in me: grown heavy in my mind like a ripe pear.' Writing *Hey Nonny* was like having a whole orchard in our heads, with the ripe fruit dropping in abundance, if only we could catch it.

We realised above all that in middle age, it was no longer a simple matter of applying energy and effort to our problems. We pushed the accelerator and nothing happened. Disasters came thick and fast. We wondered what had happened to bring our lives to this point and saw that a profound appraisal of what we had become and how we had got to this place was necessary; we found we needed to reassess the situation in the context of those who had come before us. We needed to throw a bright light on the state of women and try to differentiate between surface irritations, which so often overlie our deeper feelings, and the issues that are most fundamental to women at the beginning of a new century.

We needed to understand how it was that men had influenced our destiny, not always for the good, and how wise women who had gone before us had managed to survive (or not, as we so often discovered). For us both, it has been a form of rebellion as well as an invaluable autobiographical journey.

We have tried to approach the state of mid-life from the perspective of both fiction and non-fiction. Other women could have illustrated the same situation with equally good references, but this is our choice and we have tried to be as catholic as possible. The purpose of this book has not been to give advice but to illuminate; to ask questions rather than to prescribe solutions.

It presupposes that the reader will have some knowledge of literature and writing but we hope it will be equally accessible to the occasional book buyer. Since we are not academics, thinkers or philosophers by trade, we were aware of the problem of diluting these disciplines to make them accessible. Assume too much and we would lose our readership, assume too little and we would be insulting the intelligence of others; it has been a fine line.

We have quoted from authors both old and new, and revisited some of the classics; for instance, we found relevance and insight in Arnold Bennett's *The Old Wives' Tale* that we had missed when we were young. The political editor Martha Kearney, interviewed in *The Independent on Sunday*, has echoed our own thoughts: 'Recently I went back to *Middlemarch*, which I'd loved in my twenties. This time I found myself absolutely infuriated with Dorothea. I saw it in quite a different light.' Kathy Moyse wrote a letter to *The Independent* along the same lines: 'I read Emma Bovary for A Level. I found it tedious beyond belief because aged 17, I had absolutely no understanding of Emma Bovary's predicament. Revisiting the novel 25 years later, I found nuances of experience and emotion in the text that has completely passed me by at the time of first reading.'

Janice had a similar experience, taking her daughter to see *A Doll's House* after an interval of 30 years: 'At 16, the play made a deep impact on me – seeing a heroine who changes from plaything to independent woman. At 46, I realised how closely my life had mirrored hers.'

In our opinion, there are just too many self-help books. If this by default was what we were writing, how on earth could we justify another one? As Martin Amis has said: 'We live in an age of mass loquacity. We are all writing it or at any rate talking it: the memoir, the apologia, the CV, the "*cri de coeur*".'[6] Confession has become a national pastime and a great moneymaking exercise, as if we shall not be shriven unless we divulge all to a newspaper. Another horribly fine line divides confession and the useful dissemination of individual experience. We wanted to tell our story and those of others, not for prurience and exploitation but for the common good, but how?

We hope this book will go some way to distil what is truly important for women, i.e. the maintenance of good health, the ability to retain a sense of humour and courage and strength in adversity. We have tried to combine the poetic with the prosaic, the actual with the spiritual, and reflect the way domestic life shifts constantly between these states, to reflect the balance we would wish for.

As Andrew Motion has said, 'Poetry, like no other art, is able to combine intimate reflections with out-loud expressions. It is the hotline to our deepest feelings and to our shrewdest intelligence'. He has said he believes in poetry at times of crisis. We wonder if his wife Jan Dalley, to whom he once wrote beautiful poetry, is still reading his poems now he has a new, younger partner? Women need more poetry in their lives, although not necessarily more poets.

This was just one of the many contradictions we found. Few men are all bad. For instance, F. Scott Fitzgerald was a drinker and a tyrant to his wife, but a lyrical writer of great truths and a caring and wise father.

John Betjeman led a double life and was more than aware of its difficulties; 'Feeble, [his mistress Lady Elizabeth Cavendish] is getting very pale and washed out again. I love her. But I also love – and very deeply – Penelope and the kiddiz.'[7]

And of course, being a mistress you are not necessarily tragic and doomed. Here, Betjeman muses about a woman he observes in the congregation:

Lenten Thoughts of a High Anglican

Isn't she lovely, "the Mistress"?
With her wide-apart grey-green eyes,
The droop of her lips and, when she smiles,
Her glance of amused surprise?

How nonchalantly she wears her clothes,
How expensive they are as well!
And the sound of her voice is as soft and deep
As the Christ Church tenor bell.

But why do I call her "the Mistress"
Who know not her way of life?
Because she has more of a cared-for air
Than many a legal wife.

How elegantly she swings along
In the vapoury incense veil;
The angel choir must pause in song
When she kneels at the altar rail.
The parson said that we shouldn't stare
Around when we come to church,
Or the Unknown God we are seeking
May forever elude our search.

But I hope that the preacher will not think
It unorthodox and odd
If I add that I glimpse in "the Mistress"
A hint of the Unknown God

John Betjeman

'Having been both a wife and a mistress (although not simultaneously!) I can say that both states have their advantages and disadvantages,' says Julia. 'The main difference is that wifely difficulty can go on and on, whereas being a mistress tends to be temporary and end in tears.'

As C. Day Lewis (who should know) has written, '… once love betrays you he plays you and plays you/Like fishes for ever, so take it to heart'.[8] The rules of love can never be fathomed; women have the disadvantage in the sense that they can't compartmentalise like men. 'Giving it your best shot', applying energy and effort; methods which work well in other areas of life can count for little in love, and in fact can work in reverse; the less you do, the more you are desired. As Sonia Orwell has asked: 'Why did he love me? *And why did he stop loving me?*'[9]

The 'other woman' is rarely a tart or a floozie. She is just a woman looking for her share of happiness like the rest of us. As Joan Smith has noted, 'When a man calls a woman a whore, he usually means two things: that she enjoys sex too much, and she isn't doing it with him'. Sex interposes itself on just about everything; as Thomas Sutcliffe has said in *The Independent*: 'Sexual proficiency is now a civic duty.'

Women are under more pressure than ever before. Entire TV programmes are made about the failings in our wardrobes, the lack of decking in our gardens and the unsanitary nature of our houses. And we found while writing that there were endless family dramas that absorbed our energy and time. As Mavis Cheek recently observed on *Woman's Hour*: 'Women are still being beaten up with several sticks… they're expected to earn, have a career, bring up babies and pick up the socks'.

Fox

You said you were a feminist
And I believed you;
You told me that Germaine Greer
Had freed you.

But when the babies came along
You began to sing a different song.

So here's what I discovered
While washing your socks:
You're a male chauvinist
…Fox

Janice Warman

This book was indulged by our families as long as it was tacitly understood that their needs and requirements took precedence. There was one Sunday when Julia was struggling to get a few words down and was told in no uncertain terms by her husband that she had better set-to with the cooking *now* as he had *a report to do for the Japanese…*

In January 2005, life certainly imitated art. Julia decided the only way to get the first draft of this book done was to leave the Christmas tree up till Easter; when you take the damn thing down there is a sea of needles, the Hoover is bunged up, everything looks dusty and empty at the same time, and somehow the whole house, not just the sitting room, needs a spring clean. In her *Daphne* monologues, Daphne is most censorious when she notices that Felicity, her hapless daughter-in-law, has left a sprig of holly hanging around till Easter.

'Well, I was going to out-Felicity Felicity and be truly bad; let the gods of twelfth night strike me down with a thunderclap, let them roar, I would be typing away oblivious.' As Sophie Hannah has said, *If People Disapprove of You,*

Make being disapproved of your hobby.
Make being disapproved of your aim.
Devise new ways of scoring points
In the Being Disapproved Of Game.

Let them disapprove in their dozens.
Let them disapprove in their hoards.
You'll find that being disapproved of
Builds character, brings rewards

Just like any form of striving.
Don't be arrogant; don't coast
On your high disapproval rating.
Try to be disapproved of most.

Later we were struck by Vikram Seth's ability to focus single-mindedly on the task in hand: 'I was sunk in my novel, had no time for the dishes or the laundry and had let months' worth of important and unimportant papers accumulate into a guilt pile:

electricity bills in arrears, un-cashed cheques, outdated travel brochures, receipts, dinner invitations...' It goes on and on and on, but in the end a woman comes to sort everything out; how surprising. 'When Francie decided that things had slid far enough, she descended to restore order. If it hadn't been for her, the water would have been cut off, the bailiffs would have been called in, and even the muse would have been un-housed.'[10]

The sort of women who can carry on regardless like Vikram Seth, (make no mistake, we admire it in many ways) are those who could do that 'controlled crying' thing to get the baby to sleep when you are supposed to leave it to scream a longer (or was it a shorter?) time each night so it knows how to get to sleep on its own. Julia tried this method for all of two minutes and failed utterly, consigning herself to years of nursery rhymes until she knew the book inside out, upside down and back to front. Janice raised first a son, then a daughter to eight months old before finally realising (twice over, and how stupid is that) that the early-hours breastfeed was really just for the pleasure of her company and through the fug of exhaustion decided to discontinue it.

As a woman working from home, you are seen as a sitting duck for any number of people. The builders tell you all their troubles, the window cleaner lets it be known he takes two sugars and that his wife wants a divorce because he is selfish (how can this be?) And there is always someone banging on the back door trying to sell you some dodgy looking frozen fish. You are an ever-available agony aunt, dispenser of comfort, sick nurse, and laundress; a sort of human 118 118.

As Doris Lessing wrote in her biography: 'We all of us have limited amounts of energy, and I am sure the people who are successful have learned, either by instinct or consciously, to use their energies well instead of spilling them about.'[11] And this is echoed by Amanda Craig, a novelist who has struggled with illness herself, in her novel *A Vicious Circle*: 'all writing is made possible by a kind of surplus, not of feeling or intellect but of energy.'[12]

It is this creative energy that women find so hard to summon. It can be taken from us by friends as well as family; 'such a mistake to have friends', Sir George Sitwell once observed. We all long to paint, to write, to make music, to garden. One of Bertrand Russell's Ten Commandments, which was Julia's personal mantra when she was teaching, was 'Never discourage creativity, for you will be sure to succeed'. This is particularly true of our generation of women; even when we have created something worthwhile, we undervalue our achievements.

As Justin Cartwright has said in *The Promise of Happiness*: 'The truth is women of my generation were brought up to believe they existed through men. It doesn't matter how much you know it's nonsense, and how clearly you see that men are just as fallible, more so perhaps, deep down we have been conditioned to believe that somehow men have been granted custody of the life force.'[13]

This attitude has prevailed irrespective of cultures and class. As Virginia Nicholson reports in *Among the Bohemians: Experiments in Living 1900-1939*, even the 'liberal and enlightened' intelligentsia had the same view of women. Francis Macnamara, whose daughter was a contemporary of the Garmen girls early in the century, thought that 'girls were adequately trained if they could cook and make themselves desirable to men'.[14] And as late as 1960, Diana Melly, wife of George, attests in her biography *Take a Girl Like Me*, 'the British jazz world was as full of male chauvinists as other more conventional worlds. Men knew best and I never corrected them'.[15]

Julia was surprised to find that when she mentioned this book to a number of male friends, they became rattled and edgy. 'One old friend, a naturalised American, sent me a book on quilting.' (Stick to what you know?) Another friend said to his wife, 'What can she have to say that anyone would want to read?' and in a panic, he began to write a book himself.

'My own, by now estranged, husband said, "Will I need to sue you?" ' This is not the joke it sounds coming from a litigation addict who had a court case of some kind going on in nearly every year of our marriage. I said, 'I don't think so as you are only mentioned a few times'. He looked disappointed and said, 'I thought it was all about me'.

Janice's husband suggested a change of title – 'Return to Eden' – and a change of subject matter: a book about men and women living in marital harmony. (Perhaps next time.)

Someone else said: 'Somebody should write a book about the colossal amount of time women spend on unimportant issues – now that *would* be a bestseller!' And so it all went.

Being a writing partnership had its advantages and disadvantages. Whether we exercised our talent or not, we felt too much self-knowledge can be a bar to creativity, and most certainly that we are probably all faking it to a degree (and not just in bed).

Ballet

I knew what they meant;
I knew why I was meant to try.

I'd study myself in the mirror before I left;
I looked as if I could do it.

The black leotard, the pink tights;
The bun, that ridiculous
Pink elastic waistband.
I loved the music.
But I couldn't dance.

My ankles wobbled.
My mother frowned
At the side of the hall.

Since then I've learned
There are some things you can fake:
Wit; intelligence; blondeness;
Marriage.

Ballet isn't one of them.

Janice Warman

By the time you get to forty or fifty you are all too aware of your own limitations; it is time to quit worrying about what you can't do and concentrate on what you can:

Procrastination

Of all the advice I've been given,
Just one phrase has stuck:
"Make a start."
Whether applied to paying the bills
Or matters of the heart.

Janice Warman

In general, Janice complained Julia wrote too much and Julia complained Janice wrote too little. One way and another we batted ideas back and forth, and when one of us had a fallow period, the other rallied and took up the baton. As our individual fortunes waxed and waned we took it in turns to shoulder the load.

It was a "boys in the backroom" type of friendship; joshing, laughing and sometimes despairing. When Janice took on the editorship of a magazine in London, another friend, Susie, came to the rescue and took Julia's drafts away and produced elegantly typed chapters. 'My own personal anxiety was that I had not been a writer, not by a long way,' says Julia. 'But I was encouraged by Alan Bennett's pronouncement in *Untold Stories*: "Painters seem an altogether nicer class of person than writers, although they often make good writers themselves. They're less envious of each other, less competitive and with more of a sense that they are all engaged on the same enterprise." '[16]

Compare this with Tim Clare, writing in *The Guardian*: 'The book industry should show more appreciation for established authors, whilst disabusing those thousands of needy, bumbling timewasters of the notion that nascent masterpieces stir within their loins.' Well, you can't get much blunter than that.

All in all, it took us far longer than we could ever have imagined. As our mothers used to say, 'If a thing's worth doing, it's worth doing well', not to mention 'perseverance conquers' and other *bon mots*; not 'Daisy Pulls It Off' exactly but perhaps 'Julia and Janice win through with lots and lots of derring-do'. The writers of *School Friend* and *Bunty* had not written in vain, but it all must be done without 'showing off' in any way. We took heart from that fact that Hilary Spurling took fifteen years to write *Matisse the Master* and found a leader in *The Independent* on Emma Thompson that said: 'Her new film is out on Friday. That it has taken her seven years to write is confirmation of her integrity.' Yes, 'integrity', that sounded good; that was the reason we had taken such an age.

It took some cross-country detective work to locate our illustrator, Penny Grist; she was swept up in our tide of enthusiasm and agreed to us using all her prints in the most generous-spirited way possible, unconcerned that we were designing all the jackets even before we had finished Chapter One. We broke all the rules.

Likewise, designer Jan Moffitt was unfazed by this illogical approach and used her imagination to turn the prints into fantastic covers. It has been an infectious collaboration, with many people having *Hey Nonny* thrust upon them whether they liked it or not, but the visual aspect was critical to the essence of the thing.

There was also the question of political slant. We constantly swung from right to left and back again. Peter Snow would have been proud of us! As an early feminist, Julia read *Spare Rib*, and *Nova* (still unrivalled), and her political home in the eighties was *The Guardian* Women's Page with great female writers like Jill Tweedie and Polly Toynbee, and the brilliant cartoonist Posy Simmonds. Janice, growing up in seventies South Africa, felt feminism was a struggle secondary to the fight against apartheid. In Britain, she read *The Guardian* loyally (and was an early contributor to *Naked Ape*) until she joined its City pages, when she was amused to hear that a board member had apparently told the union in response to a query about paternity leave: 'I don't see what childcare has got to do with men, anyway.' Hadn't he read his own Women's Page?

As Eve Pollard, the former editor of the *Sunday Express*, has said: 'It was the women's pages that really educated women about health in this country; contraception, abortion and all the rest of it.' Women's pages are now either discredited or considered unnecessary, but perhaps it is time to reinvent them. Joan Thirsk, writing in *The Independent*, puts it in a nutshell:

> *Sir, I am most relieved to hear that St Hilda's College, Oxford, is to remain a single-sex college. Men cannot stop themselves from taking charge anywhere and everywhere. As a historian I have studied the phenomenon, and as an 80-year old academic I have seen it happen. If we lose our single-sex colleges, they will, at some time in the future, have to be reinvented.*

In researching this book, we have used all the broadsheets but particularly *The Independent* and *The Sunday Telegraph*. One friend, Sarah, a staunchly conservative and ex-Bow Group member, kept us up to speed about what the right were thinking and every week sent useful cuttings and snippets in the post. Obituaries were invaluable, as were readers' letters, which could always be relied upon to supply ideas that a journalist had missed.

And yet, burdened by Wendy Cope's internal policemen (or should it be policewomen?) we had doubts. South Africa is a subject never far from Janice's mind, and she was uncertain about writing a book on the difficulties of comfortably-off British women, considering how black women had suffered under apartheid – were *still* suffering the twin disasters of poverty and HIV. On her bookshelf was Antjie Krog's *Country of My Skull* – a book of evidence from the Truth and Reconciliation Commission; on its cover, a woman holding a handful of hair, all that remained of her murdered son.

On Julia's shelf was Antony Beevor's *Berlin;* she wondered, after reading about the experiences of German women at the hands of the Red Army, if there was any justification at all for complaining about the difficulties of modern times:

> *Berliners remember that, because all the windows had been blown in, you could hear the screams every night. Estimates from the two main Berlin hospitals ranged from 95,000 to 130,000 rape victims... A friend of Ursula*

von Kardorff... was raped by 'twenty-three soldiers one after the other'. She had to be stitched up in hospital afterwards.[17]

In contrast, many women have endured lives of low-grade misery, poverty and a lack of food. How, for instance, do we have the right to feel aggrieved when the dishwasher breaks down at half term, when we have never experienced war-time deprivation?

Every new generation carries its deep fears, and the post-war baby boomers lived in the shadow of the atom bomb, although its danger is now, and perhaps wrongly, discounted. Penelope Lively, in an interview in *The Guardian*, described what it was like to be a young mother in the seventies: 'I seriously didn't think I would see my children grow up.' We know from other friends of the same age that this feeling was widespread. This was an era when a 200-megaton nuclear attack from Russia was entirely possible. In the early eighties, Janice went to join the human chain between Greenham Common and Aldermaston, and persuaded her editor at the local paper (in Tory Sussex) to carry her photographs. Her sister's family, who lived in nearby Oxford, planned to park their car at the camp gates if there was an attack, as survival would be by far the worst option.

More prosaically, central heating was not universal until the end of the sixties. In the fifties, everyone woke up with ice inside their windows. Women had the worry of keeping everyone warm as well as fed. Before immunisation, measles was rife and could be catastrophic in consequence. And until the polio vaccination programme took full effect, every school in the land contained crippled children wearing callipers. To take it for granted that our children will grow up healthy (although secondary to development of the Pill) has been a major factor in the liberation of women.

Perhaps the most ambitious part of the book was to look carefully at the mental health issues women suffer in mid-life and to do what we could to de-stigmatise these problems. As well as for the utterly sane, this book is also for the clinically depressed, and a reminder that these apparently opposing states are not so far apart as we might think.

Nervous breakdowns are mysterious things and they were particularly obscure when we were growing up. Like cancer and divorce, they were unmentionable, or referred to obliquely in hushed or patronising tones. Women, and it was usually women, had them behind closed doors. Anxiety as a normal human emotion is different to anxiety as a clinical condition. We were both born with an 'anxiety gene', and yet when we were younger we found we could override it by taking action. It was when our physical energy diminished that we found we were in trouble.

In Gloucestershire, middle-aged women who cracked were sent to Coney Hill, the local psychiatric hospital. Julia has friends who were told their mothers had gone away for treatment for fictitious physical illnesses rather than nervous collapse. Even now, there are countless women who hide themselves away or are hidden.

There was and still is a sense of shame if the mind breaks. One of the purposes of this book is to try, falteringly, to demystify the difficulties of depression, anxiety and menopause, with the aim of giving hope to sufferers that these problems can be overcome. As Dr Claire Weekes says in her seminal book *Self-Help for Your Nerves*, 'The law of compensation works particularly well after recovery from nervous breakdown'.[18]

We hope many women will benefit from this book, from the working woman to the mother in track pants mucking out the guinea pigs. We direct our concerns to both the rich and the poor; although those with the least financial security understandably have the most anxiety, the woman whose husband has no financial constraints is not necessarily to be envied. As Germaine Greer has said, 'There is no job open to women more demanding than being the wife of a billionaire'. Not everyone can afford health farms, but reading, writing, rest and exercise are free.

In the post-modern/cliché-speak world, women need to be helped to re-invent themselves and find simpler and better ways of living. What we have attempted here is a kind of 'State of the Nation' address on middle age; its joys, its dilemmas and its compensations. This book is testimony to the resilience of the human heart and an epitaph for the many women who have shown courage and laughter in the face of all kinds of adversity. As Dr Johnson has said, 'The only end of writing is to enable readers to enjoy life, or better to endure it'.

Hey Nonny can be taken to the beach, read in bed, or kept on the kitchen shelf to be dipped into at time of need, and as Gwendolen has said in *The Importance of Being Earnest*: 'You will always have something sensational to read on the train'![19]

Sigh no more, ladies, sigh no more;
Men were deceivers ever;
One foot in sea and one on shore,
To one thing constant never;
Then sigh not so,
But let them go,
And be you blithe and bonny;
Converting all your sounds of woe
Into Hey nonny, nonny.

Sing no more ditties, sing no more
Of dumps so dull and heavy;
The fraud of men was ever so
Since summer first was leavy.
Then sigh not so,
But let them go,
And be you blithe and bonny;
Converting all your sounds of woe
Into Hey nonny, nonny. [1]

From *Much Ado about Nothing* by William Shakespeare

Hey Nonny heroines

What is a Hey Nonny heroine? She is someone who has suffered because of circumstance, century and male domination; who has triumphed against these odds; or who has simply showed courage in adversity.

How do you find her? You open a newspaper or randomly take a book from your shelf. She may be famous, but more often than not, you won't have heard of her. Whether public or private, our heroines are often understated, sidelined, not always at the centre of things, and many have suffered from the ability to see someone else's point of view, which has often left them at a disadvantage.

Our first choice is Marie Antoinette, who is an archetypal Heroine; her fate was decided by those with more power than her, and all she could do was make the best of frightening circumstances. At just 14, she was sent from Vienna to Versailles as a political pawn, to marry the reluctant and gawky bridegroom Louis Auguste, heir to the French throne. Due to the Dauphin's reluctance and sexual inhibitions, it was years before the marriage was finally consummated. Eventually she managed to conceive, but had to suffer the indignity of having to give birth in front of the entire Royal Court, as was then the custom.

In spite of her marriage difficulties, the exile from her family, her separation from her own children and her constant fear and dread in the face of riot and revolution, Marie Antoinette retained her composure right up to the moment of her execution.

Whatever their circumstances, few modern women can be assailed by the sheer magnitude of problems faced by the French queen in the eighteenth century. However, more than 200 years later, mothers still suffer the loss of their children. Journalist and feminist Jill Tweedie's memoir, *Frightening People*, tells the harrowing tale of how her children were abducted by her first husband, the Hungarian Count Cziraky. When she asked her parents for help, she was told by the Cleft (her father): 'Out of the question. You're not dumping the mess you've made on us.'[2]

She eventually found out where her children were being kept and sent messages and presents, but these were intercepted and destroyed. The children thought they had been deserted and rejected. It is of some small consolation that, years later, she was reunited with her children and found great happiness with her third husband, Alan Brien, before her tragically early death from motor neurone disease.

Sometimes it takes a certain type of woman to take on a difficult man and make a success of it, but Helen Dawson, *The Observer's* brilliant arts editor in the late sixties, did just that with four-times married playwright John Osborne, still best known for his groundbreaking kitchen sink drama *Look Back in Anger*. It must have taken a certain steely courage, but she nursed him through his blackest moods, encouraging him to complete two volumes of autobiography and his last great play, *Déjà vu*, shortly before his death in 1994. Their marriage lasted as long as his previous four put together, yet she always retained her own identity. As David Hare said in her obituary: 'Helen never telephoned without your feeling cheered up after, and you never saw her without wanting to see her again.'

From England to Africa, and one of the greatest female writers of the twentieth century – Doris Lessing. In her autobiography, *Under My Skin*, Lessing paints an acute portrait of the life of her mother as a settler in Rhodesia in the twenties. Her father was emotionally and physically damaged after the Great War. He had lost a leg and imagined that emigrating and starting a new life would be a healing process. He chose a nurse for a wife, Emily Maude McVeagh, who was a matron at the Royal Free Hospital in London. She was a happy, sociable woman, who loved clothes, concerts and dressing up, and she helped him to recover from shell shock and the horrors of the trenches. They settled in the north east of Southern Rhodesia, which was very wild and desolate, but the white Government was selling the land for next to nothing and loans to start farming were easy to obtain.

At first, Emily coped well with the deprivations of the bush, but as she moved into her forties, her optimism and energy diminished and she began to see that the hoped-for change of luck would never materialise, her crippled husband would never dominate the bush, and because of the weight of her disappointment, she took to her bed. She told her family it was a bad heart; and perhaps she believed this herself.

Eventually Emily made a kind of recovery, but changed from an energetic, cheerful young woman into a stern and unforgiving, always reproachful, martinet. Later in life, Doris said that she always had to go to bed for the day to recover from any visit by her mother. It is sad to realise that years of suffering and even personality change could possibly have been alleviated, if not entirely prevented, by therapy and modern drugs.

The poet Louis MacNeice's mother Lily suffered a similar depression at the same stage of her life. She was married to a clergyman and the family lived in Carrickfergus in Northern Ireland. Lily, like Emily McVeagh, was an intelligent and accomplished mother who played the harmonica and piano, invented games for her children and took them on outings and picnics. She was a devoted wife and energetic housekeeper who presided over a household that included cats, dogs, and red hens.

This was 1912, a time of great political and religious tension. Demonstrations were held all over Ulster, the Unionists were making preparations to resist Home Rule by force. The suspense of those days caused great concern to those living in the rectory and the servants had strongly held and conflicting attitudes to the crisis.

In addition, poor Lily had been ill off and on that year with gynaecological problems, and her younger son had Down's Syndrome, so life cannot have been easy, even with domestic help. She managed to take the children on holiday, but sat apart from them, looking out to sea, unable to enjoy their company or take part in their activities.

A few months later, she was told she needed an immediate hysterectomy. John Stallworthy, in his life of the poet, Louis MacNeice, does not go into the reasons why. The operation was successful, but psychologically she never recovered. Modern medicine has led to the development of oestrogen patches for use after such treatment, but none of this was available to Lily. She was sent to a nursing home and lost all interest in life. She died two years later, when Louis was only five years old, and the impact on him of losing his mother so young is evident in this extract from his poem, *Autobiography*:

My mother wore a yellow dress;
Gently, gently, gentleness.

Come back early or never come

When I was five the black dreams came;
Nothing after was quite the same

Come back early or never come.

Many of our Heroines are partners of literary men. Both Sylvia Plath and Assia Wevill took their lives as a consequence of their depression and instability, following Ted Hughes's rejection of them; Assia also murdered their four-year-old daughter, Shura.

A new biography of Wevill, *A Lover of Unreason: The Biography of Assia Wevill*, has revealed 'Ted Hughes, the late Poet Laureate, was a domestic tyrant who issued a 'Draft Constitution' to his mistress, instructing her how to carry out household chores and look after his children...' According to the authors, Yehuda Koren and Eilat Negev, Hughes's domestic instructions were probably written in 1967, when he and Wevill were living in Devon with Frieda and Nicholas, his children by Plath. He banned her from staying in bed beyond 8am, ordered her to dress straight away and told her not to catch up on sleep. The two pages of typed instructions said that she should teach the children German, play with them for at least an hour a day and introduce at least one meal with 'a recipe we have never had before' on a weekly basis. Hughes made it clear he had no intention of cooking 'except in emergencies'.[3]

Elaine Feinstein, in *Ted Hughes: The Life of a Poet*, asserts that Ted was intending to return to Sylvia and indeed would have done so, had she not taken her own life. This may have been so. Assia herself had a volatile and highly-strung temperament, with two failed marriages behind her. Nevertheless, Ted's lack of commitment to Assia, his disloyalty to Sylvia and the consequences of both, is an extreme example of what 'one foot in sea and one on shore,/To one thing constant never' can lead to.

Fay Weldon puts it another way:

> *In the days of female powerlessness the male blame game – endearments today, rejection the next – was more frequently played than it is today. Ted Hughes played the game and drove poor Sylvia to suicide (male poet: you have dared to rival me; I will choose another over you) and Assia Wevill (male poet: you have brought down dark cosmic powers to damage me: you have killed my true wife by your presence in my life: I cannot live with you).*[4]

Philip Larkin is another poet of the 'one foot in sea and one on shore' variety. Without making a commitment to either, he compartmentalised his life to accommodate both Monica Jones and Maeve Brennan. He saw Monica, who lived some distance away, at weekends and holidays; Maeve he worked with, acted as mentor to and socialised with during the week. He controlled aspects of his personality to the extent that each woman saw such a different side to him that they could have been going out with different men. He was not, however, entirely without self-knowledge. He wrote *Talking in Bed* about his relationship with Monica, and at one stage, according to Andrew Motion's biography, he was so anxious about the difficulty of maintaining relationships with both women that he blacked out and was taken to hospital.

Talking in Bed

Talking in bed ought to be easiest,
Lying together there goes back so far,
An emblem of two people being honest.

Yet more and more time passes silently.
Outside, the wind's incomplete unrest
Builds and disperses clouds in the sky,

And dark towns heap up on the horizon.
None of this cares for us. Nothing shows why
At this unique distance from isolation

It becomes still more difficult to find
Words at once true and kind,
Or not untrue and not unkind.

Philip Larkin

In spite of this, he managed to keep both relationships going for some years, and although he left the bulk of his estate to Monica, both women visited him and provided moral support in his final illness. However, Monica was destroyed after his death; ill and frail herself, she was a widow without the consolation of the title. She was too depressed to attend his funeral, and apparently hardly anyone noticed her absence.

Are poets especially prone to sitting on the fence? John Betjeman kept two women for most of his life, and according to A.N. Wilson in *Betjeman*, each one, Elizabeth and

Penelope, assumed he was going to choose her. He 'dithered and agonised'; no decision was ever made.

Like another poet/philanderer, C. Day Lewis, boundaries were set, which each of the women were not supposed to cross. It is an annoyance to us that both were such wonderful lyric poets; Lewis was also musical and had a beautiful voice.

Rosamond Lehmann was C. Day Lewis's lover. Modern psychology might say she colluded in her own downfall, (although don't we all do this for love?) She had a protracted affair with him, but he refused to divorce his wife and live full-time with Rosamond. His wife, Mary King, even when she discovered Rosamond's existence, welcomed her husband back at weekends and protected her sons from the knowledge of their father's double life. However, when he finally left her, it was not for Rosamond, who was now nearly fifty, but for the younger actress Jill Balcon. Selena Hastings describes the devastation Rosamond felt in her biography, *Rosamond Lehmann: A Life*.

> *Cecil went up to London as usual to his office at Chatto & Windus. From there he wrote Rosamond a long letter, telling her that he had fallen in love with Jill Balcon, and although he still loved his 'darling Rosie' he had irrevocably made up his mind to leave her for Jill. "I remember it said, "I can feel all your pain, every fibre of my being is conscious of your terrible pain, but I'm going to do it". Rosamond was so shocked that she instantly threw the letter into the fire. "I couldn't believe it." Immediately she sat down and wrote him a brief note demanding to see him at once. Cecil arrived and the two of them talked for hours, but nothing Rosamond said seemed to make the slightest impression, Cecil, with a show of what appeared to be 'diabolical indifference', agreeing trance-like with every accusation. "What about me?" she almost screamed at him. "Oh, I can't think of you," he replied matter-of-factly. "I'm thinking of her now."[5]*

There is something especially poignant about women who wait in the wings for years and never get the starring role. More recently, we think another Cecil (Parkinson) a particularly lowly worm for abandoning Sara Keays and his love child as he did. Does this Cecil write poetry? We hope not. *His* career, we note, carried on with only a brief hiatus; *her* fledgling political career was doomed, and through a court gagging order, she was not allowed to voice her concerns about the treatment of her daughter, who was not even permitted to appear in school photographs. Sara, who in our view is certainly a Hey Nonny heroine, told Channel 4 in 2002 that she had received 'virulent attacks' from women at the time. 'Downing Street and Conservative Central Office were conducting a very powerful and all pervasive disinformation campaign to discredit me because the only way they felt they could shore up his career was by discrediting me,' she said.

Sylvia Plath is not the only wife of a poet to be given a raw deal. In *Painted Shadow: A Life of Vivienne Eliot*, Carole Seymour-Jones explodes the myth that Vivienne was a neurotic hysteric and a drain on T.S. Eliot's vitality, who sapped his creative energy. She has come to be known for nutty behaviour like setting fire to curtains and pouring 'melted chocolate through the letter box of Faber & Faber'[6], but the truth is more complex; a conspiracy of silence has grown around the poet to preserve his image. Viv did have menstrual and hormonal problems, which modern drug therapies would no doubt have been able to address, but many of her difficulties with depression and anxiety came directly from the problems of marriage to Eliot himself. She was also a gifted writer, and contributed directly and indirectly to his growth as a poet.

Over the years, terrible things happened to Viv; she was given cocktails of tranquillising drugs which contributed to her psychotic state, was defrauded of her rightful share of her inheritance, and in later years was committed to an insane asylum by her family with the tacit approval of her husband, who never visited her. It was only on her death that her brother expressed remorse, and admitted that support and kindness would have been better for her than drugs and exclusion. 'What Tom and I did was wrong. And Mother. I did everything Tom told me to. It was only when I saw Vivie in the asylum for the last time I realised I had done something very wrong. She was as sane as I was.'[7]

The writer Hilary Mantel was not mad either, but she had a debilitating physical condition – endometriosis – that remained undiagnosed for years, while she was treated for psychiatric problems, an experience she relates in her memoir, *Giving Up the Ghost*. For seven years, Hilary had been prescribed anti-depressants and Valium, which led to frightening psychotic symptoms and further instability: 'The more I said I had a physical illness, the more they said I had a mental illness. The more I questioned the nature, the reality of the mental illness, the more I was found to be in denial, deluded... It was in the nature of educated young women, it was believed, to be hysterical, neurotic, difficult and out of control...'[8(i)]

The drugs sparked a condition called akathisia: 'It is a condition that developed as a side-effect of anti-psychotic medication, and the cunning thing about it is that it looks, and it feels, exactly like madness. The patient paces. She is unable to stay still. She wears a look of agitation and terror. She wrings her hands; she says she is in hell.' [8(ii)]

Eventually she self-diagnosed, finding her condition in a book, but by then the condition was so bad that she was forced to have a radical hysterectomy at 27, which rendered her childless and plunged her straight into menopause. 'There's one good thing anyway. Now you won't have to worry about birth prevention,' [8(iii)] said her doctor, in a breathtaking display of tactlessness.

George Orwell wrote brilliantly on inequality, unemployment and repressive and divided societies, but was deeply chauvinistic in his treatment of women, not least his wife, Eileen. The following is Simon Callow on Orson Welles, but it could have just as well been said about Orwell: 'The more he embraced needy mankind, the less able he seemed to extend his concern to the individuals for whom he was personally responsible.'[9]

His biographer, Gordon Bowker, quotes Stephen Spender in his book, *George Orwell*: 'Orwell was very misogynist. I don't know why. [He] was a strange sort of eccentric man full of strange ideas and strange prejudices. One was that he thought that women were extremely inferior and stupid... He really rather despised women.'[10]

Orwell showed a marked lack of sympathy for Eileen's serious physical problems – a lack of sympathy that may have led to her death. She suffered from protracted and serious internal bleeding and desperately needed a hysterectomy, but George expressed reservations about the expense, which caused the operation to be delayed, although he knew she had been suffering pain, fatigue and bleeding for many years.

He was out of the country when she died on the operating table. He learnt of her death via a wire from *The Observer*, and managed to absolve himself from guilt by pretending that he'd thought the operation routine and minor. From the perspective of this century, we feel enraged on her behalf; she seems so self-effacing that she is rather more Hey Nonny Martyr than Heroine. Even her last letter to him shows no sign of the distress his absence must have caused her. It is simple, direct and affectionate:

> *Dearest I'm just going to have the operation, already enema'd, injected (with morphia in the right arm, which is a nuisance), cleaned and packed up like a precious image in cotton wool and bandages. When it's over, I'll add a note to this and it can get off quickly... I feel irritated to be thought of as a model patient. They think I'm wonderful, so placid and happy, they say. As indeed I am once I can hand myself over to someone to deal with.*[11]

The letter breaks off mid-sentence as the orderlies come to wheel her into theatre. Of course, it was never completed. Having agreed to delay the operation she needed, she handed herself over to a surgeon she never saw, and died on the operating table.

Many of George and Eileen's friends felt that her death was linked to his neglect of her as well as to his chequered sexual history.

Certainly, he did not like his attentions to be thwarted, and told one girlfriend, Brenda Salkeld, that if she did not accommodate his sexual needs, it was better that they part. Brenda wisely never agreed to a sexual relationship with him and his unfulfilled passion for her haunted him throughout his life. She, unlike Eileen, lived to 98 and never married. The moral of this tale is pretty obvious. (It was Cyril Connolly, a close associate of Orwell's, who wrote: 'The true index of a man's character is the health of his wife.')

It is worth noting that Sonia Orwell, George's second wife, who worked for Connolly at Horizon and married George as he was dying, had an equally ill-starred life for different reasons. She was publicly accused of being greedy and unscrupulous and remained discredited for many years. It wasn't until Hilary Spurling wrote her lucid biography, *The Girl from the Fiction Department*, that the record was set straight. Her friends believed Sonia married Orwell because of her 'own deep unhappiness', and that 'Men who loved ideas held an irresistible allure for Sonia, who had no faith in her own worth or talents but responded unconditionally to creative drive and intellectual originality in others.'[12(i)] In fact, far from being a spendthrift, she used all the money she had to regain control of Orwell's effects so that everything she had inherited could be handed intact to his adopted son.

As Spurling testifies, 'Books remained ever afterwards her prime source of consolation, a present help in time of trouble and a fixed refuge from despair'.[12(ii)] Sonia was a Hey Nonny Heroine in the fullest literary sense.

It is wonderful to know that in later years when she was very ill, William Coldstream, who had had an affair with Sonia in his youth, 'sent a basket of pinks and bluebells, striped lilies, roses, carnations, snapdragons and sweetpeas'.[12(iii)] At least she was loved by someone. She had said of George: 'He thought if we married, he might live longer – how could I refuse?'

Kingsley Amis's humour figures strongly throughout this book, which is something of an irony given that the women he loved and married are archetypal Hey Nonny Heroines. He caused his first wife great unhappiness with his many infidelities, finally leaving her for the novelist Elizabeth Jane Howard. His letters demonstrate the enormous love and admiration he had for Jane at the onset, and how that changed over the passage of time, leading to anger, frustration and dislike on both sides. This is a love letter written in 1963:

> *Dearest dove – this is the first time I've been alone; nobody's plan, just the way things have turned out. We've had a happy time but I've been missing you. I miss your mouth and your breath and your skin and your hair and your smell and your left eyelid and your right breast and right collarbone and right armpit and the back of your neck. And all your other*

things. And your voice. And eyes. And hands and everything. I've never missed anyone like this before. I said I don't think sexy letters are any good but I keep remembering how we are together and what we do. Even thinking of things remotely connected with you makes me react physically – remind me to tell you how.[13(i)]

By 1979, things had changed. This is a letter to Philip Larkin:

On my self-pity themes, don't tempt me, son. They include year-round hay-fever, high blood-pressure so that I stream with sweat at the slightest exertion or upset, permanently-itching places on my scalp (side-effect of anti-blood-p pills) from which descend flakes of scurf the size of 1p pieces, increasing phobias that stop me travelling almost anywhere (that one's not so bad) and make me dread and hate being alone, this along with a wife who puts herself first and the rest nowhere and constantly goes out to GROUPS and WORKSHOPS and crappy 'new friends', and a total loss of sex-drive.[13(ii)]

In his memoir, *Experience*, Martin Amis describes moving day in his father's household, accurately depicting the unhappy dynamic of a couple locked in a failing relationship. As Hilary, Amis's first wife, put it: 'If you're a woman, then you are your house and your house is you.'[14] This echoes the experience of so many middle-aged women who lose their homes as a consequence of marriage breakdown, or find their husbands remortgaging the house and taking away their hard-won security.

Kingsley's letters not only demonstrate the decline of his marriage, but even more notably the frustration felt by men when their powers begin to fade, which so often results in chauvinism, anger and misogyny.[15] Revealingly, when asked by a researcher to name dislikeable qualities in men as opposed to women, he said: 'One specifically masculine dislikeable quality occurs to me: being nasty to a woman. Women can be nasty to a man all right, but a man is better equipped, with greater physical strength, greater earning capacity, not being subject to menstruation, etc., etc.'[16] An admission which is rather revealing, particularly considering how he eventually treated his second wife, Jane.

Jane found a new creative drive after their separation and faced with the need to support herself, wrote the highly successful *Cazalet Chronicles* (following a Sussex family through both World Wars, and later serialised by BBC TV) which cemented her reputation as a significant twentieth century novelist. Kingsley, by contrast, was known to say that he should never have left Hilary and lived the last decades of his life in a house shared with her and her third husband.

There are also many examples of women suffering at the hands of great painters and sculptors, but the lot of wives in bohemian and artistic society in the early twentieth century is illustrated by the obscure but tragic fate of the little-known Ida John, who has our vote for the Hey Nonny Heroine of Heroines. Ida Nettleship, a talented student at the Slade School of Art, married the up-and-coming painter Augustus John in 1901, when she was just 19 years old. This more or less put paid to her own artistic endeavours, as a year or so later she gave birth to their first child, with a second child following within 18 months. Around this time, Augustus fell in love with Dorelia Neill and moved her into the household. Ida was presented with this as a *fait accompli*. According to Sue Roe's biography of Augustus' sister, *Gwen John, A Life*: '... she knew this was the only way to save her marriage, to go along with the idea of *ménage à trois*, but Dorelia made her feel ugly and despairing.'[17]

Ida took the children away for a while, hoping the situation would improve. However, when she came back, nothing had changed; Dorelia was still there and they all moved to a large rambling house together, in Matching Green, Essex. Dorelia was unfaithful to Augustus, and Ida even had to collude in the winning back of Dorelia for Augustus, in order to safeguard her own position.

And still worse was to happen; Ida became pregnant with a fifth child. According to Virginia Nicholson in *Among the Bohemians*, 'Ida contemplated the birth of a fifth child with glum dread'.[18] (As Dorelia had been re-instated as mistress by this time, one might have thought that Ida would have been spared another pregnancy.) Following childbirth, she developed puerperal fever and peritonitis and died shortly afterwards. Her husband did not attend her cremation. 'He hated formal displays of sentiment and had reacted to Ida's death with confused demonstrations of strange exhilaration.'[19] Ida John was just thirty years old.

In life, the talented Ida was overshadowed by her famous husband, and after her death, she was swiftly forgotten. Our next subject, by contrast, heads our list of celebrity Heroines, yet she faced heartbreak and tragedy in equal measure.

Jacqueline Kennedy Onassis's life was a drama of epic proportion, but her beauty, success and fame overlay misfortune and private grief. Life with John Kennedy was a rollercoaster; she had to contend with his presidential ambitions, his health problems and his many infidelities. She suffered bouts of depression, several miscarriages and the death of her son Patrick. After her husband's assassination, perhaps to escape the Kennedy myth, or the Kennedy curse as it later became known, she married Aristotle Onassis, only to discover that being a trophy bride was no safe haven. In spite of the tragic subtext of her life, she showed tenacity and determination, and the ability to rise above desperate circumstances. Her devotion and commitment to her children was absolute, she supported the civil rights movement, encouraged the arts in America, and was devoted to books and poetry throughout her life. After Onassis's death, she returned to New York, working for the publisher Viking on Madison Avenue, and later as an editor for Doubleday. Throughout her life, she demonstrated an enormous capacity for reinventing herself and transcending personal sorrow.

Another famous American was Zelda Fitzgerald, whose fate was uncannily similar to that of Vivienne Eliot. Zelda was attractive, vivacious, intelligent and rebellious, and came from the kind of affluent Montgomery family that was well established in

Southern society. Scott was from the North, of lower social status but with ruthless ambition, and although young, was already an established writer.

In *Zelda Fitzgerald: Her Voice in Paradise*, Sally Cline describes how Scott resolved to capture the dramatic and beautiful Zelda and how determined he was to do whatever it took to get her to marry him. After a two-year courtship, he finally achieved his objective. They married in New York in 1920; she was 19 and he was 24.

Given her strong personality, it was surprising that his hold over her started from the very beginning. He took it upon himself to organise the wedding, a Catholic ceremony in the North, far from her home town. Her Episcopalian parents did not attend. It was a sombre affair, nothing like the extravaganza that would have been her wedding in the South. There, she was a sought-after Southern belle, but in New York it was Scott who was famous; she became merely his consort. She was required to be witty and beautiful – that was all; and in the spirit of the times, they drank and they partied.

But the bubble was soon to burst. Zelda became depressed, having been quickly forced into the role of a Minnesota-style wife and mother. Desperate to find some means of self-expression, she tried writing herself, and also dancing, but Scott took over her material and published it under his name, or absorbed it into his own stories. According to Jeffrey Meyers, in his book *Married to Genius*, Scott was unequivocal in his attitude to Zelda's creativity. This is what he said:

> *You are a third rate writer and a third rate ballet dancer... I am a professional writer, with a huge following. I am the highest paid short story writer in the world... I am the professional writer, and I am supporting you. That is all my material. None of it is your material... I want you to stop writing fiction.*[20]

Understandably, none of this helped her state of mind. Scott persuaded her to get some medication for her misery; this was the start of his many years of collusion with the doctors who treated his 'mad' wife.

Psychiatry was in its infancy and many 'cures' only compounded the problem. Poorly tested drugs had side effects that induced delusions and paranoia. Thus affected, Zelda was incarcerated for longer and longer periods of time and, like Viv Eliot, was encouraged to think of herself as ill and unstable, even though, like Viv, the treatment was more damaging than the condition itself. (She was told she was mad and she became so; it was a self-fulfilling prophecy.) We can only think of how both women could have recovered with modern anti-depressants, therapy and ideally escape from the damaging relationships into which they were locked.

Zelda came to a tragic end. The hospital in which she was a 'voluntary' patient burned down; she had been locked in her room, and died in the inferno.

Charlotte Perkins Gilman, another American writer, also suffered from depression, but still lived a full and active life. She wrote *The Yellow Wallpaper* in 1880, which changed the way many women were treated for anxiety, though sadly it would appear that the doctors who treated Zelda Fitzgerald and Vivienne Eliot had never read it.

In *Why I Wrote The Yellow Wallpaper*, Charlotte reveals that she was advised by her doctor to ' "live as domestic a life as far as possible", to "have but two hours' intellectual life a day" and "never to touch pen, brush or pencil again" as long as I lived.' This advice she followed for three months, she writes, 'and came so near the border of utter mental ruin that I could see over'.

She sent her story to the physician who 'so nearly drove me mad'; although he never acknowledged it, she heard years later that he had altered his treatment of what was then called neurasthenia since reading it. This, she says, was 'the best result'.[21]

Something that Charlotte, Zelda and Viv had in common with Hilary Mantel was that whether it was the late nineteenth century, the thirties, forties, or even the seventies, there was a belief that education would put too many demands on women. The psychiatrist Anthony Clare, writing about the nineteenth century, explains in his book *On Men*, 'men were [thought to be] calmed by the education they received, women overheated by it'. Clare also observes that even in the twentieth century, 'the act of resisting the status quo was seen to be symptomatic of illness in itself'.[22]

Virginia Woolf is an important role model for all women, not only because of her fame as a writer, but specifically because she wrote *A Room of Your Own*, which so accurately analysed the reasons for women's low achievements: lack of money, time and space. She was the recipient of both care and neglect by the men in her life. It is suggested in Hermione Lee's *Virginia Woolf* that childhood abuse from her half-brother Gerald Duckworth may have been at least partly responsible for her instability in later life. However, she was fortunate in her choice of marriage partner; her husband, Leonard Woolf, gave her love and stability and encouraged her writing throughout their married life.

Or was she? Some scientific studies have indicated that there can be such a thing as too much support. Although it may seem natural for a spouse to take over responsibilities for a sick partner (don't we all long for this on occasion?) it is easy to become too involved and proprietary. This type of carer has been described as the 'Golden Husband' by one neurosurgeon who observed high levels of neurosis in women with over-protective partners.

There was not much of the Golden Husband about George Carmen, whose wives became Heroines by the act of marrying him. Carmen was a high-profile celebrity lawyer, with a string of famous clients that earned him the title 'King of Libel', yet his own private life was severely at odds with the moral self-righteousness he publicly displayed. In *No Ordinary Man*, written after his death by his son Dominic, all three of his wives testify to his violent temper and controlling nature: 'After a few months of marriage, for no apparent reason, the beatings began'; 'for the next twelve years, there was no intimacy or affection at all'; 'it had never occurred to her that she would not be allowed to work any more.'[23]

> *An alcoholic, a gambler and a secret bisexual, his most appalling behaviour was reserved for his three wives, whom he beat viciously and abused verbally. Ursula Groves, his first wife, would crawl into a ball on the floor as he beat and kicked her, and emerge with bruises, black eyes and cut lips. Celia Sparrow, his second wife and mother of his only child, was punched, her head regularly hit against walls. Once she was threatened with*

two carving knifes, when Carman asked: "Which one do you want in you first?" Frances Atkins, his third wife, fought back and was thrown down the stairs where she cracked her hip.[24]

None of this came to light at the time. All three women felt trapped and worthless, internalising and repressing their emotions in the hope of a safe passage. Like Rosalind B. Penfold, who wrote the graphic novel *Dragonslippers* after enduring a similar experience, 'I stayed in the hope that things would get better... I shut down my intuition, just as I'd been shutting down so many parts of myself', it wasn't until George was dead that they were able to admit 'what began with flowers ended in abuse' and that in George's case, public and private faces were utterly polarised.[25] As *The Independent's* agony aunt Virginia Ironside has observed: 'one of the downsides of excessive charm can be the excessive cruelty that sometimes lies on the other side of the coin'. Jung put it another way: An angel abroad, a devil at home.

(In a nice postscript to this particular story, Frances Atkins, George's third wife, is now chef and co-owner of the Yorke Arms in Ramsgill, which has been declared by Egon Ronay to be one of the top 25 restaurants in the country.)

The question we have not yet managed to answer satisfactorily is aired in the first stanza of Robert Graves's poem *A Slice of Wedding Cake*, written in the fifties and therefore clearly not a new problem!

Why have such scores of lovely, gifted girls
Married impossible men?
Simple self-sacrifice may be ruled out,
And missionary endeavour, nine times out of ten

By an accident of life Julia is an expert on mavericks. 'Although not always brutal, (they can be both dashing and swashbuckling) they have a huge amount in common; shape, size, bumptiousness, litigation addiction, low boredom threshold, ability to filibuster until the cows come home and the certain knowledge that laws that apply to other people do not apply to themselves. It is rare for them to expose their own actions to any moral scrutiny and they are experts at reinventing history; their internal computers are switched to auto-delete.'

It's no accident that many of our Heroines were married to men like this, who are also poor on self-knowledge. *Spike Milligan: The Biography* by Humphrey Carpenter is essential reading for anyone who has a friend or family member who suffers from manic depression, another state not uncommon in mavericks. (See The Crack-Up.) Like Carman, Spike had three wives; the first one bolted, his second wife died young from cancer, and his third wife, Shelagh, seems to have coped but was thought by friends to be equally long-suffering. According to Carpenter, he lacked self-awareness in his relationships with women. It was suggested by Anthony Clare during an interview that 'he might not be the easiest person in the world to live with', and Spike seemed 'genuinely baffled'.[26]

Mavericks can also be outrageous liars. As Paddy Ashdown said of Slobodan Milosevic, 'Milosevic was subtle and wily, but also charismatic and charming. His biggest advantage was his ability to lie straight in your face'. Obviously their wives are heroines.

You don't hear much of Mrs George Galloway or Mrs Ariel Sharon for instance. Have they have been quietly forgotten? You do hear quite a lot about Mary Archer, but as her biographer Margaret Crick has noticed, 'Mary has long been defined by reference to her husband', but he 'has deflected attention away from Mary's considerable achievements'. Something that Julia finds harder to admit is that she only had the time and money, and indeed inspiration, to write this book because she married a maverick herself.

Many of our Hey Nonny heroines offer a sharp lesson to us. Harriet Hubbard Ayer, a leading women's editor at *The World* newspaper in New York, is no exception. She wrote a widely syndicated and popular column on beauty, grooming and etiquette as well as features on social justice and women's rights.

Following a bitter divorce, she launched a beauty business, but when one of her daughters died, she fell into a depression and was prescribed morphine for insomnia and 'nerves'. She rejected the advances of her Wall Street backer James Seymour, who, determined on revenge, laid claim to her business while she was abroad and encouraged a marriage between her eldest daughter and his son. Harriet took him to court, but the resulting press coverage, including accusations that she was a drug addict, destroyed her business. The wealthy matrons of New York cut her dead, while the marriage estranged her from her daughter.

Her reputation was in shreds and her business destroyed. Just when she thought it could not get worse, it did. Her ex-husband, financed by Seymour, fought a custody battle for her youngest daughter and had Harriet committed to an insane asylum. She was incarcerated for a year and a half in solitary confinement, with a bucket for a toilet, allowed one cold shower a week and forbidden letters. She never recovered her health.

This story is told in *War Paint*, Lindy Woodhead's biography of Helena Rubenstein and Elizabeth Arden. Both women knew Harriet; both were determined that there would be no male financial controllers of their own businesses.

More recently, Harriet's story has been mirrored by the experience of other fashion designers. Amanda Wakely is one: 'My husband was my business partner. I had begun on my own but when I married Neil took charge. I became depressed and felt pushed to the limit,' she told *The Sunday Telegraph*. Her husband, who owned 100% of the business, 'grew bored' and sold the company – and in effect her name – in May 2000.

Janet Reger, the lingerie designer, who was in business with her husband, is another. In 1981, the Regers were turning over £2m a year, but Peter Reger was serially unfaithful and their marriage collapsed. The following year, the business went under too. Blaming himself, Peter Reger fell into a depression and then took his own life. Janet Reger 'steeled herself to win everything back', including the trading name that had been sold to the liquidators. She relaunched the company and in 1998 handed the business over to her daughter. Sadly she died of breast cancer last year.[27]

All the Heroines we have written about so far have been real people, but special mention must be made of the heroines of Anita Brookner's novels. She writes movingly of the existence of quiet, often unmarried, genteel women, their lowly position in society and the restrictions this places on their lives. Her protagonists are neat, undemanding and well-mannered, but often have a deep yearning to be otherwise. No one who has ever read Brookner's early novel *Look at Me* will forget the desolation felt by Fanny, who goes to her boyfriend's dinner party expecting to be guest of honour, but finds herself openly supplanted in his affections by another woman. To add insult to injury, she knows that this woman, being more sophisticated and beautiful, is thought to be 'better for him'. She has no choice but to hide her feelings and hurt pride, even though she knows the others at the party are not only aware of her humiliation but have orchestrated it.

Brookner lectured in art history and may have gained inspiration for some of her female characters from the harem of women who worked for Anthony Blunt at the Courtauld, described so memorably by Miranda Carter in her biography, *Anthony Blunt: His Lives*. All were heroines in their own way: Else Scheerer, 'his doggedly loyal' chain-smoking secretary, Margaret Whinney, the Institute's all-purpose teacher, administrator and dogsbody, Mrs Winkle, the caretaker's wife, who lived in near squalor and had terrible feet, but who 'baked fresh cakes and buns for tea each day' and poor Phoebe Pool, who was hopelessly in love with Blunt and somehow became his responsibility from the beginning of her time as a postgraduate student in 1954 until her death 17 years later.[28]

In Brookner's novels, these heroines inevitably fall in love with the handsome hero, but he never chooses them; often they have great hopes but are jilted at the last minute. They wait patiently on the sidelines, hoping their man will notice them, leave his wife or make a commitment, but he never does. Such women work diligently, but their good citizenship is never recognised. They are rather like Philip Larkin's women – hardworking, intelligent, supportive, invaluable, but endlessly disappointed.

Failure to inspire love can, for women, be as great a tragedy as a broken heart. Madeleine St. John, who like Brookner is a novelist with perfect pitch, wrote *The Essence of the Thing*, a taut, spare novel about those twin subjects, love and loss. She lived much of her life on the margins, rather like a Brookner character: 'I had a succession of little jobs in bookshops and offices. There were plenty of jobs if you got bored.'

> *She was very ill for at least the last decade of her life. Emphysema made her a virtual recluse, though her illness did not stop her smoking. Her tin of Golden Virginia was often to be seen next to her inhaler, and later, her oxygen supply. Her reclusiveness was furthered by the fact that she lived, for the last 20 years of her life, on the top floor of a house owned by the Notting Hill Housing Trust. She called herself a housing trustafarian.[29]*

The following extract from John Betjeman's poem *Eunice* portrays just this situation:

Keys with Mr Groombridge, but nobody will take them
To her lonely cottage by the lonely Oak
Potatoes in the garden but nobody to bake them
Fungus in the living room and water in the coke

I can see her waiting on this chilly Sunday
For the five forty (twenty minutes late)
One of many hundreds to dread the coming Monday
To fight with influenza and battle with her weight.

Of course, not all single women are sad, any more than married women are always cheerful. There are numerous examples of splendid, high-powered and hard-working women, way before 'glass ceilings' were invented, who worked tirelessly in public service areas like education and health. When hospitals were more traditional, matrons ran their wards with steely efficiency.

Women's education was served well by the great headmistresses; many of them stayed single and devoted their entire lives to their school and their girls. Sheila Hancock, in her memoir about her life with John Thaw, *The Two of Us*, describes the debt she felt towards her teachers: 'Life for me was full of hope. I loved learning. Our teachers were dedicated to improving our chances at a time when good jobs for women were thin on the ground. All the professions were deemed too difficult to combine with the obligatory first priority of marriage. Which is probably why my teachers were either spinsters, who may have lost fiancés in World War 1, or lesbians. Whatever the reason, I only remember one who was married, their lives were dedicated to us girls.'[30]

If many professional women were single, it was because they would not be allowed to continue working after marriage. In South Africa, married women were not allowed permanent contracts right into the seventies: the head of English at Janice's school had to reapply for her job each year (for 20 years) simply because she was married; and her newly qualified sister Gail ran into exactly the same problem when she married in 1975.

Julia in particular reads obituaries obsessively ('now I am of an age', she says) and was recently moved by some words about an Arts Council exhibition organiser called Joanna Drew who seems to epitomise what is best and most selfless in women:

> *Joanna Drew was for over 50 years a much-loved and essential figure at the heart of Britain's art world. Nobody made exhibitions better than Drew and, by her example and personal influence, she could be said to have created the profession of exhibition organiser. She was unusual in never wanting to choose the subject or the contents herself, simply to serve the artist and selector and make the best possible exhibition for the public to enjoy. Her work gave pleasure to thousands who may never have known her name, but recognition was not something ever sought by Drew, whose modesty and lack of pretension in a world famous for large egos were exemplary.*[31]

All women have heroines in their own family and Julia's is no exception. 'My great-grandmother, Harriet Greenwood, brought up seven children virtually single-handedly at the beginning of the last century. Although she struggled with rural poverty, she was fortunate in that, although all five of her sons served in the Great War, remarkably, they all returned home.'

She is reminded of Alan Bennett's Grandma Peel, another survivor of the same era:

> *Tall, dignified and straightforward, she was in every sense a big woman who had come through the tragedies of her life unembittered and with her sense of humour intact; she had seen two bankruptcies, her family reduced from relative affluence to abject poverty, the death of her only son in the trenches, and the never-spoken-of suicide of her husband which left her with three daughters to bring up on very little, and yet she remained a funny, self-sufficient, lively woman.*[32]

One of the purposes of writing this book was to try to understand why some women seem to survive relatively unscathed and some succumb to their difficulties. We still don't know; the only clue we can offer is that with their husbands dead, these two women at least were spared what Bennett has elsewhere described as 'the hare-brained schemes of husbands'.

'My own mother, Joan Bantick, born in 1921, is also a Heroine in that her life has reflected many of the difficulties and frustrations of those who were young in the war,' says Julia. 'It is hard for us now to imagine London as it was then.' As Muriel Spark writes in *The Girls of Slender Means*:

> *Long ago in 1945 all the nice people in England were poor, allowing for exceptions. The streets of the cities were lined with buildings in bad repair or no repair at all, bomb-sites piled with stony rubble, houses like giant teeth in which decay had been drilled out, leaving only the cavity.*[33]

'Although she won a scholarship to a girls' public school, the scholarship did not extend into the sixth form and thus she was denied university. She also had to leave her job in the Civil Service upon marrying in 1947, as married women were not employed at that level. Like an Anita Brookner heroine, "she read a lot and sighed a lot" and took refuge in her garden. The greatest debt I owe her is that she taught me to read very young, and once you discover the world of books and ideas, you never have to let anyone else do your thinking for you. (The fact that I have on so many foolish occasions is nobody's fault but my own.)'

Other members of the family also shaped Julia's views. There was an occasion in her childhood that was particularly formative, which happened on her uncle's estate in Norfolk; farms in those days were quite grand and still had maids and cooks. 'I was quite young, perhaps only nine or ten, and I was eavesdropping on my mother, my grandmother, my aunt and her friend. One of my aunt's maids had insisted on going down the aisle pregnant. Worse, she had tried to squeeze into her white dress and something had happened to the baby because of the squeezing.

'Between the cluster of grown-ups there were whispers of "shame" and "how could she?" but it wasn't clear whether this shame was because the dress was white, or that she had tried to conceal the pregnancy, or that she had tried to brazen it out, or the church ceremony should have been cancelled, or that it was the act of love itself, or the terrible loss of the baby (which to me seemed quite the worst thing) that was so wrong. What was certain was that the farmhand, who surely had something to do with it, was neither blamed nor discussed.

'It was seeing other women upholding this kind of injustice, woman against woman, that was so shocking. If there was a defining moment when I knew I was a feminist, that was it. Of course they themselves could never have embraced the word, it would have negated everything they'd ever stood for.'

Janice's mother, Vera Lynne French (there's no connection – although she's roughly the same age as the Forces' Sweetheart) is another Hey Nonny Heroine. 'She was born in 1922 in South Africa, and as a child became something of a ballet star, winning prize after prize. She won a ballet scholarship to study in London, but the outbreak of the Second World War forced her to stay in South Africa, and she lowered her ambitions to follow her father into the bank.

'She was petite, blonde and glamorous, and her evening pursuit of teaching ballroom dancing – a last connection with her beloved ballet – meant she had many suitors. When she met my father, she thought the tall, red-haired former Royal Navy able seaman very good-looking.

'They married and shortly afterwards left for Britain. There, despite having grown up in thirties South Africa – where attitudes to women were a good two decades behind the UK and most women gave up work upon marriage – she worked for the Bank of England in Threadneedle Street. She even persuaded them to keep her on when she became pregnant. After my sister Gail was born she worked at Harrods, round the corner from their rented flat in a Knightsbridge garden square.

'Sadly, this independence wasn't to last: Back in South Africa my father's success grew and my mother's – a very modest one, as a bookkeeper – became relatively less important. As I grew up, I saw her independence fade, her physical problems increase, gradually closing her world in as a gardening injury – a slipped disk – cost her yoga, tennis, and modern dance; she was finally forced to give up her job at a bookshop.

'Happily, her later life seemed to bring her more joy; regular visits to London to see her daughters and grandchildren and indulge her love of ballet and the theatre. In her seventies, living between South Africa and the UK, striding around London, queuing for hours for theatre returns, and taking exercise classes with a 90-year-old instructor, she confided to me that she was fitter (and had more time for herself) than she had been at 35.

'Of course, growing up in South Africa meant that there was another example of heroism set before me every day. Like most white South African families, we usually employed a housekeeper. I remember Beauty and Hester in particular (not their real names of course): women who were, like many others, single-handedly supporting their families. Housekeepers were expected to do all the cleaning, washing, ironing and cooking, and in many cases provide childcare too. It was a heavy workload, and the hours were long. Many husbands had long since disappeared, often victims of alcoholism or unemployment, or working in the mines 800 miles away. They were separated from their children, who were in the Transkei or Ciskei, being raised by their grandparents. The apartheid laws meant it would have been illegal for their children to live with them in a white area. On a tiny salary, they paid for school uniforms and textbooks (I remember being shocked to hear that white children like me got their books free).

'Just as Jill Tweedie once said her father had turned her into a feminist, seeing the difficulties faced by these women made me solidly determined to remain independent. Of course, the best-laid plans of mice – and seventies feminists – *gang aft agley.* But I didn't know that then.'

The Baize Door

Faded green, rubbed, velvety, warm:

On one side, the new wall-to-wall;
On the other, the linoleum was worn.

At the jingling of the brass bell,
With a thwack of the flapping door,

Out came Beauty, forehead damp,
Apron skew, oval platter high with food.

We sat, majestical children, swathed
In linen. Our backs were straight.

We did not clear. We did not make beds.
We did not know where the toilet rolls were kept,

Or the clean sheets. The pool sparkled.
The trees did not shed their leaves.

Janice Warman

Comment

Oh, life is a glorious cycle of song,
A medley of extemporanea;
And love is a thing that can never go
wrong;
And I am Marie of Romania.

Dorothy Parker

Enquire within

In a time of information overload, the self-help industry seems to be accelerating out of control. It targets our vulnerability and exposes insecurities we didn't even know we had.

Why exactly is it that we need yoga, feng shui, aromatherapy, massage and meditation to help us cope? Spiritual advisers, life-coaches, makeover gurus and supernannies (all experts in humiliation, at least on TV) tell us how to live our lives. Their advice is mainly directed at female shortcomings. In general, men don't have much truck with self-help; if they have a weakness, it is surely the Internet printout, which leaves them rather less exposed.

The notion of self-help books has become so 'normal' in our collective consciousness that they have become a first line of defence. When Bridget Jones fails to receive an expected call from her boyfriend, she panics: 'Why hasn't he rung? What's wrong with me? Must centre myself more. Will ask Jude about appropriate self-help book, possibly Eastern-religion based.' Instead, Jude comes up with another idea. 'She started telling me about a marvellous new oriental idea called Feng Shui which helps you get everything you want in life. All you have to do, apparently, is clean out all the cupboards in your flat to unblock yourself.'[1]

In many houses, feng shui is urgently needed purely to de-clutter the piles of self-help books. There has been such an exponential growth of such publications that women's homes are silted up with books, magazines and pamphlets. Most of these books claim to heal the planet or the person, spiritually, emotionally or physically. Others offer what the authors consider essential practical advice. Bookshops groan with them.

What is remarkable about them is their simplicity: 'Be kind to yourself'; 'Praise yourself'; 'Be your own best friend'. Their hallmark is the repetition of the mantra and the urgency with which it is repeated. Many attempt to universalise and simplify their advice in order to elevate it to pseudo-religious status. Those who do read them pay little attention to their style: their focus is primarily on the supposedly life-changing content of the text, but their success (in sales terms at least) seems to be founded on not very much at all – much like another profitable industry. As Luke Johnson notes in The *Sunday Telegraph*: 'Ex-sports stars can earn a splendid living plying their trade at after-dinner events getting paid for a few trite mottos like "Success is a choice!" '

Deborah Ross, writing about the self-help market in *The Independent*, includes a spoof review of her own imaginary bestseller, *He's Not That Into You if He's Sleeping with Someone Else*. Astonishingly, we found that there is a book called *He's Just Not That Into You: The No-Excuses Truth to Understanding Guys*. This could spark a parlour version of *Call My Bluff* – which ridiculous book title is real?

Another book we were delighted to find was *Self-Help Nation: The Long Overdue, Entirely Justified, Delightfully Hostile Guide to the Snake-Oil Peddlers Who Are Sapping Our Nation's Soul* by Tom Tiede, a book which should win an award for the length of its title alone.

Many books are conspicuously influenced by psychoanalysis and are commonly written by therapists of one discipline or another. Elisa Seagrave, in the story of her cancer, *Diary of a Breast*, gives a list of the books her therapist wants her to read: 'The number of titles made me quite giddy: Men Who Hate Women and the Women Who Love Them; Of Course You Are Angry; Adult Children of Alcoholics; If Only I Could Quit; Marriage on the Rocks; Going Home – a Re-entry Guide for the Newly Sober.'[2]

Those who don't read self-help books often despise those who do, and yet there are few of us who have not picked up a brightly coloured paperback in a weak moment and thought, 'I'll just take a look at this one, it *might* have the answer'. The industry is as seductive as it is repelling; we soak it up like blotting paper; you don't even have to be suggestible, dim, or both to get caught up in suspect self-help credos. William Leith, whose book we return to later, has this to say about a particularly popular diet guru: 'As I look at Atkins and nod along with what he is saying, I realise what it is that's been nagging at me. It's that I want to believe in him. I want him to be right. I want this because, if he is right, I will lose weight.'[3]

Yet where is the evidence that any of these books actually work? In *Misconceptions*, Naomi Wolf articulated the ambivalence many of us have towards them, particularly during pregnancy. She bought Arlene Eisenberg's *What To Expect When You Are Expecting*: 'I quickly developed a love-hate relationship with that book; I found it obfuscating and condescending, yet I needed it. Why? Because beyond the studies, science, statistics and probabilities, it reassures.' And yet for Wolf it placated too much. 'The book seemed set to reassure me about every damn thing under the sun. Birth defects? Probably not in your case, never mind, don't fret, was the tone. Been mainlining heroin? Not good, but why not stop today! By being reassuring about everything, you simply couldn't believe any of it. And yet it had sold 80 million copies worldwide.'[4]

Rachel Cusk, in *A Life's Work: On Becoming a Mother*, felt the opposite to be true; she wasn't reassured in the least. 'The literature of pregnancy bristles with threats and the promise of reprisal, with ghoulish hints at the consequences of thoughtless actions. Eat pâté and your baby will get liver damage. Eat blue cheese and your baby will get listeria. Don't drink or smoke, you murderer.'[5]

By far the most popular subject for self-help books is female anxiety about men, which makes it difficult to counter the widely held assumption that we all have relationship 'issues'.

Yet it's not as if the industry helps us get a man; in fact, rather the opposite. Polly Vernon describes in The Observer how an unattached man goes back to a woman's flat for coffee after meeting her at a dinner party. The relationship fails to progress because he catches sight of the 50 or so self-help books on her shelves and concludes he is 'trapped in the home of a nutter'.

Nor do self-help books necessarily improve an existing relationship: it is hardly surprising that many men back away in horror when they see their partners bearing down upon them with *Men are from Mars*, or feel threatened if they see *The Road Less Travelled* placed by the bedside. It is well known that self-help books terrify men. 'My own husband also used to get uncharacteristically nervous at the sight of a poetry book,' says Julia. 'Although he did like the look of Laura Schlessinger's *The Proper Care and Feeding of Husbands*. Alas, too late to save our marriage.'

This book's premise is a kind of retro self-help, i.e. 'Men have two basic needs; if I'm not horny, make me a sandwich' or basically (yes, basically) 'you have to do sex and cooking even if you don't feel like it, if you're going to keep your husband'. Deborah Ross, in *The Independent*, interpreted the book's message even more succinctly: 'Never nag, never have a career, never say no to sex.' Simple, really.

Not that the genre is new, although anything mentioning sex would have been discreetly hidden from view by Julia's fifties mother, who presumably never bought *The Joy of Sex*. However, she did own Roderick Wimpole's *Tell Me Doctor* and *Enquire Within* by Elizabeth Craig (a leading cookery writer who, following on from Mrs Beeton, wrote The Business Woman's Cookbook for the woman 'who has to run a home as well as a career'... *plus ça change*).

Enquire Within dealt with practical subjects as disparate as boning a joint, skinning a rabbit, social etiquette, knitting patterns and crazy paving; thankfully, there was no reference to the female psyche. The rather more intimate *Tell Me Doctor* was written in the form of cosy dialogues between physician and patient, which reassured women that most of their worries were bound to be unfounded; it was the kind of book that delivered a metaphorical pat on the head. In spite of its patronising tone, this book was not completely useless. Its description of menopausal symptoms is among the most accurate we have seen: 'It is difficult to get to sleep, but soon after I drop off, I wake feeling terrified for no reason at all. My heart races like mad and I feel as if I am dying.'[6]

For straightforward factual information (as well as sheer entertainment), some of these old handbooks outdo their modern counterparts. *Enquire Within* has an excellent series of diagrams on how to fix a bow tie; there are surely plenty of modern women who still struggle with this problem on the night of the company dinner. And we were amused by the section on railway journeys, which observed: 'The railway authority is bound to carry a passenger between the places mentioned on his ticket, but not necessarily by any particular train or within any particular time.' Some things never change.

In the seventies, the self-help book industry took a great leap forward; Shirley Conran wrote *Superwoman* and life famously became too short to stuff a mushroom. This was an updated *Enquire Within*, which told you how to cut down on housework but appear to do it better. It also began to address the problem of women who worked, yet were still responsible for the running of the household.

There is also some good practical advice on how to do things that were previously considered to be in the man's domain, demystifying processes such as repairing a fuse, changing a tyre, and stocking a toolbox. This sounds revolutionary for its time, yet on closer scrutiny the content is not dissimilar to more conventional handbooks on household management. Much of it is about stains and lists; hardly new topics for the housewife. It did, however, have groundbreaking (for the time) sections on starting your own business and how to deal with rape (avoid, if possible); there is nothing on separation and divorce, although it was something that was shortly to happen to Conran herself.

We were intrigued by the method Shirley used to get her family to tidy up. 'Stand a cardboard box under the kitchen table and dump everything you find in this lost property office. After a bit they prefer to tidy up their own possessions rather than sort them out of the tangle.'[7] In our experience, this only leads to the need for a bigger box.

Shirley Conran is now in her seventies but is still dispensing brisk advice. In a recent

Observer article she said: 'There are all these men looking under sofas for their lost identity. If only they could just accept that the only thing happening is that women are no longer inferior, they wouldn't feel dazed and confused.'

Fast-forward to the eighties. This was when the industry got quite out of control and as far as we can see it hasn't abated yet. We have attempted to sort the wheat from the chaff, to see what works and why; we have gone through hundreds of books, and have made a list of the few we do think genuinely help. Most of our recommendations, however, are not from the mind, body, spirit section.

Self-Help for your Nerves by Claire Weekes is our first recommendation. It was first published in 1962, but has stood the test of time. Its style is quaint but clear and it works at all levels, whether you are experiencing low-level anxiety, physical symptoms such as dizziness in crowds or shops, full-blown panic attacks, are teetering on the edge of a crack-up, or in total breakdown. At this level of collapse, you feel you may never recover, that there is no way back, and no way out, but read this book, do what it says and we feel it could help you recover. Like many self-help books, it has a mantra: 'float, accept, let time pass', but unlike most, this mantra, properly explained, actually does help. We have both used this book and it worked for us.

Malignant Sadness by Lewis Wolpert is perceptive on the causes of depression, particularly in men, and is good on the links between the physical symptoms of disease and mental health. Wolpert, a well-known scientist and broadcaster, wrote the book after suffering a breakdown, in an attempt to understand what he had been through himself. If you have a male partner or family member who needs help, this book will be extremely useful – both to you and to them.

Anthony Clare's *On Men: Masculinity in Crisis* can be illuminating if you find yourself in a support role. As women's needs and expectations change, this book deals unflinchingly with men's resulting identity problems and the difficulties they have in adapting to their new roles. Feminism is not going away and this book attempts to describe what will happen if men do not find a positive way of accommodating it.

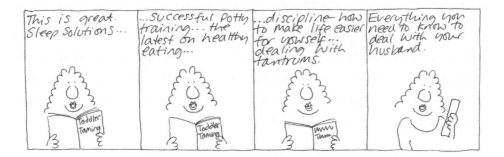

Anyone contemplating therapy would be well advised to read Anna Sands' book *Falling for Therapy: Psychotherapy from a client's point of view*. The author advises a healthy scepticism about all therapists, who are, she points out, also fallible:

> *It can feel unpleasant being analysed by someone who hardly knows you. In our everyday lives, strength of feeling is tempered by its context of day-to-day living. Our relationships arise naturally out of and are contingent on what we do together; feelings are held and balanced by the ordinariness of getting up in the morning and the business of the day. The ordinariness and the doing act as a kind of padding. In contrast, the intensity and focus of a psychodynamic relationship is out of the ordinary. There is no ballast of shared actions or common background, and the feelings that arise can be overpowering if the therapist does not act to diffuse them.*[8]

She also warns that therapy can be self-perpetuating and addictive – that in particular, isolated, depressed patients can form 'attachment problems', where the therapist becomes disproportionately important to them.

Women tend not to see illness as a failure of will – and in any case through fertility, childbirth and their role as guardian of the family's health, regularly find themselves in the doctor's surgery. A family to a forty-something woman is like a box of fireworks; she never knows which cracker is going to go off next or the size of the bang. This is when she suddenly realises what hospitals and emergency services are *really* for; heart attacks, fractured hips, punctured lungs, concussion, bike accidents and bloody noses.

Women, therefore, need to be informed about medicine. To this end, we recommend *Complications* by Atul Gawande, an insider's view of the American medical system. He is good on what patients need from doctors: 'For some patients, simply receiving a measure of understanding can be enough to control their suffering. A doctor can still help even when medications have failed.'[9(i)]

Gawande makes another important observation: 'Where many ethicists go wrong is in promoting patient autonomy as a kind of ultimate value in medicine rather than recognizing it as one value among others. Schneider found that what patients want most from doctors isn't autonomy per se; it's competence and kindness. Now, kindness will often involve respecting patients' autonomy, assuring that they have control over vital decisions. But it may also mean taking on burdensome decisions when patients don't want to make them, or guiding patients in the right direction when they do. Even when patients do want to make their own decisions, here are times when the compassionate thing to do is to press hard: to steer them to accept an operation or treatment that they fear, or forego one that they'd pinned their hopes on. Many ethicists find this line of reasoning disturbing, and medicine will continue to struggle with how patients and doctors ought to make decisions. But, as the field grows ever more complex and technological, the real task isn't to banish paternalism; the real task is to preserve kindness.'[9(i)]

He is particularly critical that mechanisms available to deal with bad doctors are often inadequate: 'Doctors are supposed to be tougher, steadier, better able to handle pressure than most. (Don't the rigours of medical training weed out the weak ones?) But the evidence suggests otherwise. Doctors are just as likely to be addicted to drugs, and are just as likely to have a serious mental disorder as the rest of the population. And doctors become ill, old and disaffected, or distracted by their own difficulties, and they falter in their care of patients.'[9(ii)]

This book helps to fill a void for women; it's thought provoking and intelligent, exposing medicine's weaknesses alongside its strengths; it's easy to navigate, and so clear you could even read it in a hospital waiting room.

It also has an excellent chapter on weight problems and the horrors of the gastric bypass operation – a procedure that is common in the US and becoming popular here too. However, by far the best book on eating problems of all kinds remains Susie Orbach's *Fat is a Feminist Issue*, which was first published in 1978, but is as useful now as it was then:

> *How we eat, what we eat, how much we eat, even whether it is okay to eat, and the relentless struggle to get our bodies the way we want them to be are still major preoccupations for women of all ages. Food and its place in women's lives continue to be painful and troublesome.*
>
> *We wish that size didn't matter, that bigness and smallness were equally appreciated. We wish that compulsive eating, bingeing, dieting, throwing up and starving were anomalies rather than the routine experience of so many women today.*[10]

Orbach is excellent on the reasons behind eating problems and how to combat them. The first thing to do is stop dieting and stop buying diet books. Gawande and Orbach agree that 95% of diets don't work, despite the $10bn spent annually in America on getting and staying thin.

William Leith, author of *The Hungry Years*, agrees; his battle with food has gone on for most of his life. His book deals with the psychology of binge eating, binge drinking and addiction in general from an excruciatingly personal point of view. It focuses on the relationship between food, sex and control; as he says,

> *Diets are not the solution.*
>
> *The problem is not the food.*
>
> *The problem is far worse than the food*[11(i)]

This book is mandatory reading for anyone trying to understand their own drinking or addiction problems, or for anyone trying to help a friend or family member, whether the trouble is incipient or full-blown. One of the problems with dependency is how hard it is to judge exactly how serious things are, especially as so much drinking and eating is done in secret. Thought processes become convoluted in the addict's mind and there is a huge amount of self-deception: 'I'm thinking that if I drink any more I'll make myself ill; I'm also thinking with a boozer's illogic that if I drink some more, my hangover will be less bad because I will sleep better.' [11(ii)]

Not many men have the extensive problem with food that Leith self-chronicles, although an ever-increasing number have male anorexia, as men become more subject to the image problems that have plagued women for centuries. It is still predominantly women who have eating disorders; men's food anxieties are often of quite a different kind. For a start, they can feel edgy if the fridge is not groaning, and food to them is often much more than just a response to hunger. Dominic Lawson writes in *The Independent*: 'When I am on holiday, it is a constant irritation to my wife – who does not share my obsession – that every day must be planned around which restaurant to go to.' We suspect this attitude is rather more prevalent than men might admit. Is it just another version of 'If I'm not horny, make me a sandwich'?

The final medical book we recommend advises on diet, but is not a diet book. It is *The Integrated Health Bible* by Dr Mosaraf Ali. It is cautious, measured and informative on preventative and alternative medicine as well as being full of common sense. One example of this is the author's insistence on relaxation and convalescence: 'Post-viral fatigue is the most common outcome of not resting for a couple of days after viral flu leaves the body weak. People are forced to rest after surgery, or a heart attack or a fracture, so why can't we rest after a viral infection, or any acute disease, for that matter?'[12]

One of the central premises of Hey Nonny is that biography and literature is often far more helpful (and frequently funnier) than traditional self-help. *Fathers and Sons*, by Alexander Waugh, is a good example of this: it is a biographical account of four generations of writers in the Waugh family, including Alexander's own father, the famously irascible Auberon, to whom self-help books would no doubt have been anathema. It is illuminating on the subject of father/son relationships, and the love, squabbles, and disappointments common to families in general. Admittedly, the

Waughs' parenting methods could be seen (at the very least) as odd:

> *My parents did not attend the passing-out parade at Mons alone I*
> *think of all the parents involved. In a way this was probably a good thing as*
> *my father would probably have worn his grey bowler or Brigade boater, and*
> *my mother, although the sweetest of women, had no sense of style. She had*
> *one fur coat, of astrakhan, but it was at least twenty years old and had lost*
> *much of its fur. It had once had rather a smart belt, but this had long been*
> *replaced by binder twine.*[13(i)]

While most mothers these days could be depended upon to avoid string round their middles, this passage illustrates the excruciating shame teenagers feel towards their parents, whose presence at school events is often anxiously checked for but who are then immediately disowned. But then, embarrassing parents are not a new problem, and neither are ungrateful children. Evelyn takes his son for a day out:

> *On Wednesday I took him to the Zoo. On Friday I devoted the day to*
> *him, hiring a car to fetch him from Highgate. I wore myself out for his*
> *amusement taking him up the Dome of St. Paul's, buying him three-cornered*
> *postage stamps and austerity toys, showing him London from the top of an*
> *hotel, taking him to tea with his godmother who gave him a sovereign and a*
> *box of variegated matches. I took him back to Highgate in a state of*
> *extreme exhaustion. My mother said, "Have you had a lovely day?" He*
> *replied "A bit dull".* [13(ii)]

From children we turn to the elderly, since Hey Nonny readers usually have to deal with both. *A Short History of Tractors in Ukrainian* by Marina Lewycka is a must-read for anyone who fears her father may be a victim of 'distasteful sexual awakening' or what John Betjeman called 'late-flowering lust'. Here is a description of the new girlfriend:

> *Then I see her - a large blonde woman, sauntering down the garden*
> *towards us on high-heeled peep-toe mules. Her gait is lazy, contemptuous, as*
> *though she can barely be bothered to stir herself to greet us. A denim mini*

skirt rides high above her knees, a pink sleeveless top stretches around
voluptuous breasts that bob up and down as she walks.[14]

Perhaps the most surprising thing about this book, though, is the compassion felt by the narrator for her father, in love with and duped by the Ukrainian girlfriend who is after a passport; and its ultimately redemptive (but not, thank goodness, sentimental) ending.

The Waiting Game, a novel by Bernice Rubens, is a wonderful burlesque on the elderly, treating old age as the black comedy it is, dealing with dementia, disinhibition, and late-onset misogyny. When one of the women gives way to hysteria, the male response is universal: ' "That's the trouble with women. Especially this lot here. What they need is you know what." "A good fuck, you mean." '[15(i)]

Set in a home for the active elderly, The Hollyhocks, it swiftly dispenses with the idea that people randomly assembled in their dotage are going to get on any better than any other group in a different age bracket. The inhabitants of the house bicker like a group of pre-school children, vie for superiority and mercilessly compete with each other for social status: 'Mrs Thackeray had been born in Croydon, but she chose Hampstead in London for her birthplace.'[15(ii)]

Classic literature can reflect contemporary realities; witness the unparalleled popularity of Jane Austen, whether in book form or in endless TV and film adaptations. We have chosen Arnold Bennett's *The Old Wives' Tale* because it is a novel primarily concerning the lives of two women, with the understanding and insight of a woman, but written by a man.

As Bennett writes in the preface, the first premise of this novel is that 'there is extreme pathos in the mere fact that every stout ageing woman was once a young girl with the unique charm of youth in her form and movements and in her mind. And the fact that the change from young girl to the stout ageing woman is made up of an infinite number of infinitesimal changes, each unperceived by her, only intensifies the pathos.'[16(i)]

The Old Wives' Tale is a page-turner that has everything: marriage, motherhood, murder and madness. Set in the mid-Victorian era, it tells the story of the Baines sisters

– shy, retiring Constance and defiant, romantic Sophia – over the course of nearly half a century. There are some wonderful characters; the villain Gerald Scales, dashing but dastardly ('a less innocent girl than Sophia might have divined that she could do anything with Gerald except rely on him') and an indolent son ('Cyril earned nothing, living in comfort on an allowance from his mother'); the largely unspoken, lifelong sibling rivalry and power struggle is well documented; 'it had been only by a wearying expenditure of nervous force that Constance had succeeded in holding a small part of her own against the unconscious domination of Sophia'.[16(ii)]

Seeing how other women have led their lives can be a revelation. Selena Hastings' biography of one of our Heroines, Rosamond Lehmann, is a vivid portrait spanning most of the twentieth century. In portraying her life, it describes every woman's life, the joys, disappointments and failures – in particular the failure of love – and in Rosamond's case, the sadness and bitterness of old age.

She made an early marriage to a man she did not love, had a happier second marriage and two children with Wogan Phillips, and then a long affair with the poet C. Day Lewis, which was happy for many years, but which ended badly. Her beloved daughter Sally died very young, after which, like many who lost relatives in the First World War, she turned to spiritualism.

Perhaps the most poignant part of the book charts Rosamond's descent into old age. She had been a beauty in her youth, so this metamorphosis was shocking. Her dress sense grew ever more bizarre: 'As her girth increased, she wore a series of tent-shaped garments in pastel colours…in which she would come sailing forth like a great balloon.'[17] A warning, if ever there was one.

However, our main reason for recommending this biography (and all her fiction, re-issued by Virago towards the end of her life) is to echo Marghanita Laski's words: 'No English writer has told of the pains of women in love more truly or movingly.'

Our final suggestion is *Slipstream*, Elizabeth Jane Howard's autobiography: a cautionary tale, which could be subtitled 'difficulties with men'. The story of her relationships illustrate perfectly the Wendy Cope poem, *Rondeau Redouble*:

There are so many kinds of awful men
One can't avoid them all. She often said
She'd never make the same mistake again:
She always made a new mistake instead.

Jane's first marriage was to the older naturalist, Peter Scott. 'I was secretly amazed that someone so old and glamorous should notice me, and I wanted to be in love with him.'[18(i)] How easy it is when young to be in love with love.

This marriage foundered all too quickly, and Jane found, like many women, that although she had no difficulty attracting men, they all wanted her for one thing. A musician: 'I went down to get the whisky and soda. When I returned it was to find him without his trousers'; a psychiatrist: 'He lunged off his chair suddenly and enclosed me in a vice-like grip'; a publisher: '…became amorous and mildly blackmailing'. [18(ii)]

She comes up hard against that universal female problem, the gap between sex and love. She was 'tired of being taken to dinner by a series of men who, baldly speaking, seemed to expect me to pay for my dinner by going to bed with them'.[18(iii)] This is a difficulty that seems to be handed down for each generation to grapple with in its own way: Do you capitulate? Pay your share? Stop going out? Pick up the bill and demand sex yourself? Answers to heynonny.com, please…

We believe that when it comes to information and education, good biographies of women, particularly writers and artists, are as helpful as the majority of self-help books. By viewing one woman's life from start to finish, we can learn much.

As Elizabeth Jane Howard says in her summing up, 'I've slowly learned some significant things – perhaps most of all the virtue, the extreme importance of truth, which, it seems to me now, should be continually searched for and treasured when any piece of it is found.'[18(iv)]

What makes each of the books we have put forward so valuable is that they are all based on personal experience and have all been written as a response to a deep-seated and passionate need to find out the truth, which seems to us, above all else, what true self-help should be about.

Advice

"Accept the stretch," my yoga teacher said.
"Then you will bend further. So!"
She meant, I think, that if you give in
You're closer to letting go.

She may be right. But I was
Younger and more supple then,
And the world hadn't dealt me so many knocks,
And my figure was nearer a ten.

But I still remember
The sun through the Clapham skylight.
That bright, still December,
And her voice: she was right;
"Accept the stretch. Then you will bend further."
And I feel closer to letting go.

Janice Warman

Pause

The question is
Whether I'm peri- or post;
Is my sex appeal
The least, or the most?

Will soya bread do it,
Or oily fish?
Or should HRT
Be my only wish?

Oh, I'm in the menopause mangle,
I'm as limp as a rag;
Night sweats and day sweats,
It's such a drag.

I go to my doctor
He says I'm too young;
He listens to my chest,
He looks at my tongue.

Patch it up, put it on,
Fat, thin, right or wrong:
Peri-, post, or right in the middle
We've got ourselves in a frightful muddle

So let's raise a glass
To post-menopausal zest:
It's got to be better
Than peri-meno-stress.

Janice Warman

Metamorphosis

We couldn't write a book about mid-life without mentioning menopause. The word is both pejorative and taboo, so we decided to call this chapter Metamorphosis – which reflects a change of state even if it's more redolent of beautiful butterflies than hot flushes. Menopause needs to be dragged out of the dark ages and have a bright light shone upon it.

There has been some progress. *The Vagina Monologues* has reclaimed another word that most people couldn't even bring themselves to say; and we note that *Menopause: The Musical* is now showing in theatres across the world.

Roughly speaking, a third of women experience hormonal problems before their periods cease, a third have more difficulties after menopause itself and some (lucky) women do not even notice its passing and simply sail through the menopause years. Menopause is merely uncomfortable for some, but for a few it is an illness in the sense that it suspends normal life; few women escape its consequences altogether.

You would think that by now it wouldn't scare people so much, but it comes right after menstruation in the list of 'm' words that frighten men. A fact used to good effect by Caroline Quentin as Maggie in the ITV series *Life Begins*, warning off the school thug who has designs on her daughter: 'I'm your worst nightmare – a menopausal woman.'

Men can be impatient with menopausal symptoms, as can women who haven't experienced them. (Imagine, for a moment, if men experienced them …it's a delicious thought.) Pre-menopausal women may be less than sympathetic towards those who 'succumb' to HRT. There is inevitably a friend keen on animal protection who is more than happy to tell you of its provenance (mare's urine), while others dismiss the alternative brigade as mumbo jumbo. But it really is hard to appreciate how disabling as many as 40 hot flushes a day can be unless you are having them yourself.

Herbal remedies have their place in the treatment of menopausal symptoms, and there are many excellent books that outline the natural approach. It's possible to cherry-pick the best remedies from allopathic and alternative medicine; herbalists have good results with menopausal clients who can't tolerate HRT, and many women find that herbal remedies can be very effective in combating specific symptoms.

Of course, they don't appeal to or work for everybody. 'I have to say that with the exception of hypericum, which I did find useful, they did nothing for me, although I gamely swallowed menopause tincture for several weeks,' says Julia.

'For women experiencing raging hormonal symptoms, there are few alternatives to HRT and it is well known that people who find certain medicines beneficial are less likely to notice side effects. In the early days of the Pill, minor considerations of breast tenderness or increased risk of thrombosis seemed negligible compared to the social advantages.'

The symptoms of menopause have little definition, can mimic symptoms of more serious illness and are often worsened by stress or even simple viruses like the common cold. This stage in life can be characterised by nothing worse than listlessness or lack of direction, and the onset can be insidious or dramatic. There is even doubt about what the word menopause means and how long it actually lasts. Peri-menopause in some books refers to the time after the periods cease as well as the years preceding, while 'climacteric' is an all-embracing term for the years of transition, which can last a month – or ten years.

Most of the major symptoms like night sweats (men, read no further) are well known but there are other disturbances which are more alarming including palpitations, insomnia, dizziness, anxiety and nausea; no two women seem to have exactly the same combination of symptoms or even have them at the same age. Neither is there is any certainty about timing. It can happen at any stage between 40 and 55, with some women still experiencing symptoms into their sixties. One study of Swedish women found that 15% were still getting hot flushes 16 years after their last period. And in some societies, like Japan, where women eat less animal protein and fat but do eat more soya – rich in plant oestrogens – menopause is practically symptom-free.

It is a paradox that before periods cease (any unlikely man still reading stop now) they often get heavier and more painful, and the womb becomes cluttered with fibroids. (Any brave man still reading, faint now.) Menorrhagia, as it's known, is hard to bear, and hysterectomy is frequently prescribed, although this treatment could now be considered as out of date. Many women do not seek help, according to the National Institute of Clinical Excellence (NICE) because they fear a surgical solution that (if the ovaries are also removed) will plunge them into menopause.

In fact, other options are available: these include (and this is far from a definitive list) tranexamic acid, which reduces bleeding; Mirena, a progesterone-releasing IUD, and endometrial ablation, which destroys the lining of the womb, using heat or microwaves, but which does not affect fertility.

As Dr. Janey Huber points out in a letter to *The Independent*: 'The vast majority of hysterectomies performed in Britain for heavy periods are both recommended by and carried out by men. I am not sure that stopping periods is the solution here so much as stopping male gynaecologists.'

And Angela Davis, in a letter to the same paper, puts forward a powerful argument in favour of leaving nature to run its course as much as possible:

While women should have every possible help with the pain of dysfunctional menstruation, the powers and cycles of nature should not be suppressed. If we deny the cycles of our body, we deny something central to our human existence. To embrace ourselves as cyclic beings within the great rhythm of the universe is an important step towards our individual harmony both spiritually and physically.

Sometimes, however, there is no alternative to radical surgery. The poet Dorothy Molloy, in what was sadly her first and last collection, *Hare Soup*, has written an evocative poem about that most forbidden of subjects. How similar it is to having a broken heart – and yet it is something that can barely be spoken about:

Burial

*I made a little coffin
for my womb,
of hardwood, lined with velveteen
and plush.*

*I went to my own funeral,
behind the garden
shed; summoned angels
to escort me*

*into Paradise. The honeysuckle
wept.
The purple fuchsia bled
upon the ground.*

I rang the blue-bells loud.
And in the hush
I cut the sod and sank the box
and topped it
with a stone. Lilies sprouted
in the grass:
Amaranthus, Agapanthus,
Amaryllis.

Snapdragons guard the spot.

Dorothy Molloy

Women who have had surgery may be given HRT to alleviate menopausal symptoms. However, women suffering from breast cancer (whether or not they are in menopause) are often prescribed Tamoxifen, which can have the opposite effect. In blocking oestrogen activity, it is a drug that sometimes causes unbearable menopausal symptoms – symptoms which patients have no choice but to withstand in order to keep their primary illness at bay.

All too often, the menopause does not arrive alone; it is not uncommon for the thyroid to under-function during these years and the symptoms of one may be confused with the other. If you have tiredness, weight gain, poor concentration and thinning hair it is worth considering asking for a thyroid function test as well.

One of the rarely remarked upon but most difficult things about menopause is not knowing how you are going to feel from one day to the next; this makes you chary of making arrangements and can ultimately be isolating.

And this is not the end of it! The body changes. There is thickening like custard and then slippage; it happens so slowly you don't notice the landslide. It's a matter of gravity and as a friend said, 'like toast burning, once it starts, there's no stopping it'.

It's not even a slow curve downwards; one day you wake up and realise you have bumped miles down the incline. No wonder we are invisible to men. As one middle-aged man of our acquaintance has said: 'The trouble with women is they get less attractive and more difficult.'

It is also hard to get the fashion thing right. We've done a lot of looks in our time, starting with stilettos and stockings (this book is particularly for those who can remember suspender belts and the colour 'American tan'), Mary Quant and Biba (fantastic clothes at affordable prices), cheesecloth and flower power, Ossie and Celia, platforms, wedges, shoulder pads, back-combing, inky eyes, with bra and without we have strutted our stuff. But where we are now, this is the really hard part. As the body changes, the fab clothes we once wore no longer flatter. It is all too easy to turn into 'middle-aged woman, size 22'. It could happen overnight. And we can't improve upon what Fay Weldon says: 'The body is wilful and usually goes the way a person very much hopes it won't.'[1]

Sometimes the marriage goes too; adultery is very popular in middle age. There is many a mother arranging her daughter's wedding with her own relationship in disarray. Or there can be a collision of hormones between an angst-ridden adolescent daughter and a hot-and-bothered mother; a combustible cocktail, especially if there is a testosterone-fired teenage son in the mix too.

As noted earlier, experience of menopause varies widely. One woman will say that she didn't notice any effect – her periods simply stopped one day. Another may suffer from hot flushes for a decade. 'You learn to dress in layers,' said a sculptor, now in her sixties, who eventually went to her doctor for HRT after a particularly monumental hot flush. 'I only ever went purple once, when we were taking people out to dinner on holiday in France. I didn't know I was purple. People kept asking how I was and I kept saying I was all right, but all I wanted to do was go outside and lie on the grass!'

A graphic designer, on the other hand, is sailing through her early fifties: 'The ending of my menstrual cycle is not something that I am sad about at all; in fact, quite the opposite. It has been relatively easy so far. I have had no hot flushes, except those experienced nightly from drinking what is possibly too much wine.'

Certainly, Julia's experience of the metamorphosis did *not* make her feel like a butterfly!

'For me the menopause started slowly. I was 43. I'd felt tired and generally lacking in energy for some months, which at first I put down to the responsibility of having very young children, and then without warning, more ghastly symptoms began in earnest. My energy levels plummeted and I found I could not sleep at all and if I did get to sleep I would wake on the hour with heart racing, acute anxiety and in a cold sweat.

'It certainly made the sleep disturbance I had experienced with the babies inconsequential, even laughable. Now I would get up in the morning and race out into the garden in my pyjamas, so urgent was my need for cold fresh air. When my legs weren't shaking they were completely wooden; other people have described this as "wading through treacle". I had strange pains all over my body and my brain had completely disengaged. Even the smallest problems were insurmountable; getting my elder child to school and home again was all I could manage in a day, and I could barely look after my younger one without help. I also felt frightened at being left alone and suffered both claustrophobia and agoraphobia.

'These conditions were so unlike me as to be unreal; previously, I had spent ten years on the Bakerloo line in the rush hour and had walked my first child five miles a day in his pushchair across the open heathland of Ashdown Forest. In short, a switch had been thrown, my metabolism and body clock was completely out of kilter; if I had been a heroin addict experiencing cold turkey, I doubt I could have felt worse.

'What would become of me, my children and my marriage? My husband was at first irritated, then concerned, then in a fury and finally in denial. There was none of that magazine-speak stuff: "If he loves you and you have an otherwise good relationship, he will try to understand your difficulties."

'Then something small but good happened; I had a chance call from a childhood friend who said she'd started on HRT because she didn't feel "all there in the head". Well, among other things, neither did I, and in spite of my brain not working something clicked. I persuaded my GP to prescribe oestrogen pills. To begin with these didn't do much, but they did make me think I could be on the right track.

'After a few months of trying out different pills and patches prescribed by an increasingly forbearing doctor, I was eventually put on a 100 microgram patch of Evorel and eureka! For the first time in 18 months, I actually felt normal. In my experience, it is not just important to make the right choice between pills and patches but the transmission of oestrogen from different types of patches can make all the difference.'

There is fierce debate about HRT; the pendulum has swung to and fro in spite of the number of high profile women who sing its praises. Teresa Gorman has been fronting the campaign tirelessly for years. According to Dr. James LeFanu in *The Sunday Telegraph*, Teresa reveals in her recent book *Hooray for HRT* that both Lady Thatcher and the late Queen Mother have been devotees. As he says, 'Need one say more?'

Women may find it difficult to make decisions about their treatment because of the conflicting advice and sensational headlines in the newspapers. There is nothing the press likes more than an 'HRT is dangerous' story – just as every new bit of research about the contraceptive pill once made the headlines. The stop-start headlines can be confusing.

Take, for example, the revelations in April 2005 that hundreds of thousands of women in the UK have needlessly abandoned the treatment because of adverse publicity. In reality, the risks attached to it are very small. It is simply the reporting of those risks that often gives them added weight.

Many women who could benefit are afraid of taking HRT and others give up too soon. Even in women taking HRT for 10 years or more (and Julia is one of them), the increased risk of breast cancer is only around 0.5%, which is less than the increased risk associated with being overweight – in fact, some studies done in the US have been skewed by the fact that so many women on HRT were obese.[2]

The consensus at the time of writing is that HRT should not be taken for more than five years, but by the time this book goes to print it is quite likely that this view will have changed. Some studies say it decreases the risk of Alzheimer's, as oestrogen is good for the brain. 'This does not surprise me,' says Julia. 'When my symptoms were first evident and I began to lose it, it occurred to me that this must be like the first stages of dementia, a kind of slipping away, which were so well documented by John Bayley in his book about Iris Murdoch, *Elegy for Iris*.'

It is strange that drugs that have led to such great improvements in women's lives are so often vilified, yet the parallel development of Viagra – available on the Internet and now over the counter at Boots – has been greeted with such joy that it is now frequently misused as a recreational drug. You don't find women taking HRT for fun. Or do you? It's been reported that hormone patches improve women's sex lives to such an extent that they will be able to continue intercourse into their eighties. Netdoctor.co.uk has reported that:

> *Ironically, many women discover a renewed or even redoubled libido if they start taking hormone replacement therapy for menopausal symptoms and not uncommonly report that their husbands can no longer keep up with their sexual demands.*

Not like the old days, when women swapped sex for gardening on the dot of 50. Perhaps men will tolerate treatments that enhance women's lives if they can see something in it for them – or will they get grumpy when prostate problems take hold and we are still feeling frisky?

Despite the debate, it is important to remember that HRT is not a new treatment; Janice's mother was on a form of it for decades and is now 84, with the bones of a 40-year-old. The paternal GP in *Tell Me Doctor*, published in 1954, allays his patient's fears: 'There are all kinds of glandular preparations; oestrogen, thyroid, and so on that will make up any deficiency, and all kinds of sedatives too.'[3] These 'sedatives' presumably meant Valium or diazepam, the addictive but once popular 'mother's little helper'.

In fact, Estrogen Replacement Therapy, or ERT, as it was then called, was first given to women in the 1930s by intra-muscular injection. But oestrogen-only therapies demonstrably increased the incidence of breast and uterine cancers, and by the 1970s, progesterone was added to mimic hormone production in pre-menopausal women.

HRT is here because women have demanded it; like the Pill, it has transformed women's lives. To demonstrate how much change was needed, it is necessary to go back a few years…to around 1840, when doctors began to investigate female fertility and the ovaries: '[The ovaries] were thought to be the autonomous control centre of sex and reproduction from which all difference between the sexes flowed. However, if womanhood was admirable and moral and the ovaries were the source of these virtues, then it followed when the ovaries stopped functioning women stopped being attractive and moral and instead became hideous. One doctor wrote, "This unwomanly condition undoubtedly renders her repulsive to a man, while her envious overbearing temper renders her offensive to her own sex".'[4]

The wives of the Lake District poets confirm that menopause in the nineteenth century was a difficult business: 'The women were now in their forties. Mary went through the menopause shortly after Willy's birth and resigned herself to the idea that she would have no more children. Dorothy, in particular, was ageing fast: "she looks nearer 60 than 50 in her profile, owing to her extreme leanness and the loss of her teeth". Sarah felt herself to be "an object of commiseration; for I am so increased in size". When

Sara Hutchinson congratulated herself on never having been a beauty and so having nothing to lose, Sarah Coleridge sighed for the loss of hers and admitted that she could not bear to look at herself in the mirror for it "is not a bit of a matter what one puts on when one is grown such a fright". Mary Lovell, who was once a "lively talented girl", had grown into a disappointed, embittered woman and she began to suffer from mysterious illnesses of a nervous and possible gynaecological origin.'[5(i)]

Without contraception, child-bearing went on into the women's forties, there being no let up on the husband's part in spite of the apparent fragility of his spouse. Women who have been prone to depression earlier in life seem particularly vulnerable at this time: When Edith Southey, wife of Robert, reached middle age she was 'beginning to show symptoms of mental disturbance graver than the bouts of depression she had always been prone to'. In a lucid moment, she told Southey she 'feared she was going mad'. She had her final child at the age of 45 and 'for many months this has occasioned so much bodily ailment and so much depression of spirits'. When her daughter died, 'she (unsurprisingly) plunged into an abyss from which she never emerged'. [5(ii)]

At the beginning of the twentieth century, we find that unfortunately not all that much has changed. In her memoir, *Eating Children*, Jill Tweedie describes what many of our mother's generation felt about being female: 'What Mother knew was that, whatever their age, the female sex was in a constant state of mental riot due to being Unwell, her word for menstruation and its all-encompassing accessories. Women were Unwell before being Unwell; Unwell; Unwell after being Unwell; Unwell while expecting; catastrophically Unwell having and enfeebled for at least three months after, or until Unwell started again. All these Unwellnesses, she would explain, came together at fifty to form one Great Unwellness lasting approximately ten years.'[6(i)]

When Jill attempts to confide in her mother about the feelings of disorientation and unreality she experiences on her own approach to fifty – 'Mother, I cried, I'm lost, I'm not myself. I don't know who I am anymore' – her mother replies that this is not at all unusual in their family: 'Mother perked up no end. "I can't say I'm surprised", she responded in the enriched voice she reserved for trouble. "Your Aunt Fay at your age, well it took five men to hold her down. Your Aunt Abbey went upstairs and didn't come down for seven years. Your cousin Eve ..." ' [6(ii)]

There is anecdotal evidence that late motherhood can trigger menopause, as it did for Mary Wordsworth. Morag Mctaggart, the mother of Julia's greatest friend, gave birth to her second child at forty and never had another period. Fay Weldon is on record as saying that she had her last child in her forties and started on HRT soon after. Miranda Ingrams, in an article in *The Times*, reports on two women who suffered severe menopausal symptoms shortly after the birth of their children.

Bridget Miles tells her: 'Now I'm 45, menopausal with three small children and I cannot cope. From a fit, lively, intellectually fulfilled older mother, I've turned into a drugged out zombie swallowing every anti-depressant and menopause treatment available. I can barely make a cup of tea and I sit there sweating, aching and bursting into tears.' Another interviewee, Christina Newell, also 45, is completely ruined by the relentless misery of an unexpected early menopause. 'I'm exhausted, I can't sleep, I suffer from hot flushes, my legs and hips ache constantly and the hormones are raging.'

Menopause can be a melancholy time for childless women. In *Giving Up The Ghost*, Hilary Mantel (one of our Heroines) laments her childlessness as she passes fifty, particularly as her friends are becoming grandmothers: 'The time I fell in love is the time I should have acted. I miss the child I never had. I know what Catriona would have been like. She would be nothing like me at all. She would drive a car and sing in tune and know about things like making curtains.'[7]

The journalist Jan Masters wrote in *The Times* about the disappointment of not having children and says she feels that to many people 'involuntary childlessness is about failure', but to many women, it is just as easily 'a product of misaligned life moments'. Many women will recognise the reality of being 'easily drawn to alpha males who are yet to develop their nesting instincts'. Commitment-phobe men can be a problem to today's women, as shotgun weddings are more or less a thing of the past.

Perhaps it is just as important for young women to read this book, take heed and make hay while the sun shines. However, as Deborah Orr has observed in *The Independent*, 'Women have little choice if they wish to succeed in their education and careers, but to defer the having of children as long as they can'.

There is another strange phenomenon that is seemingly counter-intuitive. Sometimes women who have reconciled themselves to childlessness finally hit their stride in their early forties. We have several friends who far from finding their fertility in decline, suddenly conceived naturally when they were least expecting it; sometimes this is a long-awaited second child, and sometimes it's the first. The painter India Jane Birley, interviewed in *Harper's Bazaar* in 2005, describes her transformation from a state of mourning over not having a child – 'in painterly form it would be awash with blue-black ink' – to her 'miraculous conception'. 'I didn't know I was pregnant for ages, I thought I had a serious disease.'

The average age at which women have children is constantly rising. They often wait until they are financially secure, or to be sure they are with the right partner. Helen Fielding, creator of the ultimate thirty-something singleton Bridget Jones, is a case in point, having given birth to her first child at 43.

If this trend continues, first-time motherhood and menopause could become a common combination, replacing the traditional empty nest syndrome.

Whatever happens, you are damned if you do and damned if you don't. Women who have children later are often thought of as selfish and ambitious and older mothers receive the same disapproval ratings as pregnant teenagers. Older fathers escape this opprobrium, although as Polly Toynbee pointed out when the story of 'menopausal mum' Patricia Rashbrook broke:

> *Oh yuk! A mother at 63! The woman's a child psychiatrist, shouldn't she know better? How selfish! How grotesque! Here we go, the old war cry goes up again against wicked women who defy nature and refuse to accept their fate. Well, defying nature is often human progress. Mother Nature was never women's (or men's or children's) best friend. Red in tooth and claw,*

she murdered mothers in childbirth by the million, leaving children orphaned at a tender age as often as not. Kindly nature slaughtered young children in great battalions too. She left great regiments of women infertile, to their despair. So let's set aside the "nature knows best" nonsense. Defying nature is often a victory.

...It is an enjoyable coincidence that The Guardian *ran a feature on old fathers, after news that sperm isn't what it was after 40. The gallery of elderly dads included John Humphreys, Rod Stewart and the scary sight of Rupert Murdoch. "These ubermensches can still do it!" But women? Oh no, oh yuk!*[8(i)]

Did anyone comment on the fact that Patricia's husband was of a similar age to her? Not that we saw. Polly's colleague, Zoë Williams, argued that the outcry showed equality between the sexes is still far off: 'Any cultural flashpoint regarding the sexuality of older women, from Edwina Currie admitting her affair with John Major to this 62-year-old giving birth, scratches the surface-morality and underneath is "Ew! Put it away! How could you be so disgusting?" I don't think, as cultural mores go, that it's one to spend a lot of time pioneering against. But it's an interesting insight into how far gender parity has yet to advance, all the same.' [8(ii)]

Body Shop founder Anita Roddick has said: 'The older you get, the more radical you become.' So – have a baby, take a younger lover, change your life, court controversy: after all, menopause is metamorphosis: it has the power to help you transform yourself.

However bad you are feeling, there is light at the end of the tunnel; however terrible your symptoms or your circumstances, recovery can and will happen and when we are through it all and out the other side, there is 'post-menopausal zest' to look forward to – the term coined by the great anthropologist, Margaret Mead.

We can't believe any man can still be reading this but here comes the last straw; (look away now!) because there's something else to celebrate: a farewell to sanitary pads and tampons. As Deborah Ross has written in *The Independent*: 'Mini, Regular, Maxi, Everyday, Every Other Day, Incredibly Thin, Incredibly Fat, Super, Super Plus,

Overnight, Teatime, Elevenses, Long, Super Long, Extra Super Long'; it's goodbye to all that, subterfuge, embarrassment and all.

Then there is sex. Diane Keaton has said in *The Week*, 'You are suddenly free from it. And thank God for that'. Or as Beryl Bainbridge, who is now in her sixties, put it: 'I have recently abandoned sex, as at my age I consider it uncomfortable and undignified.'

However, not all women live without it or want to; apparently STDs are growing fastest in women over 45. 'When I first read this,' says Julia, 'I believed it to be the knock-on effect of husbands/partners playing away, but now I'm not so certain, having got up to a bit of Hey Nonny myself recently. Or, as Sophie Hannah has it in *Before Sherratt & Hughes Became Waterstones*:

> *I've seen a few customers looking dismayed,*
> *Too British to voice their objection,*
> *But how can I help it? I like to get laid*
> *Just in front of the poetry section.*

'I now feel sure there must be a body of women out there having fun without need of contraception whose husbands are divorced, dead or in retreat. Maybe it's not necessarily a good thing to hang onto stale relationships – is it in fact possible to be married for too long? Can freedom from marriage be as liberating as freedom from parenting? And think of what you can do if these things happen together!'

And how liberating not to have to worry about contraception. Think of Diane Keaton's joyous cry in the film *Something's Gotta Give,* when Jack Nicholson asks what she is planning to use: 'Menopause!'

Julia recently congratulated her mother on her sixtieth wedding anniversary and said she didn't think many of her own generation would achieve the same. Her mother said: 'Perhaps it's just as well. I would never enter into a lifetime commitment with anyone again.'

But then, remaining single can be disadvantageous too. As Fay Weldon points out: 'No-one wants mothers to remarry...Leaving aside matters of love, loyalty and companionship, without a partner for an excuse, a woman quickly gets roped in to do baby-sitting, emergency dashes to hospital, fund-raising, caring for aged parents (decades out of her life), collecting others from stations.'[9] In fact, families put any number of obstacles in the woman's way.

Jill Tweedie, who suffered so many reversals in her early life (see Hey Nonny heroines), had a happy last marriage to Alan Brien before her tragically early death. This is what she said about him: 'He loves me for what is lovable in me and distances himself from what is not. He looks at me carefully with the world's eyes as well as the eyes of love. I know him to be accurate in his assessments and so I know where I am.' And she quotes the song:

At seventeen
I fell in love quite madly
With eyes of a tender blue
At twenty-four
I got it rather badly
For eyes of a different hue
At thirty-five
I flirted rather sadly
With two or three or more
But when I thought that I was past love
It was then I met my last love
And I loved him as I'd never loved before.[10]

It is heartening to know that such happiness is possible. And in all likelihood it is happening everywhere; you only have to witness the number of older couples walking hand in hand. Even accounting for revisionism, there are plenty of gravestones that read: 'To my dear wife, much loved and missed.'

And there is more evidence: According to an article in *The Independent* in 2004, 'In Britain, one of the most dramatic falls is in suicide among women age 45-75, which now stand at one third of the level in the 1960s'. Divorce rates may have soared and tensions between family and career sharpened but women are less desperate, not more. Women no longer feel stifled by bad relationships or are too scared to leave. More sex, less sex, no sex; at least from now on, it's up to us.

Finally, we offer an entry from a correspondent in Simon Hoggart's book on Round Robin letters, *The Cat that could open the Fridge*: 'My periods seem to have stopped at last. I'm overweight and hope that I don't gain more. I have been looking for a camper van.'[11]

If there is a point to this chapter, it is to reassure our readers that this last option is *not* inevitable.

Things

There are worse things than having behaved foolishly in public.
There are worse things than these miniature betrayals,
committed or endured or suspected; there are worse things
than not being able to sleep for thinking about them.
It is 5 a.m. All the worse things come stalking in
and stand icily about the bed looking worse and worse and worse.

Fleur Adcock

Sleep

Women are the sex who don't sleep.

This is not an issue when you are young and in love ('Not to sleep for pure joy'); when you are a student, it is easy to party or work through the night. But when you have children it is a different matter. And to any 'woman of a certain age' it can be a great problem; in fact, the fear of not sleeping can be worse than the insomnia itself.

There are many reasons for disturbed sleep in women: premenstrual bloating, headaches, moodiness and abdominal cramps; pregnancy with nausea, heartburn and pressure from the baby on the bladder; menopause with hot flushes, palpitations and night sweats. More women than men suffer from night time pain, such as migraine, tension headaches, rheumatism and arthritis.

New research shows that lack of sleep is as damaging as poor diet and lack of exercise, can alter metabolism and hormone function, damage the immune system, raise blood pressure (higher risk of heart attack) and lower insulin production (risk of diabetes). Too little sleep also means you produce less growth hormone, which controls levels of fat and muscle. So it can even make you put on weight...is there no justice?

Most of us will already have been through years of young babies and children waking at night and will have stumbled red-eyed through too many days, whether at home or at work. And we know why sleep deprivation is such an effective form of torture; leaden-limbed and fuddle-headed, we would readily have signed any confession offered to us when our children were young.

For Janice, with young children and a freelance career, nights were when most work was done. Sleep was a luxury; and occasionally a deadline meant working right through the night.

When she returned to work at *The Guardian*, her son still breastfed at 2am and rose for the day at 5.30am; by the time she arrived at work after a two-hour commute, she'd been up for five hours. A (male) colleague observed the carpetbags under her eyes and remarked: 'You're the only one here on the night shift as well.'

Dick Davis uses children as an apt analogy for insomnia:

6 a.m. Thoughts

As soon as you wake they come blundering in
Like puppies or importunate children;
What was a landscape emerging from mist
Becomes at once a disordered garden.

And the mess they trail with them! Embarrassments,
Anger, lust fear – in fact the whole pig-pen;
And who'll clean it up? No hope for sleep now –
Just heave yourself out, make the tea, and give in.

Dick Davis

It's not surprising to learn that new mothers get two hours less sleep a night than their parents did. While their own mothers may have been able to catch up on their sleep during the day, parents today are often tired out by trying to juggle work with a new baby.

Susan Johnson says in her book, *A Better Woman*: 'In the darkness I closed my eyes and tried to sink into the deliciousness of long-awaited sleep. I had dreamed of sleep while standing with my eyes open, pushing Caspar's pram back and forth, back and forth. I had physically yearned for it, as if desiring a lover to come into me. I had prized a night of unbroken sleep more than world peace or permanent happiness and now after more than one hundred nights of unbroken dreams, sleep would not come to me.'[1]

A lack of sleep can be a precursor to breakdown; the children's author, Anne Fine, describes in *The Week* how a long depression she experienced in her twenties was triggered by sleep deprivation following childbirth: 'Oh the tiredness, when you are actually almost hallucinating from tiredness in the day. You reach a level of physical anxiety where you fall asleep absolutely exhausted – when you are finally allowed to fall asleep – but you wake at 2 am and even though your skin is crawling with tiredness – as if you had lice all over you – you still cannot sleep because you are worried about the baby.'

Yet there are sometimes compensations for keeping strange hours. Julia was once feeding her baby son very early one autumn morning. Sheila Pollock's poem perfectly conjures the memories of that time:

Mother and Child: 5 am Feed

Still half-asleep I see
Your rat-like jaws draw hard;
Pink and vacant gums grasp your life-valve
With a strange and frightening desperation,
I wince and turn my face away
And wait to feel your tiny violence
At peace against my heavy breast.

Sheila Pollock

'I had been up with him about six times that night and was so tired I could hardly stand, and fearful that although I had hardly slept the sun was already rising but I remember looking out of the window and seeing a flock of goldfinches on the frosted lavender heads in the garden. With my infant son in my arms and the confetti colours of the birds in the early light, it was like a benediction. Whenever I see goldfinches now I experience the same sense of hope; even an individual bird is a talisman.'

In family life, general anxieties are bound to intrude and issues which seem manageable in the daytime take on a different perspective in the small hours, like the demented elderly parents escaping at midnight in *Bridget Jones's Diary*: 'Granny turned schizophrenic and took all her clothes off, ran into Penny Husbands-Bosworth's orchard and had to be rounded up by the police.'[2]

Teenagers tart themselves up for going out at about the time you want to tuck in and then confidently drive off in your car, having only passed their test the week before. Husbands are often restless with waterworks problems or night starvation and stumble triumphantly about the bedroom at 3am with fruitcake and cups of tea. Thus replenished, they start manically e-mailing. Sometimes no two nights a week are the same. Late night and early morning phone calls never bring good news. As Fay Weldon has said in her memoir, 'The harsh tones break into sleep, the hand goes out for the bedside receiver – *What fresh hell is this?* With any luck it's an early call from an airport – the prodigal child on his gap year is unexpectedly home. *Come and fetch me.* But mostly it's a sudden illness, a rush to hospital, death, news that can wait till dawn, but not a moment longer.'[3]

And even when you are both in bed there is often disparity between the sexes about the time it takes each of you to actually get to sleep, as Judith Holder explains: 'He hits the pillow and he's asleep instantly. There is nothing more annoying when you're up with a hot flush and thinking about when you're going to have time to get some king prawns by Friday evening with the person next to you making a noise as loud as a hedge trimmer. Then he wakes up and says he didn't have a very good night. Hello?'[4]

Julia's tale is similar: 'Even when you have finally dropped off to sleep with the aid of eye patches and earplugs because your husband is watching an old Clint Eastwood film you wake with a start to find the light full on, the husband snoring and the TV running. Or you have gone to sleep a full hour before him to be brutally woken when he comes up, has a noisy shower, fiddles with his organiser and flaps *The Daily Telegraph*, shouting with irritation when he discovers you have your earplugs in.

'And men also object to hot water bottles. They like to be the dispensers of warmth and comfort, regarding rubber items of this nature (in fact rubber items of all natures!) as unwanted intruders. And they don't like it when your sticky HRT patch mysteriously transfers from you to them in the middle of the night.'

Cherie Blair unwisely revealed to *The Sun* Tony's sexual stamina. No wonder she has said elsewhere there is nothing she loves more than an early night with a good book. Most men don't like books in bed as it may mean they are not getting enough attention (unless they are half way through the latest Wilbur Smith or Ian Rankin which requires *total* concentration). As Hanif Kureishi writes in *Intimacy*: 'She says: "Are you coming upstairs?" I look at her searchingly and with interest, wondering if she means sex – it must be more than a month since we've fucked – or whether she intends us to read. I like books but I don't want to get undressed for one.'[5]

Magazines are always full of articles about sleeping. However, your chances of emerging drowsily from a warm bath surrounded by scented candles are slim; about as unlikely as foods like brown rice or lettuce sending you off to the land of Nod. Although this last one does have a literary precedent; in the opening lines of *Tale of the Flopsy Bunnies*, Beatrix Potter debunks the myth: 'It is said that the effect of eating too much lettuce is "soporific". I have never felt sleepy after eating lettuces; but then I am not a rabbit.'[6]

Some 'experts' tell us we should have 'vigorous exercise' in the evening (although not just before bedtime) but this is difficult if you are at work, loading the dishwasher or supervising the homework; 'have more sex' (even when after all the above it's the last thing on your mind), open a window (the better to hear barking dogs and aeroplanes) or keep to a routine (tricky unless you live alone).

If we are still in doubt, there are countless TV programmes to advise us. Here is Thomas Sutcliffe on Professor Robert Winston's *How to Sleep Better* (BBC TV): 'Perhaps unsurprisingly the snorer discovered that strapping a bra on back to front and stuffing the cups with tennis balls did not deliver quality "shut-eye".'[7] *Shattered* was described by John Preston in *The Sunday Telegraph* as 'Big Brother plus sleep deprivation' and 'was very close to watching people being tortured for entertainment'. Since hallucination and tearfulness are states women routinely endure at different stages in their lives, they may not find this particularly entertaining.

Very often it is the husband's behaviour that makes the woman sleep badly. Alan Clark says complacently in his diary: 'Jane slept badly (how many good nights does she get per year? Three maybe.) Poor little soul, she carried all the problems of my (ir)responsibility' , and 'Jane lay awake last night for two hours (she told me this morning) in a mood of depression so black she could have killed herself' .[8(i,ii)]

Others who find sleep easy, often, irritatingly, claim a clear conscience. There is a Russian proverb: 'The less you know, the better you sleep'. It is in the early hours when sleep often becomes a distant, unobtainable goal – in fact an obsession. The more you invoke sleep, the more elusive it becomes. Wendy Cope's poem highlights what happens when relationship problems hit rock-bottom in the middle of the night, often compounded by sexual rejection.

At 3 a.m.

the room contains no sound
except the ticking of the clock
which has begun to panic
like an insect, trapped
in an enormous box.

Books lie open on the carpet

Somewhere else
you're sleeping
and beside you there's a woman
who is crying quietly
so you won't wake.

Wendy Cope

Sleep problems are not wholly confined to women. Men can be just as susceptible, particularly those who do a lot of travelling, like John Preston in *The Sunday Telegraph*:

> *Two weeks ago I was in India. Last week I was in Bulgaria.*
> *Somewhere between the two I started suffering from the worst insomnia I*
> *have ever had. In Bulgaria I bought some sleeping pills in a pharmacy. Just*
> *one of these pills, the pharmacist stated confidently, would lay me out cold*
> *for a minimum of six hours. But it had no effect at all, apart from giving me*
> *a strange sense of amnesia.*

*Back in England, I bought some "Sleepy-Time" tea from the local
health food shop. Again, useless – as well as disgusting. When I looked up
the pills I'd bought on the internet, I read that they were "the world's second
most notorious date-rape drug after Rohypnol". As a last resort I sat in a
hot bath and took a double dose of the date-rape drug, knocked back with
an extra large cup of "Sleepy-Time" tea. Nothing. After four days of this, I
feel as if I've got sludge going round in my veins and a herd of bison trapped
inside my head.*

Justin Cartwright in his novel *White Lightning* muses on the general problem of night
thoughts. Do we ignore them at our peril?

*Why are our shafts of doubt tipped with poison at night and why do
we look disparagingly on our optimistic, daytime, gullible-bumpkin selves?
No doubt it's a simple matter of diminished blood supply or hormones
taking a rest, but this is not so reassuring either. Which chemicals are the
true ones? Which state of mind accurately reflects the facts?*[9]

Our terrors during broken sleep are magnified when we are ill and can slow our
recovery. Julia remembers that whenever she had a fever as a child, in her nightmares,
giant cotton reels would skid and criss-cross, crashing and banging into each other like
dodgem cars.

Actress Jane Lapotaire records her own difficulty in sleeping in *Time out of Mind*, her
account of recovery from a brain haemorrhage:

*Sleep continues to elude me. Or my body does its jump and jolts me
into consciousness again. Exhausted as I am, the moment my head sinks
into the pillow, my brain reruns all the scenes of the collapse that I can recall
... I can't shake off the terror of wondering how I'll manage to get through
the day if I don't sleep... I take my sleeping pills but sleep evades me all
night long. There is not one second of respite from the churning thoughts. In
desperation I get up and begin to make lists of what I'll need in the new flat,
what I'll have to sell or dump. It just makes bad worse...* [10]

The inability to sleep after bereavement can make coping with the rush of grief even more insupportable. In *A Grief Observed*, C. S. Lewis describes how loss of sleep compounds his profound sense of loss: ' "I must get a good sleep tonight" ushers in hours of wakefulness. Delicious drinks are wasted on a really ravenous thirst. Is it similarly the very intensity of the longing that draws the iron curtain, that makes us feel we are staring into a vacuum when we think about our dead?'[11]

Nor is it only middle-aged men who can't sleep. In *The Strings are False*, Louis MacNeice describes how he felt when his first marriage ended: 'I did not sleep very well these days. In a bed in a big yellow room with a ten foot skylight (we had this room built to our own design) I felt the sky encroaching, tried to dodge it: sometimes it was a falling tent and sometimes too silent and sometimes full of voices; I would open the door quickly and no one would be there.'[12]

According to *The Guardian*'s Tim Dowling, sleepers can be divided into Bush or Thatcher camps. It was Thatcher who set the gold standard on sleep, managing on a mere five hours a night, while George Bush is early to bed. Julia is definitely a Bush type (or was when she had to be up for the school run): 'You refuse to watch any film that starts after 9pm, you eat supper in your pyjamas, you don't even listen to hear who is on *Question Time* in case you might be tempted.'

Janice, on the other hand, had her time clock permanently reset by night shifts at the *Financial Times*. 'I would finish at 2am after four deadlines. I would then be whisked home by cab, but it was impossible to go straight to bed: if you finished work at 5, could you be in bed, asleep, by 5.30?'

'Even now, I simply can't go to bed early and even if I don't have an article to finish will often stay up late, often pointlessly watching a late film. As I have to be up at six for the school run (or my own journey to London, or most likely, both) I don't get much shut-eye. My husband, on the other hand, is in bed by 10 at the latest.'

Tim Dowling also frets that he is not part of a bedtime compatible couple. 'My wife goes to bed at least an hour before I do, sometimes more. We never say so, but we regard each other's nocturnal habits as the height of selfishness.' It is true that marriages can fail on this incompatibility; but this is not about sleep *per se*, or even plain exhaustion, it's about sex, control, abandonment, loneliness, all of which are inextricably involved with our ability to sleep.

Next to the knotty problem of sleeping apart. Traditionalists will state, 'If a woman leaves a man's bed the marriage is over'. But what is worse for a marriage – separate bedrooms or no sleep? Men may think that it is a reflection on their sexual prowess or lack of it, often forgetting the nights they chose to spend in the spare bedroom when their children were babies.

The initiation of sexual activity in the early morning is not always welcomed by those women who have just got to sleep. Robert Tucker writing to *The Independent* testifies: 'My wife has placed me on warning that unwelcome amorous advances between 11pm and 7am should now be regarded as a breach of human rights.' It's all a far cry from those student halls of residence when it seemed possible for two to sleep in the narrowest of beds and still be bright-eyed the next day.

Sleep and sex are inevitably linked, with 'bed' often used as a euphemism for sex. In fact, the shared bed is a relatively recent habit that was originally caused by lack of space, in marked contrast to the stately homes of England, which had their separate bedchambers at opposite ends of the house. The shared bed was commonly used solely for procreation, though Maria Theresa, mother of the ill-fated queen Marie Antoinette, strongly advocated the marital bed to her teenage daughter to solve the crisis of her unconsummated marriage – and the consequent, critical lack of an heir:

> *Louis Auguste was helped by the custom of the French court by which married couples did not necessarily share beds. This became an enduring bone of contention between the Empress and her daughter. Maria Theresa who believed in the marital bed herself, attached enormous importance to this spending-the-night-together, presumably hoping that passion might strike the Dauphin in some unguarded moment in the middle of the night or the early morning.*[13]

Rather more recently, building work caused one couple we know to sleep temporarily in separate beds. She remarked how much better she felt; *he*, on the other hand, retorted that he felt a lot worse and that she must not regard it as a good idea.

Male and female insecurities about sex are enough to inhibit either partner's good night's sleep. Hint that your partner might be boring at your peril. Kate, in Alan Ayckbourn's *Bedroom Farce*, tentatively suggests the female point of view:

> M: *You don't get bored with me, do you?*
>
> K: *No. No. Not often.*
>
> M: *What, you mean – when we're – in bed? Here?*
>
> K: *Not often …*
>
> M: *Well, that's nice.*
>
> K: *Only once or twice.*
>
> M: *Bored?*
>
> Kate: *No, not bored. You know, it's just I have my mind on other things.*
>
> M: *You mean, other men.*

K: No. Ordinary things like, shall we have a carpet in the hall or shall we stain the floorboards. That sort of thing.

And Malcolm speaks for the chaps:

Nobody ever told me before I was boring. And I've been with a few, I can tell you.

K: Yes, I know, you've told me.

M: They weren't bored. None of them were bored. No woman who's been in bed with me has ever complained of boredom. That was the last thing on their mind. If I were you, I'd start worrying that there wasn't something wrong with you.[14]

Of course, we have never been bored with our partners and our partners have certainly never been bored with us!

Some people go to extraordinary lengths to get a good sleep, though readers may feel Tony Benn's method a step too far, not least for his fellow train passengers:

Caught the 7.30 to Chesterfield and slept all the way. I have a marvellous system. I have two balloon cushions, one fits up my back and the other stops my head from wobbling. I've got an airline eye-mask, and two foam rubber arm-rests, and I leave my ticket on the table and I'm usually sound asleep for an hour. Sometimes I set the alarm clock so I don't go to Sheffield, which has happened.[15(i)]

Tony Benn is also a menace at home with his clock. Later in his diary there is an entry that says, 'Caroline was disturbed all night by my talking clock, which announces the hour every hour because I've forgotten how to switch it off. So I'm going to have to hide it in the bathroom at night'. [15(ii)] (Janice, on the other hand, has a Blackberry that announces every incoming email unless turned off – easy to forget if you're creeping into bed at 1am...)

Julia had the same annoying experience with her husband's watch which beeped on the hour, and his Psion organiser which during a supposedly romantic weekend break roared into life at 3am because he had just come back from a business trip and left the wake-up call on Istanbul time, and again two hours later to remind him it was their wedding anniversary. This turned into a torturous weekend of sleep deprivation rather than romance and relaxation. The same kind of thing happened again recently even though they are now separated. (Funny, that...) 'The phone rang at 5.30am and I thought somebody must have died, but I could hear his voice and Russians talking. He'd dropped his phone in a meeting and it had auto-dialled.'

The trouble is that if sleeping in the same room is all about sex, the paraphernalia that are often employed to achieve a good night's sleep are death to sex; earplugs, eye-masks, sleeping tablets, along with reading glasses, reading lamps, even ear-phones for TV or radio. Maybe it's why other rituals replace sex. The second couple in *Bedroom Farce* resort to sardines in bed for excitement:

Delia: Let's be really really wicked...

Ernest: Eh?

D: Let's eat them in bed.

E: In bed?

D: Sardines on toast in bed, do you remember?

E: Good lord, yes. You've got a memory. Sardines on toast in bed, yes.

That's right. Are you sure it wasn't baked beans?

D: No, not baked beans. Sardines.

E: Yes, quite right. Sardines. All right, we'll go one better. I'll go and hot them up while you get into your jim-jams.

They end up quarrelling about who gets to sleep on the of damp patch (and not for the usual reason):

D: Darling, you're getting fish on the sheet.

Now we're going to reek of fish all night. I don't think this was terribly bright idea of someone's.

E: Oh well. You only live once. What the hell.

D: Well, it's on your side. You have to put up with it.[16]

And so we are really no further forward on the subject of sleep (we warned this was a book which would provide no answers!) except we need it like we need food and water. The only true way to get a good night's sleep is to change your life to remove some of its stresses, but it is another paradox that you may not have the energy or insight to do so unless you have slept well in the first place; terribly wrong judgements can be made when we are tired. So do whatever it takes. Be as selfish as you like. Spend a week in the spare room (you can always institute visiting hours!) Or take tablets if necessary. It's not a moral failing.

Robert Graves' *Not to Sleep* was dedicated to the actress Ava Gardner, and written when he was 68, and not in the first flush of youth at all.

Not to Sleep

Not to sleep all the night long, for pure joy,
Counting no sheep and careless of chimes
Welcoming the dawn confabulation
Of birds, her children, who discuss idly
Fanciful details of the promised coming –
Will she be wearing red, or russet, or blue,
Or pure white? – whatever she wears, glorious:
Not to sleep all the night long, for pure joy.

This is given to few but at last to me,
So that when I laugh and stretch and leap from bed
I shall glide downstairs, my feet brushing the carpet
In courtesy to civilised progression,
Though, did I wish, I could soar through the open window
And perch on a branch above, acceptable ally
Of the birds still alert, grumbling gently together.

Robert Graves

And those 'twin' poets W.H. Auden and Louis MacNeice are also philosophical about how important it is to somehow learn to put all disasters and losses behind us. This is from the *Song of the Master and Boatswain* by W.H. Auden:

The nightingales are sobbing in
The orchards of our mothers,
And hearts that we broke long ago
Have long been breaking others;
Tears are round, the sea is deep:
Roll them overboard and sleep.

Or if you prefer, Louis MacNeice says:

Sleep and be damned and wake up good

Or try sex and sardines…whatever works for you.

One final piece of advice: shoot the messenger. Don't have a telephone by the bed at all.

The Ted Williams Villanelle

Watch the ball and do your thing,
This is the moment. Here's your chance,
Don't let anybody mess with your swing.

It's time to shine. You're in the ring.
Step forward, adopt a winning stance,
Watch the ball and do your thing,

And while that ball is taking wing,
Run, without a backward glance.
Don't let anybody mess with your swing.

Don't let envious bastards bring
You down. Ignore the sneers, the can'ts.
Watch the ball and do your thing.

Sing out, if you want to sing.
Jump up, when you long to dance.
Don't let anybody mess with your swing.

Enjoy your talents. Have your fling.
The seasons change. The years advance.
Watch the ball and do your thing,
And don't let anybody mess with your swing.

Wendy Cope

Health and safety

As Chekhov has said, 'Any idiot can face a crisis – it's day to day living that wears you out'. Most women in middle age have a brush with mortality.[1] This can be in the form of a chronic condition such as arthritis, or something potentially more devastating like breast cancer. At a stroke, good health can no longer be taken for granted. Sometimes even a minor physical condition can lead to depression and anxiety. Even if it were wise to separate physical and mental problems, they are usually so inextricably entangled and symptoms are similar in several illnesses; for example, it can be hard to distinguish menopause from depression, depression from M.E... so circular are these conditions that it is often impossible to get to the root cause. Back pain is a good example of an illness with physical and psychological causes. It can be confusing for all concerned when we are no longer, as Janice says, *What it says on the tin*.

What it says on the tin

I no longer do exactly
What it says on the tin;
I'm no longer so malleable
And no longer so thin

I'm afraid my guarantees
Have all run out.
I'm inclined to brood,
Liable to shout.

Janice Warman

Tradition has it that women have better health care because with regular gynaecological check-ups and pregnancies they see their doctors more often. But it is also true that they spend more time taking their children to the doctor and chivvying their husbands to seek treatment. They often discount their own symptoms – and their symptoms are often discounted by the medical profession.

A friend who was tired, listless, and had dropped to six stone in weight mentioned it in passing while at an appointment for her daughter. 'Count yourself lucky – most women would kill to be as thin as you,' snapped her doctor. Subsequently we heard his wife weighed 16 stone; *quel surprise*. And Harriet – let's call her that – soon found out she was seriously ill. Not from her own doctor, but from another who walked into her kitchen shop and took one look at her while buying a Le Creuset casserole dish.

Obviously, not all doctors fall into this camp. 'When I said I was worried I might be wasting his time, my GP simply said: "Any breast lump is an undiagnosed breast lump until it has been examined" – and referred me immediately,' says Janice. Nevertheless, it's a sad fact that women often tend to put their own needs last, and are tentative at best when asking for help. Here, as in all other areas we cover, it's vital to combat that tendency fiercely.

Not that Janice took her own advice, having steadfastly ignored abdominal pains for 48 hours as she was busy – a son returning from India, a daughter's orthodontist appointment, a tax return (and a book to write). The result was a weekend in hospital on a drip, and very nearly losing a perfectly healthy appendix.

It was certainly being the wife of a famous (possibly the famous) politician that wore out Clementine Churchill; having already spent the war years in Downing Street, she found herself doing another stint there in her seventies. Mary Soames, in *Clementine Churchill*, describes her mother trying to cope: -

> *To her family she would be generally 'tricky' and demanding.*
> *Nervously restless, she would fuss endlessly over what seemed to others to*
> *be trifling matters; above all, when she was 'down', the present held no*
> *enjoyment, and the future loomed with problems great and small.*[2]

Time was when illness was not openly discussed. One of the benefits of a freer society is that many people are writing about their experiences in order to help others. The actress Jane Lapotaire, writing about her recovery from a brain aneurysm, talks to her therapist about life before her near-death experience:

> *How do I tell this young woman what fifteen years of being a single*
> *parent feels like? The hamster-wheel of shop, cook, clean, work, child,*
> *work, clean, cook, shop. Any theatre performer knows the pole-axing*
> *exhaustion of eight performances a week. Or the opposite, the gut-grinding*
> *worry of being unemployed and the accompanying how-do-I-pay-the-*
> *bills refrain.*[3(i)]

Jane undoubtedly had to keep going for the sake of her child; her story is a warning to women who never stop. And families are often less than kind. Jane's foster mother said: 'Now look what you've brought on yourself.'

Her day of reckoning began badly: 'I wake feeling ghastly. Nothing new in that. I've woken feeling ghastly for years. Tired, achy, lifeless, all symptoms of overwork. I have painkillers with muscle relaxant, painkillers that give me a lift, and painkillers with sleep aid.'[3(ii)]

We should take note. In fact *Time Out of Mind* is not just relevant to those who have had an aneurysm. The sensations described could be experienced by someone recovering from M.E., a damaged nervous system or profound depression: 'London had flashed past, a blur of intolerable noise, strobing lights and swarms of people, which had, even from the comfort and protection of Ann's car and her little mews flat, overpowered and undermined me. Then the train journey, more traffic, more people, noise outside, perpetual movement, perpetual stimulus that beat my spinning exhausted brain with blow after blow.'[3(iii)]

Another actress, Sheila Hancock, describes a similar stage in her life: 'I had pushed my body to excess and now it had given up on me: in quick succession, I had breast cancer, gallstones, shingles and a dodgy cervical smear.'[4]

Yes, we do bring some things on ourselves. Half of all cancers – equivalent to 135,000 cases a year in the UK – could be prevented by changes to lifestyle according to Cancer Research UK in 2005, although more often than not, illness seems to strike out of the blue. Allison Pearson in *I Don't Know How She Does It* describes the death of her character Jill:

> *She died peacefully at home in the small hours of Monday morning. The cancer swept through her like a forest fire. The surgeons were in first, and after them a SWAT team of pharmacologists and radiotherapists all trying to contain the blaze. But the cancer was unquenchable …breasts, lungs, pancreas. It was as though Jill's energy was being used against her; as if the life force itself could be hijacked and redeployed in the fell purposes of death.[5]*

It's widely accepted in the field of animal husbandry that stress lowers the immune system and makes livestock more likely to fall ill. And it's finally beginning to be acknowledged in humans too. We know that stress is a factor in illness, though exactly what amounts to 'stress' in humans is arguable, and what we regard as stress would have been laughed off by our parents. In *Fifty Years of Hancock's Half Hour* by Richard Webber, the comedy team Ray Galton and Alan Simpson describe their working practices in the 50s: 'In our heyday we were writing forty shows a year and taking a month's holiday. Stress didn't come into it: I don't think we'd heard of the word in those days.'[6]

In *Dr Sweet and His Daughter* by Peter Bradshaw, the hero tries to explain to his elderly parents that his young daughter has been upset by the unexpected return of his wife:

> *'Well, Alice coming back like this at Christmas has stirred up quite a lot of nerves. There've been broken nights, thumb-sucking, sleepwalking and bed-wetting. Mum, look I'm just – I don't know. I'm just saying that both Cordie and I are quite stressed.' But Dr Sweet saw instantly that this emphasis on stress was misjudged; John and Rosemary were from a generation that didn't see stress as an occasion of leniency.[7]*

One generation is often intolerant of another and memories are short. In Rachel Cusk's *The Lucky Ones*, the mother is unsympathetic to her daughter who has recently given birth: 'She's absolutely fine', said Mrs Daley irritably. 'She's just like any other mother with a new baby. What sort of strain could she possibly be under? She's got one tiny baby and everyone falling over themselves to help her. I never had any one worrying that I was under strain, or making sure that I was all right.'[8]

Stress has become a blanket expression for anything ranging from catastrophe to a little local difficulty. We are more stressed out by stress than any other generation. As Anna Purslove says in *Harper's Bazaar*: 'We're stressed out, according to the many surveys (another modern irritation in themselves) conducted on the subject, by too much work, not enough work, having children, not having children, sex, no sex, and both wealth and poverty.'[9] The old adages hold true… people can quite literally drive you mad, bring you out in a rash and give you a headache.

There is even supposed to be good and bad stress in the same way there is both good and bad cholesterol. Good stress to us means the creative excitement that leads to achievement and imaginative endeavour. Bad stress is created by prolonged pressure and powerlessness, causing the adrenaline levels to remain high over too long a period. Research into stress at work shows that those at the top, with more responsibility, but crucially, more power, have less stress than the powerless drones at the bottom. This would explain why many women, at home as at work, are subject to high levels of stress.

Many jobs have also become far more difficult as society has changed. Research reveals that 72% of teachers (most of whom are women) had considered quitting their jobs because they were worn out by pupils' disruptive behaviour – swearing, vandalising property, throwing eggs at staff and spitting.[10]

It's in middle age when everything happens at once… somehow a health disaster triggers further health disasters, the opposite of success breeding success. The following example is from Simon Hoggart's *The Cat That Could Open The Fridge* (a guide to the scary world of Christmas round robins):

Terry had his two-yearly colonoscopy. They removed two polyps, but found his diverticular was inflamed, so he had to have antibiotics for it, he was also going to a physio for a backache when he fell on the brick pavement in the garden, breaking his right hip (he had been up the ladder clearing away the guttering, came in for coffee, then went out to prune shrubs, and fell). We went by ambulance to the private hospital not far from home, but because he takes Warfarin they could not operate til the Friday... at the end of August we were just getting back to some type of normal life when Terry fell on the tiled floor in the kitchen, did not break anything, nasty cut on the corner of the eye and huge bruises and lumps on both knees due to Warfarin... We do not entertain anymore, used to enjoy the odd little dinner parties, we just have tea or coffee and biscuits. I cannot walk very far because of my back problem when trying to nurse Mother when she broke her hip, which she never got over.[11]

This is a far cry from the usual smug tones of round robin letters, but haven't we all had years when life falls apart like a broken string of beads? If we couldn't laugh, we really would go mad.

Stress, like sleep problems, has even come to be an acceptable form of entertainment. Thomas Sutcliffe reviews two such programmes in *The Independent*. 'The Stress Test took on the case of a woman struggling to maintain two jobs, five children and evening coursework, and *Supernanny* which meant being parachuted into the home of a single mother whose children communicated almost entirely by means of screams and punches. In both cases you couldn't help thinking that the most effective form of stress relief would have been reliable contraception.'[12]

And in a review of *Spirituality Shopper* (surely an oxymoron), Sutcliffe suggests that 'instead of choosing between various spiritual practices in order to bring tranquillity into her life, what would really transform it would have been to get her partner – a shiftless, pony-tailed layabout she worked all hours to support – to help with the housework.'[12]

The miracle is that women don't suffer from stress-related illness more often. The writer Rebecca West (1892-1983) may not quite have been the average woman, but as her personal chronology in her *Selected Letters* reveals not only did she live through two World Wars, she experienced all of the following – heartbreak, bereavement, estrangement from her son and dementia in her husband, while her own precarious health included tuberculosis, an ectopic pregnancy, jaundice, fibroids, phlebitis, gall bladder problems and cataracts. Somehow or other she managed to withstand all these brickbats and reversals of fortune to become an acclaimed novelist and journalist of international standing who reported on the Nuremburg war tribunal. Her life must surely be a prime example of adversity acting as a catalyst for achievement.

After stress comes fat. Britain is the fat man (or woman) of Europe. Yet as women we are obsessed with our weight and need to stop dieting. The Conservative MP Anne Widdecombe was asked to write a diet book (after appearing on a celebrity diet programme whose name escapes us) and apparently said it would only consist of four pages, each carrying a single word: EAT. LESS. EXERCISE. MORE. But somehow such common sense seems beyond us. While the health of the nation has generally improved, the rise in obesity levels has had a profoundly negative effect on general health. Walk into the foyer of any NHS hospital and you will see all the characters from *Little Britain*.

We fall hook, line and sinker for diet books of every persuasion. As Amanda Craig says in her novel, *A Vicious Circle*: 'We are becoming more and more like America, where you can tell how low someone's income is by the size of the clothes they wear.'[13] And according to Susie Orbach: 'Class society is exposed. The poor are fat. The rich are aspirant, controlled and thin. Above all the fat woman wants to hide. Paradoxically, her lot in life is to be perpetually noticed.'[14]

Nor do we take any notice of Government directives. As Deborah Orr reports in *The Independent*, 'The Government has spent £5.7 million on promoting healthy eating, with virtually no impact whatsoever'. Yet we do not see MPs taking the lead. How can a cabinet that includes Gordon Brown, Charles Clarke and John Prescott tell us we are too fat? There are also strange shapes in opposition; Christopher Soames comes unavoidably to mind. There is also a double standard. A paunch may be seen to lend men gravitas, but women feel the need to succumb to the expectation that to be in control, they must be slim. Women's size is also more often remarked upon. As Ann Widdecombe has said, 'I have probably had a lot more comment about my circumference than John Prescott has had about his circumference'.

American scientists who spent $42.5m on a survey to prove the benefits of a low fat diet were frustrated by the fact that the women, all volunteers over 50, failed to stick to the diet and therefore skewed the results! By the time they are adults, 95% of women are unhappy with their body shape, nearly the same number have been on a diet, and as Susie Orbach and Atul Gawande agree, 95% of diets don't work. Many women see obesity as a cosmetic rather than a health problem, and fail to realise that yo-yo dieting is worse for your health than not dieting at all.

> *Whatever the regimen... liquid diets, high protein diets, grapefruit*
> *diets, the Zone, Atkins or the Dean Ornish diet... people lose weight readily,*
> *but they do not keep it off.*[15(i)]

In America, gastric bypass operations are not uncommon and are even paid for by the publicly funded Medicare. Yet as Atul Gawande says in *Complications*: 'For the very obese, general anaesthesia alone is a dangerous undertaking. Obesity substantially increases the risk of respiratory failure, heart attacks, wound infections, hernias ...almost every complication possible, including death.' [15(ii)] The American neurosis, particularly obvious in New York, is compounded by the need to be exquisitely dressed and thin as a pin, while surrounded by the world's best restaurants and mountains of food on all sides. The American way of eating is well illustrated in Madeleine Albright's biography *Madam Secretary*: 'Like many Americans, I tried a variety of exercise and diet programs. When I was on the plane, the crew did its best to accommodate whatever regimen I was on. They found room for a portable stair stepper and weights and always had tuna fish and the right kind of crackers. They heated my homemade cabbage soup when I was on a diet featuring that gourmet dish, and they obeyed my order that KitKat chocolate bars be banned from my cabin. No matter what, however, during each trip there was that special moment when exhaustion overcame discipline and my favourite taco salad smothered in everything arrived, along with smuggled-in KitKats.'[16]

Because so many of us are overweight, even the concept of gluttony has had to be redrawn. Obese people are not greedy; they are 'victims of low self-esteem'; and supermarkets are blamed for stocking the wrong kind of food. However, many large women often eat in secret. In Maggie O'Farrell's novel *The Distance Between Us*, the character Mair is one such closet eater:

> *Mair loved eating – but only in secret. She found it difficult to eat if anyone else was there. Mair hated being watched, hated the idea that someone might count the flapjacks she was consuming or hear the small constricted noises she made when she swallowed.*

> *Huw was perplexed by the half-eaten sandwiches he came across occasionally, greened with mould, stuffed into a drawer of the dresser. He assumed it was one of the children. He would tell his wife and she would tut and fling them into the all-consuming mouth of the stove.*[17]

It is an unfortunate fact that metabolism slows in middle age and a certain amount of weight gain is inevitable. Each generation has its different methods of dealing with this. Julia's grandmother said she kept her figure because she always wore a good corset.

(Presumably this was because she experienced stomach pain if she ate too much?) Now the pantie-girdle seems to be making a comeback; Roland Mouret calls it a 'waist restraint'. Kylie Minogue laughs off the suggestion that she has a 16-inch waist in one of her 'Showgirl' corsets. And then there are always Trinny and Susannah's 'Magic Knickers' – in their latest form, a vile flesh-coloured thing that runs from just below the breasts to just above the knees. A corset by any other name? But certainly not one you'd want to be seen in!

Perhaps we should simply take the advice of the world's oldest person, Hendriki van Schipper, aged 114, who attributes her old age to eating a herring and drinking a glass of orange juice every day. Annie Knight, a former suffragette who died recently at 111, put her long life down to a diet of porridge, no alcohol and the occasional sweet. Britain's oldest twins proclaimed their double century due to fruit and vegetables, early nights and the odd drink. Michele Hanson has said about her mother:

> *I blame her healthy lifestyle: no smoking, no drugs, hardly any drinking, just the odd Martini and lemonade, only homemade food, lots of dancing, living mainly by the seaside and not a single mouthful of McDonalds in her whole life. That is the way to be nearly a hundred. If that's what you really want.*[18]

Reading about healthy eating can often have the opposite effect. Alex Jamieson, a vegan chef, was asked by *The Sunday Telegraph* what she had for breakfast. She said she had a 'breakfast shake of a banana, frozen blueberries and strawberries, Vitamin C powder, powdered dehydrated greens and sea veg, flaxseeds' and all this after a 45-minute early morning hike. It made us want to sit in a comfy chair all day wolfing down coffee and croissants. The dietician reviewing her food intake felt the same: 'Oh please… pass me a pork pie!'

Longevity is common in writers however – surprising, given the sedentary nature of the occupation. Authors whose work we have extensively quoted, such as Elizabeth Jane Howard, Doris Lessing, Rosamond Lehmann, even Iris Murdoch (in spite of Alzheimer's) all reached a great age.

In A.N. Wilson's book, *Iris Murdoch As I Knew Her*, he points out that 'eating disorders' are not just the province of the young: 'One of the things which sustained her writing was a regular intake of sweet food, milky drinks and farinaceous snacks. When she was working, she would break mid-morning for a foaming cup of Horlicks, often accompanied by Mr Kipling cakes or by sweets such as Mars Bars or Crunchies; and this explained, I think, the fact that while she continued to put on weight, she seldom displayed much interest in food at the table.'[19]

Rosamond Lehmann also eschewed a healthy diet. Selina Hastings, her biographer, writes: 'When I stayed with her it was understood that I always did the cooking and I quickly learned that what she loved was rich nursery food, particularly very sweet puddings with plenty of cream.'[20] Perhaps there is a certain stage in life when it no longer matters what you eat. Jenny Joseph in her seminal poem *Warning* declares when she is an old woman she will eat 'three pounds of sausages at a go, or only bread and pickle for a week'. The historian Brian Wormald also did not go gentle. According to his obituary in *The Independent*, his motoring came to resemble that of Mr Toad, and in retirement he lived on fried bacon and bananas and smoked and drank into his late eighties. Spike Milligan also lived to an advanced age; according to his biographer Humphrey Carpenter, he would 'fortify himself with jam doughnuts (three at a time)' when he was climbing out of depression.

(There must be something about writers and doughnuts. When Elizabeth Jane Howard worked in publishing with C. Day Lewis, they had a habit of bingeing on doughnuts to cheer themselves up. In her memoir *Slipstream*, she describes how their boss Norah would burst in on them without warning: ' "Eating again!" She would accuse, looking at the greasy paper bags held down by doughnuts like paperweights.'[21])

Not that everyone's weight problems are self-inflicted. Hilary Mantel's biography, *Giving up the Ghost*, chronicles in detail how she metamorphosed from a slim twenty-something to a matronly figure due to thyroid problems, a hormone imbalance and undiagnosed endometriosis:

In my late twenties I have a narrow ribcage, a tiny waist and a child's arms fuzzed with white-gold hair. At twenty-nine I am cast as a ghost in a play. But then my life will change. I will be solid, set, grounded, grotesque; perpetually strange to myself, convoluted, mutated, and beyond the pale. All of us can change. All of us can change for the better, at any point. I believe this, but what is certainly true is that we can be made foreign to ourselves suddenly, by illness, accident, misadventure, or hormonal caprice.[22]

According to Nigel Slater in his memoir *Toast*, food can be used as a weapon as well as a pleasure. His (wicked?) stepmother was a far better cook than his own mother. ('Joan's lemon meringue pie was one of the most glorious things I had ever put in my mouth: warm, painfully sharp lemon filling, the most airy pastry imaginable (she used cold lard in place of some of the butter) and a billowing hat of thick, teeth-judderingly sweet meringue.'[23]) But as Anne Chisholm in *The Sunday Telegraph* writes, 'The huge and delicious meals she provided were, Slater implies, her way, along with sex, of ensnaring and controlling his father. It is also implied that her cooking killed him; he grew fat and died suddenly from a heart attack when Slater was 16.'

Which brings us to men's health. In general, middle-aged men fall into two camps: the hypochondriac will Google his symptoms, although seldom actually visit a doctor; health websites are visited by men almost as much as pornographic ones.

Having had cancer and anxiously awaiting a possible re-occurrence can lead to heightened neurosis. Alan Bennett in *Untold Stories* describes his fears: 'Did you get cancer in the elbow, I wondered as mine was quite painful. Was the thumb a site?'[24]

Another worrier, Martin Lukes, e-mails his wife in Lucy Kellaway's *Who Moved My Blackberry?*:

Jens – Am feeling worse by the minute. I've just googled bowel cancer again and found that one in 18 men in their mid-forties have it – it's the second biggest killer in men. My athlete's foot has also flared up horribly. Do you think this is connected to the other symptoms?[25]

We have a friend whose husband takes her on 'medical holidays' so they can be examined thoroughly inside and out. This same man is also systematically replacing his own body parts as they wear out. Being an inventor, he is a dab hand at refining his own design.

In the other camp are men who say they are as fit as a fiddle and feel that no lifestyle changes whatsoever are necessary. In *Case Histories*, by Kate Atkinson, there is a middle-aged man named Theo who is a case in point:

> *Theo had begun to try to walk more. He was now officially 'morbidly obese', according to his new, unsympathetic GP. Theo knew that the new, unsympathetic GP – a young woman with a very short haircut and a gym bag thrown carelessly in the corner of the surgery – was using the term to try to frighten him. Theo hadn't considered himself 'morbidly obese' until now. He had thought of himself as cheerfully overweight, a rotund Santa Claus kind of figure.*[26]

As we've said, men frequently have wives and mothers who make their doctor's appointments and supply their vitamins, so it's not surprising that married men are healthier than single men (though the reverse is true for women).

Not that all men listen to their wives. Diana Melly describes a holiday spent in Egypt with her husband, the maverick jazz musician George:

> *He had completely ignored my dietary advice – taken from the guidebook – and the whisky, the large quantities of meat and unwashed fruit now combined to create havoc with his bowels and he spent the entire flight home in the lavatory.*[27]

On to fitness; there are three important rules when it comes to exercise: that it must naturally fit into your life, you must enjoy it, and you must keep it up. Spasmodic exercise is like yo-yo dieting; it's a waste of time. A regular walk to the station or a weekly gardening or lawn mowing session is better than occasional visits to the gym.

If just getting to the yoga class becomes a pressure then the whole thing is self-defeating. It is also a fallacy that you get more exercise living in the country, where you have to jump into the car for everything. Julia was never so fit as when she commuted from Richmond to Baker Street – and Janice than when she lived in Balham and worked at *The Guardian*. A brisk walk to the station and endless treks up and down broken escalators were more aerobic than any step machine.

As Judith Holder maintains in *Grumpy Old Women*, for some reason it's now mandatory for middle-aged women to be fit and appealing. She says: 'It's not as if you can just knuckle down to a big box of Quality Street and turn into Peggy Mount, as your mother did, with no one batting an eyelid. These days you have to try to retain your figure by spending hours in the gym. People say "You look well", which is code for "You look a bit fat".'[28]

Plus keeping fit can lead to its own kind of neurosis. Jude in *Bridget Jones's Diary* goes home early because she has to get up at 5.45am to go to the gym (and see her personal shopper) before work starts at 8.30am.

As Bridget says, 'it is easy to make resolutions… stop smoking, drink no more than fourteen alcohol units a week, reduce circumference of thighs, eat more pulses, go to the gym three times a week not merely to buy a sandwich',[29] but almost impossible to keep them.

Even if you work from home it's hard to fit in the time to do sit-ups. Just changing into the right clothes is a bind… although it is possible to do the school run in baggy old yoga trousers as long as you don't have to get out of the car. Somehow the more changing of clothes you have to do, the more time it all takes and the less you seem to achieve in the day overall, and the control on your life starts slipping away which becomes another stress in itself. 'I can wear the same outfit for hoovering, mucking out the guinea pigs and riding my bike,' says Julia. 'But this wouldn't work if I lived in a town, and the track pants certainly don't keep the mystery in a marriage. Because not only does society decree we keep fit; we must somehow still look charming for our partners.'

The Lucky Ones features a husband anxious about his wife's appearance: ' "Are you going to spend the day in your dressing gown?" said Colin. "I don't think it's unreasonable of me to expect my wife to make an effort when she sees me off to work in the morning".'[30] Do we really have to wear high heels and put a ribbon in our hair at 7am?

In fact most women probably exercise without realising it. Muscular strength for instance; surely lugging the Hoover up the stairs counts? Flexibility… reaching into the back of the car for the old apple cores – we can tick that box.

Diana Melly often escaped from her marriage problems by walking her dogs: 'While I walked them I could sometimes walk away from my confused, unhappy feelings. It's very easy to accept sympathy from animals. With friends you feel some responsibility: to get better, not to be a bore, to respond in some way and to reassure them that they have said the right things. With the dogs I could be alone, which I often needed to be, and never feel lonely.'[31]

'Housework to Keep You Fit' is supposed to be news now. Supermarkets, rather than reducing the amount of junk food they stock, are designing new hard-to-push trolleys so we can work out while we shop. How thoughtful of them.

Deborah Ross in *The Independent* has the answer to the feel-good factor at least. She attends an aquarobics class to cheer herself up: 'My classmates are mostly big older ladies in caps that tie with a popper under the chin and those swimsuits with bust supports like steel girders. I believe that such swimsuits are only available from a very secret place as you never see them in shops. Anyway they make me feel quite young and sprightly.'

There remains the vital task of ensuring our children get enough exercise. Successive governments selling off local government playing fields is shameful, and the creeping compensation culture discourages 'dangerous' activities such as climbing trees, sports like rugby and adventure holidays or school trips. Ever increasing traffic and the perceived danger of paedophiles has made us reluctant to allow our children to travel to school alone.

Alistair Cassel's solution in a letter to *The Independent* is ingenious: 'There is a simple answer to cycling to school with lots of stuff – a bicycle trailer. For several happy years I accompanied my own children to school with my "bike-hod" bobbing faithfully along behind, laden with bags, violins, cakes etc.' But we know what our daughters would say: 'No way Mum, people will think I'm a saddo.'

The irony is that we wear ourselves out taking our children to physical activities that they were once able to incorporate into their daily life. We should use this energy instead to encourage governments to put in more cycle tracks and reinstate school sport. What we really need is a Jamie Oliver of the football pitch to raise consciousness and shake up government departments.

It is also important to set examples for our children to follow. Each of us have had our role models: Janice's mother, a former ballet dancer, taught ballroom, took modern dance classes and played tennis, while her father played squash well into his seventies, often against much younger partners whom he took delight in trouncing. Julia's father cycled to and from work, rode his bike until he was 80 and lived to the age of 85.

As women, we owe a lot to the bicycle. 'Bicycling', declared the American suffragist Susan Anthony in 1896, 'has done more to emancipate women than anything else in the world'. The bicycle changed everything: it got them out and about (often without a chaperone), made them strong and healthy, and prompted them to try new modes of dress. Once a few pioneering bicyclists had cast aside their stays and petticoats in favour of bloomers and short skirts, women from all walks of life started following suit.

P.G. Wodehouse would walk four miles to get the newspapers every day, and was always doing physical jerks and press-ups. He lived to a great age, although it may have been his blameless life – apart, perhaps, from his foolish decision to record broadcasts for the Nazis after his release from internment in France in 1941. He was a faithful husband in a long marriage, and Robert McCrum in his biography describes his early relationship to a chorus girl called Fleur as 'Plum's one wild oat'.[32]

Although it is never too late to start exercising, old age is likely to be difficult to manage unless we try to get fit before we get there, but we mustn't feel that it is unattainable unless we join a gym. Just walking a lot will do the trick. But one thing is for certain... we won't be striding across the hills in our seventies if we can't do it in our forties.

Penelope Betjeman, poet and wife of John, was a larger than life character who roared and strode until the day she died. She foresaw the couch potato epidemic back in the fifties. 'There are new gadgets advertised every day so that everything can be done from your armchair, so why not go right down into your grave now if you are never going to get up again?'[33]

It would be impossible to examine women's health without looking at the issue of breast cancer. How can we reduce the risks? The current advice seems to be common sense; eat a healthy, low fat diet with plenty of fruit, vegetables and olive oil. Exercise regularly and cut down (or cut out) alcohol. Examine your breasts regularly and have regular mammograms; catching the disease early helps to defeat it. The rest is down to genes, age or luck.

About 1 in 10 women will develop this disease at some stage in their lives, but we have concentrated here on the testimonies of two women who have written books about their experiences. One, Ruth Picardie, died tragically young; the other, Elisa Segrave, survived. Ruth's book, *Before I Say Goodbye*, edited by her husband after her death, takes the form of a column she wrote for *The Observer* and e-mails she sent to friends as her treatment progressed.[34] She describes the consuming nature of the disease.

> *My whole life seems to have been taken over by illness. This week, for example:*
>
> *Monday: trip to Suffolk to see healer, Matthew Nanning.*
>
> *Tuesday: appointment with Michael Baum (head of cancer treatment at UCH); secondary breast cancer group meeting at Guy's; appointment with Guy's.*

Wednesday: appointment with complementary practitioner (biomagnetic therapy).

Thursday: day off.

Friday: acupuncture.[35(i)]

This extract shows that you will try anything when you are completely desperate; and being only in your thirties with two young children, how could you be anything else? Ruth struggled to keep a grip on mental disintegration and in trying to cope, she said everything out loud: ' "Great! I'm going to die of cancer," wrote Ruth in one of her last columns, "but I'm going to go bonkers first." ' [35(ii)] Although many treatments can be exhausting, at least by trying to be pro-active, you may feel more in command of the progression of your illness. Later, however, it all becomes too much even for Ruth:

Luckily I have now come to my senses. The expense, the exhausting round of treatment, the sense of failure (I kept forgetting to bring mineral water to be healed; I would 'lose' my Chinese herbs) was part of it. But the thing that finally made me give up on beards was the revelation that complementary medicine does not work! Three months with Dr Charlatan, and the disease had spread to my bones. Six months on Golden Seal Comb and Five Leaf Amachazuru tea, and tumours developed in the liver and lungs. Three months of New-Age bonging, and I ended up with a brain tumour, despite confident declarations from all and sundry that I was on the mend. To be fair to the beards, mainstream treatment from arid white-coats has utterly failed, too, but at least it's a) free, and b) you don't have to listen to Vangelis in hospital.[35(iii)]

Sophie Hannah acidly echoes these sentiments:

Healing Powers

My foot is blue and bloated.
The swelling won't go down.
My limp is duly noted
As I hobble through the town.
I pass a Reiki master.
Of course! I should have put
The two together faster:
Healing powers, my foot.

I take my sore size seven
And place it in his hands.
It's ten now. By eleven
I'll be sprinting to the sands.
I ponder such remission.
My tears, like magic, dry.
Pure chance or superstition?
Healing powers, my eye.

My walking looks much better –
I jump, I jog, I hike,
Reluctant to upset a
Reiki master whom I like
But the pain is most dismaying
And I must confess, I put
New conviction in the saying:
Healing powers, my foot.

Sophie Hannah

Ruth finds other ways of keeping her spirits up; she discovers shopping: 'Essentially, after months of careful research, I have discovered a treatment that is a) cheaper than complementary therapy, b) a hell of a lot more fun than chemotherapy and c) most important, incredibly effective! Retail Therapy!' [35(iii)] Ruth first splashes out on Bobbi Brown make-up to heal her damaged psyche. 'The other problem – my enlarged liver – I believe has been solved by my later splurge at Whistles sale (blue skirt, lilac shirt). Even if the dread organ doesn't shrink, the clever bias cutting hides most of the lumps.' [35(iv)]

We can't all have Ruth's courage and black humour but this is one good way to look death in the face. None of us know how we will react until a given situation presents itself. If we had terminal cancer, would we rail 'against the dying of the light', 'go gentle' or prefer to remain in denial until the end?

Elisa Segrave's book, *Diary of a Breast*, deals among other things with the problems of serious illness in a domestic setting; money worries, problems with ex-husbands, single parenthood and chemotherapy, and in one particular passage, the kindness of strangers.

Here she is staying in London for her treatment and it is her birthday:

> *The babysitter could only stay till midnight. I rang Miranda and begged her to stay the night in my house. Having agreed to this, Miranda then rang saying she had a very bad period and couldn't come. I saw my new neighbour and asked if she knew a babysitter. She told me to wait a minute, went into the house and came out saying her husband would stay with the children. Their kindness is quite staggering'.* [36(i)]

While you are having treatment, you often find that in addition to the stress of your illness, life can slide out of your control:

> *When I returned home, I found that Mr Bigg had come over to complain about Toby. Apparently Toby had been round every day after Mr Bigg's spaniel bitch which is on heat. This morning at 6 am Toby scratched the putty off his kitchen door trying to get at her.*

I am not in control of my own house. Also, I feel extremely ill. I am in a panicky state and I keep feeling hot and cold. Emily is doing her best, but Paulo is very selfish and is obviously annoyed he is not being waited on hand and foot, as he is in his parent's house in Italy. Fortunately the Douthwaites, pensioners who live in the bungalow next door, come over later:

When Mrs Douthwaite's there everything seems calmer. Joseph does his homework at the kitchen table with her and Lucy goes off to ride her pony. I must be looking odd, as Mr Douthwaite, a man of few words, asked 'Are you alright?' [36(ii)]

Susan Johnson, author of *A Better Woman*, a memoir about motherhood and illness, also discusses the organisational problems of bad health. When she requires an operation, she 'put it off because it's actually quite hard to organise a six-week absence from your life while you recover and someone else stands in for you, getting your children up and dressed, cooking dinner, running the house, helping you to put on your own socks'.[37]

'I know from my own experience,' says Julia, 'that when leaving hospital you are often given a sheet that says you must not go back to work for a week. However, there are no instructions for housewives who find that as soon as they are home their family expects meals, the supermarket shop and the school run to resume immediately.'

We all have friends with cancer now. How can we help them? Virginia Ironside answers this problem in her 'Dilemmas' column in *The Independent*.

What ill people want is a barrage of low-grade, quiet and unfailing sympathy going on in the background like a soothing drone, a drip-feed of kindness. A small bunch of flowers sent every few weeks could hardly be taken amiss. And, on meeting, a hug with an extra squeeze at the end is always welcome – non-verbal communication is often best at this point. The odd postcard with a little joke on it, or just a few kisses would be nice. And certainly the occasional phone call – perhaps once every ten days just to ask how her friend is feeling, and whether there's anything she can do.

Deborah Hutton, Vogue health writer and journalist, died of lung cancer aged only 50, in spite of having smoked only briefly in her teens. She wrote a useful book about what others can do in the way of support for the cancer victim, entitled *What Can I Do to Help?*, which is a comprehensive book of useful, practical advice.

It is important to end this section on an upbeat note; breast awareness, digital screening and better drugs have dramatically improved the prognosis for breast cancer. It is no longer necessarily a killer. What is lacking is intelligent reporting on these drugs that enable women to make informed choices to improve their quality of life. As you get older, it becomes harder to keep your health in your own hands and it becomes vital to know which medical interventions, whether surgical or medical, are useful and to have some clear idea of the relative risks.

At the moment we simply do not know what to believe. *The Sunday Telegraph* recently reported a study by Oxford academics that said:

> *Scientists are routinely cherry-picking the results of clinical trials so that they can present the findings they want. The research which assessed the published results of more than 100 scientific trials, also found that inconvenient findings were often not disclosed to the public. In several cases the stated purpose of the trial was altered as it progressed so that acceptable findings, rather than inconvenient results could be published.*

★ ★ ★

How do women balance up conflicting information and relate it to their own lives? Returning to weight issues, the latest health warning is not just about fat *per se*, but where the fat is. You can now have a body scan which will show if you are fat *inside* – something even thin-looking people can be. And apparently if we let our middle go over a metre we are in danger of imminent heart disease. Now women are dashing about in a mad panic with tape measures. (Still, as Julia points out, she is the same height as Ariel Sharon but eight stone lighter. And even he did not have his catastrophic illness until he was 77.) Statistics (damned statistics) can be impossible to interpret and when you are ill there always seems to be a plethora of articles about your condition, all with conflicting messages. In *Diary of a Breast* Elisa Segrave reads *The Independent*:

> *Statistics show that in women whose cancer has spread to armpits, 62% who had extra treatment survived at 7 years, compared with 50% who did not and 35% of treated women survived at 15 years compared to 23% who did not.*

> *Did this mean that 62% survived who'd had treatment and 50% who'd also had treatment did not survive, or did it mean that the 50% who'd not had treatment did not survive? I became frantic with worry.*[38]

Well, wouldn't anyone?

A recent study in Copenhagen says that stress *lowers* your breast cancer risk by depleting your oestrogen. How can women possibly know what to believe?

Even if you're in perfect health, you're bound to become more obsessed about your looks as the years roll by. Faddy diets don't work, but plastic surgery is increasingly popular. It's our view that undergoing a general anaesthetic for anything other than sheer necessity is madness. There is a big difference between plastic surgery after an accident or mastectomy, and for purely cosmetic reasons. Even plastic surgeons themselves say surgery will not save a marriage, nor will it mend an unhappy life.

Women should not be afraid of senescence; we should not feel that like the old radio jingle we have to 'keep young and beautiful if you want to be loved'. As Johann Hari says in *The Independent*: 'The fashion and cosmetic industries are carefully calculated to locate the gap in our self-esteem and crowbar it open.'

The ultimate in ghastly TV is a US-made programme called *The Swan*:

> Each week, two ordinary women who were unhappy with their appearance were brought before a panel of cosmetic surgeons, dentists, hairdressers, stylists and life-coaches who would transform their looks into the all-American ideal. Tears aplenty followed as the participants were subjected to traumatic surgical procedures and isolated from their families. It was all deemed worthwhile several weeks later, when the women, with bouffant hair, cleavage-revealing frocks and lashings of make-up were allowed to look at themselves in the mirror.[39]

Channel 4's *Ten Years Younger* is much the same. As another *Independent* columnist, Philip Hensher, has written, we love these programmes in a car-crash kind of way.

Surely it's time to challenge the assumption that appearance is more important than health. (And yet... should there be a distinction between women who take HRT to look better and those who take it to feel better?)

We're with Dr. Rowan Williams, who in 2006 was quoted in *The Independent* as saying: 'By following lifestyles defined by a refusal to accept our mortality, we run the danger of becoming beset with a sense of anxiety, unreality and psychological fragility. A healthy human environment is one in which we try to make sense of our limits, of the accidents that can always befall us, and the passage of time which inexorably changes us.'

Jenny McCartney reports in *The Sunday Telegraph*, 'Once seen as extreme and dangerous, surgery is now promoted as just another beauty product. Women talk of saving up for another "boob job" as if it were a holiday'. By contrast, it is cheering to read what Jerry Hall said about cosmetic surgery: 'I'd never have plastic surgery. I think it's disgusting and grotesque. Anything that interferes with your health is really a big mistake. If you sleep well, have a happy disposition, drink plenty of water, get fresh air and exercise you're gonna look good, or as good as you can look.' Cameron Diaz also thinks along the same lines: 'The embalmed look just doesn't suit me.'

There are many other detractors from cosmetic surgery. Norman Hutchinson, the portrait painter, told *The Sunday Telegraph*, 'women get more beautiful as they get older', and asserts that 'facelifts denigrate women and make them lose their essence, their soul'. Anyone who has seen Cher attempting to smile on *Parkinson* would agree; she only has just enough facial skin left to grimace. The tragedy is that someone with her innate talent and beauty should have felt she had to go to these lengths.

And where do you draw the line? As Sue Arnold has observed in *The Independent*: 'The combinations of taut dewy complexions and bee stung lips with wrinkled hands covered in liver spots is macabre. A friend had been sent to the surgeon by her husband who said she was beginning to look like an old hag and she should have something done about her wrinkles before he traded her in for a new model. When the friend woke up the morning after the wrinkle treatment her entire face had blown up like a football and turned bright green.'

If you want to be put off plastic surgery, this passage, from William Leith's *The Hungry Years*, should do it. Leith is in theatre as his friend is having a face-lift:

Anne was on her back, on a trolley. She looked like a corpse. She looked like a dead old bloke. She had tubes coming out of her mouth; a machine was breathing for her.

The first thing the surgeon did was to make a hole under Anne's chin and insert a cannula, which looked like a thick needle. The cannula was attached to a clear plastic tube. After a moment or two, a bubbly pink substance, like strawberry milkshake was sucked back through the plastic tube. This was the fat. This was the double chin.

In the end, she might look younger, or better; she might have fewer wrinkles and a taut neck. But on some level – physical, mental, spiritual – she looked like she was paying for it.[40]

Plastic surgeons are the most unregulated of specialists; any general surgeon can undertake plastic surgery, and there are many horror stories. Olivia Goldsmith, author of *The First Wives Club*, had a heart attack and died during a facelift in America; in Russia, two doctors left a 24-year-old woman in a coma following what should have been a minor procedure for liposuction.

Movie stars no longer feel they have to hide their Botox and cosmetic surgery. Sixteen-year-olds are given liposuction as birthday presents; a procedure that is pointless unless you also eat less and exercise more. A recent follow-up patient study revealed that within a few months, nearly half were fatter than they were before the surgery.

Jemima Lewis in *The Sunday Telegraph* abhors this American way of grooming and celebrates the English way of beauty:

Our teeth are still crooked and yellow, our bodies soft and sinew-free. Instead of looking elegant or fit, we excel at originality, throwing on mismatched collections of clothes like children plundering a dressing up box. We are messy and inharmonious – and sometimes downright ugly – but at least we look like individuals.

Even Jane Fonda, who has had plastic surgery herself, is now campaigning to stop her fellow actors following suit. She said in a lecture given to Britain's Women's Institute: 'I grew up feeling that in order to be loved I had to be perfect, which is terrible, because nobody is perfect... I hope all of you like me will come to the realisation that we need to show perfection to the door.'

Make-up guru Bobbi Brown was asked in *The Times* if looks improve with age. 'I think that women can certainly look great as they get older, but the trick is to change your brain. You have to love yourself because, unfortunately the most beautiful years of a woman's life are when she is too young to realise. Don't look in the mirror; act like you look good and you will. Don't worry about age. You just have to learn to look at yourself differently as you get older.'

Cosmetic surgery is no longer the province of women. Even George Clooney (perfect, in Janice's view) has apparently had his eye-bags done. Investment bankers, who presumably don't have time to visit the gym, are using their large bonuses to have a little fat trimmed off. But it seems that many have over-optimistic expectations; even the president of the British Association of Aesthetic Plastic Surgeons says that some men would be better off eating fewer crisps and drinking less beer.

And so to face creams: the poor woman's alternative to plastic surgery. Because we are told that we are too old, too fat, too spotty, too wizened, or just plain unattractive, (sub-text: and will never get a man), we are in perpetual search of a skin product that will solve our life problems. New moisturisers are as seductive as self-help and diet books; we are, against our better judgement, always prepared to try another one. We've come a long way from the Ponds Cold Cream used by our mothers, but it is the hype that has advanced, not the ingredients. As Helena Rubenstein said at the beginning of time: 'Never sell it too cheap, it won't move off the shelves.' How many of us have got pots of cream in our bathrooms that cost a fortune but have been abandoned? Elizabeth Day points out in *The Daily Telegraph*, 'the beauty business thrives on disappointment'.

Make-up also has a special place in women's hearts. At its best it is an armour against the world and can certainly give you a lift. Providing of course that your 15-year-old daughter hasn't swiped the lot and gone off to a party, as Janice's did one New Year's Eve. And what solace new Bobbi Brown make-up gave Ruth Picardie in her last days.

Beauty treatments can be more problematic. Several *Sunday Telegraph* readers have reported on misunderstandings at health spas: 'Thalassotherapy. The word promised hedonism, classical decadence, salty bubbles, clinging seaweed, languorous mermaids even. Instead there was a brisk German nurse, who ordered me to strip and stand, arms raised, at the far end of a tiled chamber, where I was buffeted for a long time by a riot-strength water-cannon. My screams upset the other patients and my treatment was discontinued.'

Another reader reports: 'I once waited on a cold marble bench wearing nothing but a shower cap. A masseuse of Hungarian shot-putter proportions emerged to usher me into the treatment room. She gave me a withering look. "Why" she barked, "are you wearing your disposable knickers on your head?" '

The challenge is to find a lifestyle compatible with our strengths and limitations. It's a process that must be constantly re-evaluated and it is much easier said than done.

Seamus Heaney, in his poem, *Weighing In*, deals with the stoicism required in so many life circumstances:

And this is all the good tidings amount to:
This principle of bearing, bearing up
And bearing out, just having to
Balance the intolerable in others
Against our own, having to abide
Whatever we settled for and settled into
Against our better judgement.

E. Jane Dickson describes a friend who has nursed a sick child over a number of years: 'The reality is there is no lifestyle decision she can make that will dramatically cut her stress levels because real stress goes beyond lifestyle.'[41] The stress women face in coping with disabled children lies both in their love for them and in bearing a burden that lasts a lifetime. In addition to the caring, you have to fight for everything if you have a disabled child, because if you don't fight you don't get help. To think facials and lifestyle gurus are going to help women through these seemingly unending difficulties is an insult.

Women often make more progress in understanding their illnesses by discussing their problems among themselves and sharing information than they do from their doctors. As we've said, the symptoms of depression, anxiety, M.E., nervous exhaustion, and hormone imbalance are similar yet equally vague; cause and effect can be so easily muddled. Virginia Woolf, in her forties and probably in a state of peri-menopause, 'quite suddenly had a fainting fit. A long period of ill health followed, characterised by "that odd amphibious life of a headache". That autumn almost any effort brought on further headache, and she was condemned to her old regime of milk-drinking and woolwork, bed at 5pm and visitors rationed to one a day'.[42] Whether her symptoms were viral, hormonal or psychological would have been hard to determine, then or now.

Doctors are increasingly devoted to their own specialities; GPs are the only non-specialists left and so hard-pressed that it would be unfair to criticise them for failing to get to the bottom of things. 'I'm sure it must be exhausting for overworked doctors, faced with a surgery full of miseries, to come up with a way of shuffling them in and out of the door in the twelve minutes or so each patient is allotted,' says Janet Street-Porter.[43]

One of the reasons that alternative practitioners are so popular is because they consider every aspect of a patient's health and give you time to talk about your fears as well as the physical symptoms themselves. Here at Hey Nonny we keep an open mind about alternative therapies. Janice is a user of homeopathy and acupuncture: 'I think it works if it works for you. I like the idea behind Chinese medicine: that the idea is to keep the patient in a state of health. Every sick patient is a failure. It's the ultimate form of preventative medicine.'

Alternative medicine seems to be good for maintaining health and conventional medicine for when you fall ill in spite of it. Homeopathy proved effective for chronic back pain and depression in one study that concentrated on how it performed, rather than how it actually worked.

Surely Prince Charles is right when he says integrating different practices must be right; taking the best of mainstream and alternative medicine and making both available. The antagonism that exists between health practitioners of different persuasions just isn't helpful to the patient.

And moderation is vital. We are now so worried about melanoma that we hardly go in the sun at all and ignore the health benefits of sunshine, in particular the manufacture of vitamin D. (Studies have linked vitamin D deficiencies to heart disease, schizophrenia and cancer.)

So much of Hey Nonny is commonsense revisited, reminding ourselves of things that deep down we know already. And to recognise we can't do it all. (One headmistress friend's children think all vegetables come in microwave trays from Marks & Spencer, but she takes her daughter on great shopping trips; as a parent we can't be remembered for everything.)

We highly recommend considering the following tip from Rebecca Ash, taken from her book *The New Spend Less Revolution*:

> *Become lighter in everything you do or own. Enjoy having less in your drawers, less in your wardrobe, less in your car. Your unconscious mind is weighed down by everything you own. It stores up knowledge of everything you own. Whatever things you have in your home, you also carry round in your head.*
>
> *"The more you have, the less you are."*
>
> *Karl Marx*[44]

It is often also hard to know how to best support ill members of the family without becoming sick yourself. As Susan Sontag has said (and she suffered much serious illness), 'there is the kingdom of the sick, and the kingdom of the well, and neither can envisage the other'. And one of Jane Lapotaire's doctors says in *Time out of Mind*, 'People, brain patients, get scared. Families feel helpless too. People always withdraw if they feel helpless'.[45]

Many women are shocked and hurt by their husband's indifference or unhelpfulness when they are ill, in spite of being the recipient of devoted care when it's the other way round. It was Sarah Stickney Ellis who in the nineteenth century said: 'Men, engaged in the active affairs of life, have neither time nor opportunity for those innumerable little acts of consideration which come within the sphere for entering into the peculiarities of personal feeling, so as to enable them to sympathise with the suffering or the distressed.'[46]

Men are so often at an emotional loss, but do what they can. In the TV drama *Footprints in the Snow*, based on the novel by Julia Hill, the husband's only positive response to his wife's illness was to build her some cupboards that she couldn't reach. And it is not only husbands who can be unsympathetic. Family advice is not always helpful. In *Something in Disguise* by Elizabeth Jane Howard, Alice is staying with her in-laws following a miscarriage: 'What she found unnerving was how much everybody else seemed to expect her to feel, and what a lot they seemed to know about it. She'd spent ages listening to the various things that Leslie, Mrs Mount, and Rosemary told her she was feeling.'[47]

Some of the best health advice we've ever read is that given by the Royal Physician Sir James Clark in a letter to Princess Alice, written in 1862: 'I cannot feel satisfied to let Your Royal Highness leave this country without giving you a few hints and cautions to guide you on the subject of your health.' He mentions 'the necessity of healthy fresh air', 'before going to bed ablution with tepid water should never be omitted, and the eyes especially should be carefully bathed. The feet also often require bathing at night. It will be your own fault if you have either corns or chilblains. A warm bath also, once a week at least, should never be omitted when it can be had'.

Finally he advocates something that is free to us all, princesses and commoners alike: 'Your Royal Highness will I trust keep up the habit of daily exercise in the open air. Walking is the best.'[48]

We must remember this.

Be near me when my light is low
When the blood creeps, and the nerves prick
And tingle; and the heart is sick
And all the wheels of Being slow

From In Memoriam by Alfred Lord Tennyson

The crack-up

F. Scott Fitzgerald's autobiographical short story, *The Crack-Up*, written in 1946 about his experience of breakdown, is illuminating on the subject of personal disaster in middle age. He defines breakdown very simply: 'Now a man can crack in many ways – can crack in the head – in which case, the power of decision is taken from you by others! Or in the body, when one can but submit to the white hospital world: or in the nerves.'[1(i)]

In Scott's own case, it was his nerves: 'nervous reflexes that were giving away too much anger and too many tears.' Scott had lived too hard. He was only 39, but he was exhausted. 'I found I was good and tired. I could lie around and was glad to, sleeping or dozing sometimes twenty hours a day and in the intervals trying resolutely not to think. I had begun to realise that for two years my life had been drawing on resources that I did not possess but I had been mortgaging myself spiritually up to the hilt.'[1(ii)]

There is an irony in our quoting Fitzgerald. Perceptive as he was about his own mental state, he was rather less sympathetic to his wife Zelda, who herself suffered a breakdown (see Hey Nonny Heroines). Nevertheless, women will recognise his description, and the image is a powerful one: in the same way that there comes a point where your debts become insurmountable, so you may reach the point where you are simply so emotionally worn out that you have nothing left to give. And sometimes both eventualities occur at once. Many women find they are trapped by circumstances, lessening energy, and by their duties to others. Whatever their financial circumstances, women in mid-life, particularly if they have families, are likely to have less freedom and fewer options than they did in their twenties.

Depression can arrive spontaneously, or it can be triggered by external events – children leaving home, a failing marriage, the death of a parent, severe physical illness, overwork, or simply too many life changes occurring simultaneously. Statistically, women are twice as likely to be depressed as men.

The symptoms of depression are well known – continual low mood, hopelessness, low self-esteem, tearfulness, feelings of guilt and irritability, lack of motivation, suicidal thoughts, anxiety and a reduced sex drive. However, sufferers themselves are often the least likely to realise what is happening to them.

Depression can present itself in many ways, not all of them obvious. Take these symptoms, for example: fatigue, visual disturbances, pins and needles or numbness; problems with short-term memory, concentration, reasoning and judgement, mood swings, emotional outbursts; muscle spasm, weakness, loss of coordination, clumsiness; loss of balance, dizziness, vertigo, tremor. They could be caused by clinical conditions ranging from multiple sclerosis to anxiety and depression.

As a result, any but the most perceptive doctor may often see a patient who seems to be one of the 'worried well', whose physical symptoms may never add up to anything serious, but who may be referred again and again for specialist investigations that reveal nothing. That anxiety and depression affect the immune system is now a given; sufferers may, therefore, be constantly ill with minor complaints.

Neither the patient nor the doctor may be aware of the real cause, as the human mind is all too efficient at hiding its own problems from itself. In consequence, depression can be very hard to understand, for the sufferers themselves as for uncomprehending onlookers. As Dr N. Yognathan, a consultant psychiatrist, said in a letter to *The Guardian*: 'The dilemma I face in my daily work is how to balance the psychiatric, scientific model with a more dialectic, artistic approach to mental health.'

However, if you have experienced clinical depression, you will know that it is as far from being fed up as a sprained little finger is from a broken leg. Unfortunately, a broken leg generally elicits far more sympathy and genuine help from your family than an illness no-one can see. Julia, after an attack of disabling (but invisible) labrynthitis, tried posting this notice on her fridge: *My leg is still broken.* The point was entirely lost on her family, who continued to expect service as usual.

As women we assume that as we get older, our responsibility for our children will lessen, but in fact all that happens is that our concerns change. Mothers often have more anxiety about exams, gap years, drugs and nightclubs, than they ever did about potty training or starting school. In fact, women as a sex tend to do most of the worrying. According to Julia Briggs in *Virgina Woolf: An Inner Life*, an example of the typically 'Laingian' dysfunctional family was 'one where one member bore the burden of chaos, doubt or anxiety on behalf of the others'.[2] In our experience, this is often the mother; very often, she would also have borne the burden of the 'dysfunctional family' as a child, too.

We may be in the midst of what feels like a life-and-death struggle for our own sanity, while our family around us is proceeding as usual: GCSE's, A-levels, dating, breaking up, learning to drive. Children and husbands may be understandably distracted with their own concerns, most of which are stressful in their turn. They may not notice that you are not well, particularly if you have never before demanded attention, and if until now, as Mary Chapin Carpenter reminds us in her song *He Thinks He'll Keep Her*, everything has 'run right on time, years of practice and design/Spit and polish till it shines...'

In Hanif Kureishi's novel *Intimacy*, the narrator's mother has clearly given up on the spit and polish. She is recalled as an abject creature, who seems to be loathed rather than pitied, and it's hard to read the following passage without wondering why he had so little sympathy for one so obviously reduced:

> *Mother was only partially there. Most of the day she sat, inert and obese, in her chair. She hardly spoke – except to dispute; she never touched anyone, and often wept, hating herself and all of us: a lump of living death. She wouldn't wash: there were cobwebs in all the rooms: the plates and cutlery were greasy. We hardly changed our clothes. All effort was trouble and she lived on the edge of panic, as if everything was about to break down.*[3]

There are many further examples in literature of a lack of compassion or understanding – here in Arnold Bennett's 1908 *The Old Wives' Tale*, concerning the ailing Maria Critchlow: 'She naturally had no sympathy from Charles [her elderly husband] who now took small interest even in his own business, and who was coldly disgusted at the ultimate cost of his marriage. Charles gave her no money that he could avoid giving her…It appeared that for many months she had been depressed and irritable. She did not sleep for whole nights…She had noises in the ears and a chronic headache.' Mrs Critchlow next tried to kill herself by stabbing herself with a pair of scissors. 'There was blood in the shop. With as little delay as possible she had been driven away to the asylum. Charles Critchlow, enveloped safely in the armour of his senile egotism, had shown no emotion, and very little activity.'[4]

Another woman took the same option, with more success: 'A funeral came by of a poor woman who had drowned herself, some say because she was hardly treated by her husband; others that he was a very decent, respectable man, and she but an indifferent wife. However this was, she had only been married to him last Whitsuntide and had had very indifferent health ever since. She had got up in the night and drowned herself in the pond.'[5]

During mid-life, our identities as individuals are under siege as never before. We seem to exist only in relation to others, and the struggle to re-establish ourselves and to forge an identity can be as difficult, if not more so, than when we were teenagers. This should be a time to pare down, re-evaluate and perhaps find 'it's all right to be slow':

Yet to learn

I've yet to learn
How not to go too far;
I've yet to learn
How to give up.

In fact, the going getting bad
Seems to spur me on.
I throw my weight into the harness
And plod on up the hill

Never realising that
Freedom lies around the corner;
There's grass in the valley
Below

Never realising that giving up
Can be good;
That it's quite all right
To be slow

Janice Warman

But very often it's at this stage that depression and anxiety can attack from left field; just when all our energies are needed to hold everything together: career, household, children, parents, family, even the pets, which seem to live a dramatic life in our households at least, when it seems the worst possible moment – but when would be a good one?

It is not unusual for family members to experience completely different realities simultaneously. We may have what Rebecca West once called in a letter to Arnold Bennett a 'dreadful summer of misfortune' – yet our children may look back on that same summer as an idyll of long, golden hours. Women often shield their families from the worst of things.

And when you are facing a nervous breakdown, families are not always supportive; they may even be angry with you for not being well. The ability to refer others' troubles back to oneself is extremely common: A friend's aunt lost a mother and a sister in quick succession. 'Why do these things always happen to me?' she enquired of her surviving family. We would like to think their answer was short and to the point. And it is not unknown for a partner to say: 'What have I done to deserve this?'

Anxiety and panic attacks – surges of overwhelming fear that flood the system with adrenaline – can be equally terrifying. Physiologically, they mimic what happens when you face a real threat and need strength to fight or flee: without the need for either action, you are left trembling, dizzy and sick. Diana Melly (wife of the jazz musician, George) describes what happened to her in vivid detail:

> *The ground seemed to be tipping away from me like something in a painting before perspective was discovered. I sat frozen on the bed, but*

slowly the explosive feelings began to subside. It was as if I had been under water with my lungs bursting and my heart and blood racing. The first panic attack is the worst; you do feel you must be dying. Nothing afterwards is ever quite as bad.[6]

Panic attacks were no bar to success for Stella Rimington, who went on to hold what was surely one of the most stressful jobs in the country, as the first woman director of MI5. Here she is in her late twenties:

The first few months of married life were very difficult. For a year or so I had been suffering from a recurrence of the claustrophobia which I had suffered from quite acutely in my teenage years and now which made it very difficult for me to travel to work on the underground. I had to sit or stand close to the door or I would start to sweat and gasp and feel faint. If the train stopped for any length of time in the tunnel, I found it very difficult indeed to keep control.[7]

Janice had her first panic attack in Act Three of Gluck's *Iphigenia* at Glyndebourne. 'I was in the middle of a row, flanked by my husband, our American friends, and their guests, an MP and her husband. Suddenly the light and the music began to fade – it was as if I was going blind. I could barely breathe, I couldn't hear, and I could barely see. It was as if I was looking at the stage down a long, narrow tunnel. I thought I might be dying, as it truly seemed that all my systems were shutting down, although there was a shred of common sense in there somewhere that told me I wasn't. I clung onto my husband's arm and told him – actually I can't remember what I told him. He offered to get me out of there but the thought of disrupting the entire theatre with an invasion of paramedics was too much. I just clung on and did slow, yoga breaths. I didn't see or hear the entire second half – it was all I could do to keep breathing – and can barely recollect how we got out of there and drove home.'

As the panic attacks became more frequent, Janice (rather reluctantly) started taking Seroxat (paroxetine) alongside her therapy. She felt it was far from a cure-all, and according to BBC TV's *Panorama*, possibly addictive:

Thank you to Paroxetine

Thank you to Paroxetine;
Paroxetine has kept me clean
My nose don't run
My step is keen
My family seems like new
If Panorama has it right
I may never sleep another night
If I come off of you

But hey, I'd rather hold on tight
Keep my nerves clean;
Serves me right,
For ever choosing you –

But oh Paroxetine,
Thanks to you,
I don't really care
What I do

Janice Warman

'I was already having cognitive therapy and reading every book I could lay my hands on, so I was addressing the problem by every means at my disposal. But there came the day when my therapist took one look at me and said I was to see my GP without delay.

'I could not have been more reluctant. I had always turned to alternative medicine first, except for the serious stuff. I hated the idea of a mood-altering drug and felt that submitting to it made me a failure. But it was an unmitigated blessing. It was as if a huge weight had been taken off my shoulders and I could stand up and look around me at last; it enabled me to see clearly what had been happening to me.

'That's not to say there were no side effects – I had some nausea to begin with, as well as sudden temperature spikes which had me tearing my jumper off. Both passed. Like Robbie Williams (our only point of similarity!) my weight ballooned, though at the time this seemed supremely irrelevant. And it was tricky to get the dose exactly right; too little and the panic attacks would return; too much, and I felt dull and exhausted. And I can't emphasise enough that continuing with therapy was essential. The anti-depressants meant that the therapy was more effective – because I was in a better state of mind to work with my therapist.'

'When I cracked up, I tried to do everything I could to get back to the land of the living,' says Julia. 'I tried rest and a lot of it, therapy, (my son took one look at the therapist who came to the house and said "Who's that madman in the sitting room?" I said, "Actually darling, he's the only one of us who's *not* mad"); as much exercise as I could manage, cranial osteopathy, homeopathy, tonics, vitamin supplements, yoga, healthy organic eating, conventional anti-depressants. My GP asked: "If you do all these things at once, how will you know what works?" My response was that it didn't matter what worked, as long as something did.

'In the event, it was probably a bit of everything, although I was particularly grateful for the Seroxat which calmed me down without actual sedation and friends both old and new who came to my aid. Some listened *ad nauseum*, some wrote me letters to remind me of the person I'd once been and hoped to be again. I was particularly in debt to the friend who recommended *Self-Help for Your Nerves*, which was invaluable for my recovery (see Enquire Within) and became my Bible.

'Because I was furious with myself for allowing the illness to take hold (something I have since learned to reconsider), I needed to prove to myself that there was something I could do to make myself better. Action of some kind, any kind, was needed for me to start feeling even a bit better.

'As a footnote, I was hopeless at the yoga, I'm sure the Seroxat sledge-hammered the homeopathy, and when I had a shorter subsequent bout of depression I got better with Seroxat, rest and exercise alone. By this time, I'd run out of money for facials, therapy and cranial adjustment; it was a "no frills" recovery and it seemed to work just as well.'

The psychologist Dorothy Rowe has written many excellent books on depression but in an article in The Independent, she is critical of certain anomalies in the mental health field. She is concerned that the wide spectrum of normal behaviour is being eroded by spurious psychiatric labels; that 'quiet, compliant women can be diagnosed as mentally ill for being what society expects them to be, yet aggressive, sexist men are to be protected from the stigma of mental illness'.

While it is true that some people collapse more readily than others, the point at which people give up in the face of problems is likely to vary with the extent of their engagement with them in the first place, as well as their psychological capacity to cope. For example, one member of the family may collapse after a prolonged period of looking after an elderly relative, while another member may have ignored the problem in the first place or told themselves it was nothing to do with them. They may have thereby safeguarded their own mental health, but society would not function properly for long if everyone was like this.

Depression can come with no warning and for apparently no reason. But very often it is triggered by life events. Sometimes there is a final straw, something that, though unfortunate, should not have been a disaster. For the writer Adam Nicholson, it was a mugging.

> It was not the attack itself for which I wept and sweated that night but for everything of which it seemed, however irrationally, a culmination: the failure of my first marriage the year before, my guilt at my own part in that failure, the effect my leaving would have on my three sons by that marriage, the failure or near-failure of a business I had been involved with for five

years, which I had also abandoned, unable to work properly any longer,
leaving it in the hands of my cousin and co-director at the one moment he
most needed my help. If I had been a horse, I would have been shot. I
should have been shot. I had broken down.[8]

We've established that women are twice as likely to be depressed as men. Statistics also show that while the lack of an intimate, confiding relationship is important, the rates of depression are highest in unhappily married women. It is not uncommon for a wife to take medicine to enable her to cope with her husband's mood swings; and of course, it's quite possible that his mood swings may be caused by an undiagnosed depression. One Ayurvedic practitioner told Janice: 'If I could only treat the husbands, I wouldn't need to see the wives at all.'

Women approach depression differently, according to Lewis Wolpert, whose *Malignant Sadness* we recommended in Enquire Within: 'Women, when placed in a situation that gives rise to emotional distress, respond with a style that emphasises excessive self-analysis; they often weep and talk endlessly to friends, and write in diaries about their feelings. This is in stark contrast to men who use distraction to cope with similar problems, ignoring them altogether, or working harder, playing sports or drinking alcohol.'[9]

Mary in Amanda Craig's *A Vicious Circle*, inconsolable at the end of a love affair, bears this out: 'Every letter, scribbled between shifts or at three a.m., would begin with violent humility, followed by the realisation that for Mark there was no impulse of remorse. This understanding came to her slowly, and at first she could not believe it. Yet she could not stop writing. It was like being on a treadmill: fury, despair, hatred, desolation. Every letter-box was a temptation, another return to the wheel of fortune.'[10]

Kingsley Amis seems to agree:

From A Bookshop Idyll

We men have got love weighed up;
Our stuff
Can get by without it.
Women don't seem to think that's good enough;
They write about it,
And the awful way their poems lay them open
Just doesn't strike them.
Women are really much nicer than men:
No wonder we like them.

Kingsley Amis

Are women really much nicer than men? Well, we'd be the first to admit – not always! And of course, some years later he changed his tune. In a letter to *The Sunday Telegraph* he responded to a review of one of his novels: '...my novel "Stanley and the Women" does not argue that "all women are mad". No, as a leading character puts it, they're all too monstrously sickeningly TERRIFYINGLY sane. Not that it makes a lot of difference to those at the receiving end, admittedly. Or to a feminist.'[11] Novelists, male and female, are often subject to depression. Does 'an examined life' go with the territory, or do they attempt to stay sane by the act of writing itself? Does the writing cause the instability, or is it the writer's sensibility that makes them more attuned to external events?

However paralysing it feels at the time, depression can be a creative space, too: Nora Ephron (scriptwriter of *When Harry Met Sally and Sleepless in Seattle*) turned her husband's affair and the breakdown of her second marriage into a scintillating book and a film, *Heartburn*: 'My mother taught me many things when I was growing up, but the main thing I learned from her was that everything is copy...As a result, I knew the moment my marriage ended that someday it might make a book – if I could just stop crying. One of the things I'm proudest of is that I managed to convert an event that seemed to me hideously tragic at the time to a comedy.'[12]

Sometimes for the creative woman there was an upside to physical exhaustion. 'Sara Coleridge's post-natal depression had freed her from many of the responsibilities of housekeeping and motherhood. She had fallen into the childhood habit of letting her mother look after things while she lay on the sofa "reading from morning to night".'[13(i)] Of course, few women today would have that luxury: when women collapse, families can implode. (And the washing-up doesn't get done, either.)

Sara also saw the link between breakdown and creativity: 'My nervous trials have been the source of some of my most valuable mental acquisitions.' She even wrote a forerunner to Hey Nonny, an essay on *Nervousness*: 'She had understood from observing her family and her own personal suffering that depression was a complex phenomenon. It manifests itself by so many different symptoms that the sufferers themselves are puzzled what to make of it. Those who perceive only how it weakens the mind are apt to forget that it also weakens the body.'[13(ii)]

Paula Danziger, a children's writer who died in 2004, used her experiences of growing up in what would now be called a dysfunctional home in her books for teenagers. Nicholas Tucker, in her obituary in *The Independent*, describes her home life: 'Danziger had to put up with the verbal aggression of her deeply frustrated father while her mother sought shelter in passive acceptance, enlivened by occasional bursts of binge shopping. She vowed from the age of seven that whenever her father yelled at her or made fun of her weight or clumsiness she would later use this in a novel.' And this she did in *The Cat Ate My Gymslip* in which her own experience is lightly disguised: the story tells of a 'sarcastic and unloving father tolerated by a beaten down wife who prescribes tranquillisers for herself and huge bowls of ice-cream for her daughter, so exacerbating the weight problem mocked by the father in the first place'.[14]

Paula Danziger did for children what we are attempting to do for adults. 'She had the first belief that certain stories can significantly help a child by describing their problems – and then some possible solutions.' This was a trend successfully continued by Jacqueline Wilson with her children's books that tackle divorce, fostering and even manic depression with insight and sympathy.

What these women have discovered is what Amis has accused them of: that writing can be a salvation. Wendy Cope has said she wrote her first poems after starting analysis; and Doris Lessing confessed in her autobiography, *Walking in the Shade*: 'The reason for my not having been personally mad or in breakdown is, I think, partly that any inclination towards it has been staved off by writing about it.'[15]

The writer Elizabeth Buchan has said: 'I think I am lucky to have had a creative life. Most of my anguishes and neuroses go into that so it has been, in a way, a firewall for my family.'

The act of writing restores order to experience. Julia started writing at a young age 'because I felt I wanted my life to amount to something, and in some strange way felt this would help. I felt my family had such low expectations of me that I had to do something to bump up my self-belief. Of course this I understood later; at the time it was pure survival.' Janice wrote as a matter of instinct, both creatively and for her livelihood; it was only when life struck her a series of blows that she clammed up – the opposite to 'happiness writes white'.

The medication debate is a heated one. In *Love is Where it Falls*, Simon Callow's memoir, he describes his doomed relationship with his lover Aziz, who rejected medication and took his life: 'The stability Prozac brought him bored him, he lost his edge.'

Seroxat is alternately said to be addictive or lifesaving, and there are warnings about its near-relative Effexor (venlafaxine) which is known to be extremely difficult to come off. Perhaps this is because anti-depressants are still seen as an optional extra; people perfectly understand the need for insulin or heart medication and yet, as Andrew Solomon points out in his excellent book on depression, *The Noonday Demon*:

> *I am often asked in social situations to describe my own experiences, and I usually end by saying that I am on medication. "Still?" people ask. "But you seem fine!" To which I invariably reply that I seem fine because I am fine, and that I am fine in part because of medication. "So how long do you expect to go on taking this stuff?" people ask.* [16]

Advice like this is wrong-headed and dangerous; it can also reinforce any feelings of shame and hopelessness.

> *Just like insulin, thyroxin or heart medication, anti-depressants are simply correcting a chemical imbalance, this time in the brain. Neurotransmitters are produced naturally by the body and transmit signals between the cells in the brain. During depression the neurotransmitter systems, particular the chemicals serotonin and noradrenaline, don't seem to work properly; anti-depressants, like the newer Selective Serotonin Reuptake Inhibitors (SSRI's) work by stimulating these chemicals so they are more active. It's as simple as that.* [17]

We should warn that it's not always easy to come off them, and that if you can't, it's not a failure. When Janice had trouble reducing her dosage, she was told very firmly by a friend's husband, a psychiatrist, that she wasn't to beat herself up about it, she clearly wasn't ready, and she was to go back up to the minimum dosage and carry on seeing her therapist. 'It was the best thing I ever did. My panic attacks, which had restarted, eased off, and six months later, I cut back slowly and came off them quite easily.'

Yet despite changing attitudes to medication, this stigma remains. The following are letters published in *The Independent*. All are clearly grateful for the benefits of their particular drug of choice; none has chosen to give their name.

> – *I for one would be in trouble if Seroxat were not available next time the black dog turns up at my door.*

> – *The Prozac has transformed me from a bear into a human being. It literally saved my life. If I had not gone to the GP and been diagnosed and treated I would be dead.*

> – *For most of my adult life I have suffered from agoraphobia. My husband and I have not had a holiday, day at the seaside or cinema visit for almost 30 years. My entire married life has been lived within a few miles of our home. Two years ago I asked my doctor to prescribe Seroxat. He suggested I start on a daily dose of 10mg and increase to 20mg if I had no side effects. After two weeks I began to feel less anxious in situations which normally would have triggered panic. In a few weeks I was able to visit two towns we last visited in 1977, I decided to remain on the 10mg dose as it was effective. To someone who has never experienced the devastating effect of chronic low-level anxiety, the expansion of my universe will seem trivial. It isn't.*

Nick Foulkes, writing in *The Sunday Telegraph*, admits having taken anti-depressants for ten years, 'and I have found them an enormous help; indeed, I probably owe my life to them. I used to be afflicted by bouts of the most crushing depression: I'd lie in bed in the early hours, paralysed by fear and unhappiness; I saw transience, futility and death in everything – and that was the good days. Since taking SSRIs, however, I have rediscovered, if not euphoria, then at least what it feels like to be happy. It's as if a mist has lifted.'

Women can find some male depressive behaviour, such as the MP Mark Oaten's dalliance with rent boys, particularly hard to fathom. (Solomon's book is particularly revealing on this subject.) Has 'understanding' gone too far? The problem page in *The Daily Mirror* advises a woman who has discovered her husband wearing her clothes and visiting gay bars that he had 'just decided to explore a new side of his sexuality'.

And so to the causes of depression – where they can be determined. Somerset Maugham said: 'The greatest tragedy of life is not that men perish but that they cease to love.' And when we consider the divorce statistics, it is no surprise to learn that marriage breakdown is one of the commonest triggers of depression in both sexes.

In Amanda Craig's *A Vicious Circle*, Tom and Adam are in conversation: ' "I should think losing your lover and your home would make most people pretty suicidal. She's not normally neurotic or depressive, I'd say." "*Cherchez l'homme*. It's always that way with women, isn't it?" '[18]

Anna Kavan, in her novel *Asylum Piece*, writes a perceptive description of a failing marriage, how women in particular feel when their hopes for the future are dashed; how hard it is to look back and see the moment of change, how indiscernible the start point of fragmentation:

> *Who shall describe the slow and lamentable cooling of the heart? On what day does one observe the infinitesimal crack which finally becomes a chasm deeper than hell?*
>
> *The years passed like the steps of a staircase leading lower and lower. I did not walk anymore in the sun or hear the songs of larks like crystal fountains against the sky. No hand enfolded mine in the warm clasp of love. My thoughts were again solitary, disintegrate, disharmonious – the music gone.*[19(i)]

She goes on to describe the practical reality of such fragmentation, feelings which will be familiar to women who find separation and divorce forced upon them:

> *One is forced into a position of inactivity, of passive waiting, of nerve-wracking suspense, with absolutely no relief except an occasional visit to one's official advisor – an interview which is just as likely to plunge one into utter dejection as to buoy one up with fugitive hopes...*
>
> *And through all this one is expected to carry on one's personal existence as usual: to work and to perform social and family duties as if the background of one's life were still perfectly normal; this is what is hardest to bear.* [19(ii)]

Different losses seem to affect different parts of the brain; heartbreak seems to inhabit its own country. Joanna Trollope, in her novel *Marrying the Mistress*, has her heroine describe it somewhat apologetically: 'I have never quite been able to live up to Guy, you see. I've never quite been able to be what he wanted me to be, what he made it very plain he wanted me to be. The things I'm good at he can't see the point of.'[20]

The moods of one partner can have a devastating effect on the mental health of another. And if we are considering curmudgeonly husbands, the one who springs to mind most readily is, naturally enough, Kingsley Amis. Here is Elizabeth Jane Howard on living with him (after the first flush of love had gone): 'The moment we were alone, Kingsley's irritation with me was like the atmosphere before an impending thunderstorm. I dreaded being alone with him.'[21]

'You can be broken by a lifetime of such treatment caused by a man constantly finding fault,' says Julia. 'A lifetime of tutts and sighs, small subtle signs from the man that the woman is just not up to scratch, can be as damaging to the female psyche as discovering he's having a fling with his secretary.'

Certainly a bad marriage can prompt breakdown as much as a stressful divorce. Anyone who has had a difficult, overbearing partner has only to read Elizabeth von Arnim's *Vera* for an accurate psychological profile of a particularly sinister example.

Lucy Entwhistle marries Everard Wemyss after her father's death and the death of Wemyss' wife Vera, whom he has driven to kill herself. At first she does not realise the full extent of his character, explains Xandra Hardie in the introduction: 'She loves Wemyss because he is protective, and for his schoolboy sense of fun which diminishes the thirty years difference between them, and because like Henry VIII, he is immutably there. His tyrannies are so small and ludicrously domestic. Servants race, timed by his watch, from door to door....He is, it seems, too ludicrous to be threatening. His love is childlike, and must therefore be innocent, so he must be harmless.'[22(i)]

Like Daphne du Maurier's *Rebecca*, Vera's presence seems to grow through the novel, and slowly Lucy realises what Wemyss is like: 'If Lucy does not behave like his adorable, obedient baby, Wemyss' protectiveness turns into violent anger. Only a parade of guilt restores his love and good humour, otherwise he sulks. He sinks in a sea of self-pity and resentment at not getting the kind of love he so desperately needs...' [22(ii)]

One partner may be aggressive (anger can be a symptom of depression) and the other may withdraw; and it is not always the man who is the tyrant, although it was Hitler who said: 'The greater the man, the more insignificant should be the woman.' Certainly his relationship with Eva Braun would seem to bear this out. Her recently discovered 1935 diary makes disturbing reading: she seems to have spent the majority of her time anxiously waiting for rare visits from him and then quite often being ignored. A previous mistress killed herself, as did his niece, Geli Raubal, with whom he also had an obsessional relationship, according to Angela Lambert's biography of Eva Braun. Eva herself attempted suicide twice, first by shooting herself in the neck and then by taking an overdose of sleeping tablets. The last entry reads: 'I have made up my mind to take 35 pills this time, and it will be "dead certain"[23].' Of course, she survived to live a sequestered life with Hitler, never appearing with him in public (it was considered politically expedient for him to appear single) and to commit suicide alongside him the day after their marriage in the Berlin bunker on 29th April, 1945.

Wemyss himself would probably have been described by psychologist Oliver James as having Borderline Personality Disorder: 'BPDs shift between extended periods of dejection and apathy and have frantic spells of anger, anxiety or excitement. Offended by trifles, they're readily provoked to contrariness; they report proneness to affairs yet they invariably identify their partner with the sexual problem. Intimate contact leaves

BPDs feeling battered because their omnipotent and narcissistic fantasies are constantly banging at the ceiling of reality.'[24]

The late Irish novelist John McGahern writes of a similar patriarch in *Memoir*, one many will recognise: 'Nobody was going to dictate to him what he could do or couldn't do in his own house, he told her in his fury... His general moods were so changeable that apart from a passion for contrariness, he never knows his mind from one minute to the next. Even when the decision was his alone, he would try to turn it round in blame on someone else once it started to go wrong...All our energies were concentrated on surviving under our father.'[25]

Women today are luckier than their mothers, who struggled with the nameless feeling that something was missing in their lives, and which often caused depression. The journalist and broadcaster Joan Bakewell describes her mother in her memoir, *The Centre of the Bed*: 'Over the years, trying to understand her despair, I have wondered whether she ever considered that being thwarted of a chosen and fulfilling career had any bearing on her later mental state. I judged my mother harshly as a difficult woman. Now I can see clearly that she was clever, she had hopes and training, and it took her nowhere.'[26]

The ability for one generation to help another is often limited. In her memoir, *Janey and Me*, Virginia Ironside describes life with her mother, the once formidable (but later alcoholic) Janey Ironside, doyenne of the Fashion School at the Royal Academy of Art: 'Woodstock was happening and hippies were dancing in the streets with flowers in their hair. The truth for me was that most of the time I sat alone in my flat, worrying about my mother. She became fat, slow and dazed with antidepressants, and spent her time sitting at home, her neck swaddled in a bulky scarf, eating sweet biscuits and drinking tonic water all day.'[27(i)]

Nor could Virginia's grandmother offer any help: '[She] lived in a mansion block down the road, and although sympathetic, she was unable to be any support. She had her own anxieties, loneliness, age and forgetfulness, and although she had plenty of theories about [the TV programme] the *Mind of a Murderer*, she had no clue about addiction and depression.'[27(ii)]

Women who don't suffer depression or anxiety may have to cope with relatives who do. Michele Hanson's *Living with Mother* will be familiar to many:

> *I open the front door and see a desperate figure. Is that the first Mrs Rochester standing screaming and wailing at the top of the stairs in her nightie with her hair awry? No. It is my poor mother in a panic. Where have I been, why am I so late, she thought I was dead! But how, on a dog walk? Easy, thinks my mother: crashed on the way home, drowned in a pond, gobbled up by Rottweilers. She is the Anxiety Queen on overdrive. She knows that if there is a psychopath on the loose, he is bound to home in on her only child.*
>
> *She cannot help this. It runs in the family.*[28]

Life still holds all sorts of unforeseen difficulties for women, but it's worth remembering that it is far less restrictive than it was. Many women in the near and distant past suffered nervous exhaustion and breakdown, who today would have found freedom in work, travel or even love. And many would have benefited from effective contraception.

Edith Southey, wife of the poet Robert, lost her fourth child just as the little girl began to walk and talk, but was prevented from sinking into uncontrollable grief by the fact that she had another child at the breast who required all her attention. Altogether, however, she lost four of her eight children and with each death sank into a more permanent state of depression. Like Cherie Blair (though undoubtedly with fewer staff) she had her last child at 45. Although her poor physical condition and continued pregnancies had put their marriage under strain, Southey himself seemed oblivious to the principle of cause and effect.

In fact, nearly all the women of this poetic circle seemed to suffer from 'nerves' of some kind, perhaps the combination of unfulfilled artistic temperaments as well as too many pregnancies and bereavements. Once these women were married, they were in effect taken prisoner; 'They led stifling lives within the four walls of their houses, their lives bounded by child rearing and domestic concerns without any prospect of escape': 'Divorce and separation were rare, expensive and socially ruinous for women, who were usually forced to stay in unhappy, sometimes abusive relationships.'[29] This situation hardly changed until the development of the contraceptive pill and the emergence of the feminist movement in the 1970s. Another reason that liberation was so essential, perhaps even the paramount reason, was its positive effect on female mental health.

Post-natal depression was no doubt rife, but almost certainly undiagnosed. Even today, as many as one in seven women suffers from a mental health disorder during pregnancy or after their baby is born, yet only 30% of women with postnatal depression are diagnosed. Take 41-year-old Paula Talby, who killed her two boys and herself in 2007. Paula had suffered post-natal depression after the birth of her second child, but was thought to have recovered.

Some indomitable female spirits were not so easily overcome or just luckier that they had an escape route. Christina Patterson, in an article about early pioneering women in *The Independent*, describes the life of the travel writer Isabella Bird: 'Isabella, a 23-year-old clergyman's daughter who suffered from insomnia, restlessness and a host of vague aches and pains was prescribed a long sea voyage in 1854. "I am well", she wrote to a friend, "as long as I live on horseback, go to bed at eight, sleep out-of-doors, or in a log cabin, and lead in all respects a completely unconventional life".'

This was in marked contrast to Kath in Pat Barker's *The Ghost Road*, the third novel in her trilogy on the First World War:

> *The whole course of Kath's life had been constriction into a smaller and smaller space. As children, they'd both had a hundred acres of safe woods and fields to roam in, but from that point on his life had expanded: medical school, round the world as a ship's doctor, Germany, the Torres Straits, India, Australia, the Solomon Islands, the New Hebrides. And over the same period, the little girl who'd rambled all day through woods and fields had become the younger of the two Miss Rivers, scrutinised by her father's parishioners, the slightest breach of decorum noted, and then, after father's retirement, a small house in Ramsgate, deteriorating health,*

confinement to the house, then to the bedroom, then to the bed. And yet she
was no more intrinsically neurasthenic than he was himself. But a good
mind must have something to feed on, and hers, deprived of other
nourishment, had fed on itself.[30]

Many women, past and present, have found therapy useful. Elizabeth Jane Howard, after her separation from Kingsley Amis, recalls: 'Therapy was giving me a steadier view of myself. I could see my faults and weaknesses more clearly and could forgive them, which in turn meant I was in a better position to do something about them. Some people will dub all this indulgent self-absorption, but, in fact, feeling good, or at least better, about yourself enables you to be of more use to other people.'[31]

Kingsley himself doesn't appear to have derived much benefit from the therapy he had before the end of his marriage to Jane. Since the treatment involved having his 'erections measured by a machine call a plethysmograph' and the wearing of a 'nocturnal mensurator' – a device for measuring 'penile tumescence' – perhaps this is not surprising. It did, however, lead to his brilliant seventies novel, *Jake's Thing*, about an Oxford Don in pursuit of his lost libido.

Therapy can do harm as well as good. A distressing number of suicides occur among patients who are already seeing a health professional, although naturally it is difficult to quantify which of them might have taken their lives without therapy. There is some evidence that patients treated by untrained people do just as well as those treated by experienced psychotherapists; empathy and understanding are so often random and instinctive.

In some cases, the best therapy may simply be practical assistance. In *Self-Help for Your Nerves*, Claire Weekes cites the case of a farmer's wife who became lonely and depressed following a lung infection: 'Had she realised that her troubles were the expression of exhaustion following pneumonia, she would have been saved much additional suffering. As it was she became bewildered and afraid of her condition and visited a psychoanalyst. She made an unfortunate choice, was inexpertly analysed and an odd collection of small, pathetic guilt complexes were exposed. The analyst made much of this and so did the patient, so that she now found herself with a bunch of problems to solve. She became apprehensive and distressed and developed a protracted nervous breakdown.'[32]

Sally Brampton, a *Sunday Telegraph* journalist, had several bad experiences of therapy. ' "Does it upset you," she was asked, "when you get angry with me?" If I said no, I was in denial. If I said yes, I had issues around anger.' Even in therapy, it seems, you can't do right for doing wrong.

In *Bridget Jones's Diary,* her friend Jude runs into a similar problem:

> *Jude arrived in vixen-from-hell fury because Vile Richard has stood her up for the Relationship Counselling.*
>
> *"The therapist woman obviously just thought he was an imaginary boyfriend and I was a very, very sad person."*
>
> *"So what did you do?" I said sympathetically, banishing a rogue disloyal thought from Satan that said, "She was right."*
>
> *"She said that I had to talk about the problems I had that were unrelated to Richard."*
>
> *"But you don't have any problems that are unrelated to Richard," said Sharon.*
>
> *"I know. I told her that, then she said I had a problem with boundaries and charged me fifty-five quid".*[33]

Sarah Standing, a *Daily Telegraph* journalist, thinks a Book Club is better value than a therapist: 'My solution is much simpler and cheaper. I just bore the members of the book club with my problems. In fact all nine of us do this. We don't do it all the time, certainly not to the exclusion of reading, but vast chunks of our monthly meetings are spent having frank and often revealing conversations about ourselves and our problems.'

Even Book Clubs are not straightforward to organise however. Jenny Withers, heroine of *Martin Lukes: Who Moved My Blackberry?* finds her husband appears not to appreciate its importance as an alternative to therapy:

> *Jens – I know it's your book club tonight, but I don't think I'll be able to make it back in time to hold the fort. I need to prepare something for Keith and BSM on revocation. With respect I don't think you quite grasped the point of this, this morning – you were too busy giving orders to Svetlana and looking for Max's cricket jumper.*[34]

Unfortunately Julia's own book club experiences had no therapeutic value and ended the week she hosted the meeting in her own home. 'My children, ages 5 and 7, were told to keep quiet upstairs; left unattended, they larked about and broke a window. My husband came home earlier than expected, sulked at the lack of supper and went to bed. When I finally went up myself he glared at me and said, "What do you do down there, just natter?" '

Book Club

> *My tame, domesticated wife*
> *Tugs slightly at the strings of life*
> *When, once a month, she flies the coop*
> *To join a book discussion group.*
>
> *No men allowed! This silly rule*
> *I think is chauvinist and cruel.*
> *"Who needs," I shrug in my defence,*
> *"Their gossip laced with Lit. Pretence?"*

But when it is her time to host
It's then it irritates the most.
Ignored! My fragile ego scarred!
A writer scorned! A poet barred!

I prowl the house, aloof and numb
But furtively, each time, succumb.
And with a patronising sneer
Against the door I lay an ear.

The moral is: What men deride
Is that of which they are outside.

Gus Ferguson

The journalist Jemima Lewis had a more positive experience of therapy, however. 'Quite why it works is hard to say. Part of it is just the act of going. Doing something about it puts you back in the driving seat.' And she rightly says, 'Talking to friends is no substitute: they get bored and restless and they're hopelessly indiscreet'.

We believe speaking to friends can help, and we certainly couldn't have survived without ours, but it is essential to choose your adviser with care. Too many confidantes and too many points of view can make you even more confused. Here is Anna Sands, in *Falling for Therapy*: 'What therapy needs is a touch of poetry, because poetry speaks most eloquently of the power of love and pain. The poet shares how he feels, and what it means to be alive. Although I am, in the end, alone, I do not feel alone.'[35]

Lewis Wolpert found that the best psychiatrists were the ones who gave hope, but were also honest about the stony ground on which their advice fell: 'She was extremely reassuring, telling me again and again that depression is self-limiting and that I would recover. I did not believe a single word.'[36(i)]

His doctor was right and he went on to write a book about his experience. But depression did recur and his first experience of recovery did not help him: 'My therapists assured me I would recover. I did not believe them. My experience of recovering from my previous depression was no help at all. I had learned nothing. When a friend urged me to read my own book I was not even amused.' [36(ii)] As it turned out, with medication and cognitive therapy, he made a full recovery once again; we certainly found his story encouraging.

Our view – which of course is informed by our own experience – is that finding the right therapy can be a process of trial and error. We were both lucky. Others, as we've said here, have been less so. Its success is dependent on finding the right person for you, no matter what the school – cognitive therapy, transactional analysis, psychoanalysis, or another. And the difficulty can be that at a time when you are making a crucial, possibly lifesaving choice, you are probably least able to do so.

It is all too easy to find someone who only reinforces your own tired point of view. Jeremy Clarke, writing in *The Sunday Telegraph*, strikes a warning note. He describes how he almost became addicted to being listened to: 'With an hour to talk freely about myself I'd revisited the same old bruised places, like a dog returning to its own vomit. What a self-pitying bore I was.'

And even counselling can be over-used. Recently a stewardess friend was on a flight to the Far East that hit turbulence and dived several thousand feet, causing trolleys to crash and lockers to fly open. No-one was seriously hurt but there were a few cuts and bruises, mainly among the staff. A team of counsellors were lined up as they landed, but as Jenny said, 'It was the last thing we wanted; all we needed was to get to our hotel room and have a shower and a cup of tea.'

Fay Weldon has been critical of therapists who give their clients 'permission' to leave their spouse, or form an alliance against them: she wrote a novel, *Affliction*, after this happened to her. And in Lucy Kellaway's *Martin Lukes: Who Moved My Blackberry?* Jenny receives an e-mail from her husband, who is consulting a life-coach: 'I know what you think of Pandora, but I've been doing some interesting work with her on my relationships, and looking at the ones that drain my energy compared to the ones that boost it. My relationship with you, regrettably, falls into the first camp. Pandora clearly thinks we should split up, you aren't bringing anything to the party, if you will. Frankly I'm beginning to see where she's coming from.'[37]

However, there are times when ignorance can be bliss. Mary Evans writes to *The Times*: 'Knowledge is not necessarily a solution. If I believe that my husband adores me, whereas, in fact, he regards me as a part of the furniture, who would benefit by my having this explained to me?'

At best, therapists are philosophers and can open doors. They are there to promote the understanding of human nature and how to live productively and wisely.

Louis MacNeice, in his *Easter Returns*, points out how out of suffering good can come:

the stone
Is rolled away once more, the grooved
Sad earth still finds her own
Resurrection in corn. As man can find
The same green shooting from the
Wounded mind.

Elsewhere, in his poem *Autumn Journal*, written at the outbreak of war and a time of personal crisis, as a love affair was ending, MacNeice bears witness to the tenacity of the human spirit:

I must go out tomorrow as the others
Do
And build the falling castle;
Which has never fallen, thanks
Not to any formula, red tape or
Institution,
Not to any creeds or banks,
But to the human animal's endless courage.
Spider, spider, spin
Your register and let me sleep a
Little,
Not now in order to end but to begin
The task begun so often.

Janice was told, when in the depths of despair, by a friend: 'You realise, of course, that you will be glad that this has happened to you. You will come out of this so much stronger than you were before.' Of course, she didn't believe it. But both statements were true.

Perhaps this is a good place to end. For the mind is at base, tough – and barring severe trauma, it can and does recover from the most extreme abuse. We all have unknown reserves when put to the test. Some of us never have to draw on these in our lifetime, but for those who do, we offer this chapter to show some of the ways it can be done.

Panel 1: Things are dreadful between Ian and me. All he do is argue and shout and cry.

Panel 2: I've asked him to go to Relate with me but he won't.

Panel 3: I mean, there's no point in going on my own, is there?

Panel 4: I'll go with you.

Black Dog

Churchill
called it
The Black Dog.

But this one's
been a cure.

With her quivering
gaze,
her absolute
attention.

Her happy
expectation.

Food.
Walks.
Sticks thrown.

That you'll
be there
in the morning.

Janice Warman

A Woman's Work

Will you forgive me I did not run
to welcome you as you came in the door?
Forgive I did not sew your buttons on
and left a mess strewn on the kitchen floor?
A woman's work is never done
and there is more

The things I did I should have left undone
the things I lost that I could not restore;
Will you forgive I wasn't any fun?
Will you forgive I couldn't give you more?
A woman's work is never done
and there is more

I never finished what I had begun,
I could not keep the promises I swore,
so we fought battles neither of us won
And I said "Sorry!" and you banged the door.
A woman's work is never done
and there is more.

But in the empty space now you are gone
I find the time I didn't have before.
I lock the house and walk out to the sun
where the sea beats upon a wider shore
and woman's work is never done
not any more.

Dorothy Nimmo

What women do

What exactly is it that women do? No-one has the faintest idea, and no-one is at all interested. If you were to ask a man with a stay-at-home wife he would regard it as some kind of trick question. The husband of a friend recently said to her, 'What have you ever done?' (Not much, just raised four children.)

Julia's children have said, 'Why don't you get a job? All you do at the moment is the washing'. When her husband asked how she spent her day, he glazed over before she'd even got halfway down the list.

Twelve Things I Don't Want to Hear

Assemble this in eight straightforward steps.
Start with a fish stock, made the day before.
The driver has arrived but, sadly, drunk.
We'll need some disinfectant for the floor.

Ensure all surfaces are clean and dry.
There's been a problem. Madam, I'm afraid!
We'd better have the manhole cover up.
Apologies, the doctor's been delayed.

I'd love to bring a friend, he's so depressed.
They've put you on the camp bed in the hall.
There's just one table left, perhaps you'd share?
I know it's midnight, but I had to call

Connie Bensley

Whether we do paid work or not, to our husbands, parents and children, it may appear that we do not do very much, and they often put little value on the things we are good at – unless perhaps it's a strawberry meringue. Julia's husband remarked: 'My first wife made pavlova, my second wife made trifle', and as the second wife observed, the woman who was unsuccessfully trialled as third wife only made flap-jacks.

Pavlova be damned. Some women run pell-mell back to work for just this reason. Janice found going back to work part-time at *The Guardian* after having a baby was, in many ways, bliss: 'People talked to you in whole sentences, colleagues brought you cups of coffee and collected your dry-cleaning. You could engage your brain. At the end of the day you had something to show for your labours. Compared to the utter chaos of life with a new baby, it was a breeze.'

Many of us will remember our mothers not doing very much. Like Sunday lunch, a sweaty, all-day affair over a hot Aga, with washing up to follow; like driving us to ballet or riding, waiting in the car for hours, listening to *Women's Hour*, eyes staring into the middle distance; struggling with a huge supermarket shop, trying to make the chequebook balance, or rushing to post the housekeeping cheque through the door of the bank so the grocery cheque wouldn't bounce. Hemming our uniforms; darning our socks; doing the school run; like us, juggling home and work, a struggle that in the utter self-absorption that is childhood, we simply didn't notice.

It's only now that we understand. Now that we too are bag ladies: 'Life is one long succession of bags … swimming bags, work bags, charity shop bags. Not to mention the bag lady, me, who hefts them about.'[1]

Now and then something reminds us what it is we do – and how much it would cost to replace us. It's £63,000, since you ask, to provide the cooks, cleaners, chauffeurs and nannies to do the work of a single housewife (according to the US Bureau of Labor Statistics). And we doubt that any woman reading would be surprised to learn that women are often more productive than machines. The bursar of a public school considered buying a £20,000 shirt ironing machine, but he found that his ironing lady and her part-time helper (who washed and ironed 2,500 shirts a week) were more efficient.

However, here is a small compensation for women who can't remember what it actually is that they do. For some, buying this book will be worth it for this list alone. It was created by a business set up to do it all for you; their services, as you may imagine, were not cheap.

Cleaning
Washing
Ironing
Washing up
Tidying
Gardening
Shopping
  – food, clothing, uniform, birthdays, Christmas
Dry cleaning
Repairs
Library
Dog walking
Vet visits
Find
  – reputable builders, handymen, plumbers, electricians, decorators and wait in for them

Household admin:
– Utility bills
– Filing, making and reminding of appointments
– Typing, photocopying
– Post, delivery & collection
– Chasing up general enquiries

Cars
– clean, fill with petrol, arrange servicing

Relocation
– House viewing
– Removals
– Finding schools
– Registering with doctors & dentists
– Arranging children's activities

Babysitting
  – find babysitters, organise babysitting circle

Entertainment
– Organising & catering for dinner parties
– Office parties
– Booking restaurant tables/hotels
– Booking theatre tickets

We tend (often mistakenly) to think that things are easier than they once were. Grocery shopping online with timed slots for home delivery may be wonderfully convenient (unless they forget the loo rolls or bring you bumper packs of unwanted crisps), but if you lived in the country where Julia grew up in the immediate post-war period, vegetables, milk, paraffin and fizzy pop were all delivered to the door as a matter of course. The laundry man returned sheets and pillowcases neatly wrapped in brown paper parcels, although clothes were washed at home, first pushed through a mangle and in later years heaved with giant tongs across the twin-tub.

As with so many things, we've merely gone full circle. Women like Janice's neighbour Jean, now in her seventies, sat by the phone with lists for the butcher, baker and grocer, who all delivered weekly. She certainly never had to wrestle an overwrought toddler round the supermarket or bribe him with sweets from the display by the till.

Julia says: 'I remember the pastry being rolled out and cut in neat circles to fit the patty pans, and the royal icing on the Christmas cake being spread with a hot knife. Such sights are long gone. What memories will my own daughter have? I do make occasional desserts, but the Christmas pudding is micro-waved in 5 minutes, not mixed in October and left steaming in a basin for hours. I am more creative in the garden but that too is taken for granted. It was only this year when I was occupied with writing that the children said, "What's happened to the flowerbeds?" '

Everyone seems to think that women do nothing, which means they are endlessly available. This is a transcript of a friend's answer machine over a single day. It is the last day of term and her daughter's birthday (cake, presents, party, etc). She drops her children at school, takes the car to be serviced and gets home to find the following message from her elderly aunt:

Jennie... it's about half past nine. When you come in will you give me a ring before I go out with the dog? I want to discuss all sorts of things. Ring me when you get from wherever you are because it's always this ruddy answer machine.

10 minutes later:
Jennie, do ring me as soon as you get it. I am getting sick of this
wretched answer phone. What would happen if Celia went under a bus?
Or I went under a bus? You'd never know. Who cares? I will be going
out in about half an hour.

20 minutes after this:
I know you are not away. This ruddy answer phone. I'll try and ring
you on the mobile but then you'll have to ring me back because it's too
expensive.

10 minutes further on:
I'm absolutely fed up. I am sure you are not away. I'll leave my mobile
on, no I won't leave my mobile on. But I NEED TO GET IN TOUCH
WITH YOU!

None of this, of course, would ever appear on a CV, and those women who have chosen to raise their children full-time can find their lives full of seemingly pointless duties.

Cartoon by Susie Rotberg/Snooze@btinternet.com

Here is just one day from Julia's year: it was a 'chores day' to free up the next day for writing ... well, that was the theory:

··

The building society is shut because of a 'security failure'. I go to buy cat and bird food at the pet shop but they don't take credit cards and I daren't write a cheque until the cheque for the new pony trailer has gone through. The cats will have to eat the spare tin of sardines in the kitchen cupboard, which is past its sell-by date. Then I go to the garage to buy a trailer number plate and discover that the garage doesn't do number plates any more as they make for 'too much paperwork'. They suggest Halfords. Warned that I will need identification, I present car registration document, utility bill and driving licence. However, I do not know the precise size of the number plate, as I didn't know they varied and my driving licence is no good, as it is the old sort without a picture. I go home, measure the old number plate and bring in my passport. By the time I return there is a new man on the desk who says the utility bill cannot be accepted as it is a cesspit emptying bill and it should be gas, electricity or water. And so on...

The trailer is for my daughter so she can ride at shows, so what contribution has she made to the process? Answer: nothing. On my return, still without the number plate, I go into her room and back out again. On the floor there is a wet towel, some dirty clothes, an old breakfast plate, milk gone sour in a glass, two dead mice in an advanced state of rigor mortis and an old apple core. As well as failing administratively and domestically, I don't seem to be passing on the right value systems, let alone health practices.

··

To be brutally frank, even today – with so many women in the workplace – society simply couldn't function without the unpaid labour of millions of us. Like the solicitor we know who takes one day off a week to fetch ponies for Riding for the Disabled. Well, someone has to do it, or the RDA would not exist. And the majority of carers are women; how many men do you know (and yes, they do exist) who have given up their jobs to look after a parent, handicapped child, or sick spouse?

Without these women, Margaret Thatcher may yet be proved correct. There will eventually be no such thing as society.

Betty Friedan put a name to the 'nameless, aching dissatisfaction' felt by countless 1950s housewives in her revolutionary book, *The Feminine Mystique*. Here is a Nebraska woman with a Ph.D. in anthropology:

> *A film made of any typical morning in my house would look like an old Marx Brothers comedy. I wash the dishes, rush the older children off to school, dash out in the yard to cultivate the chrysanthemums, run back in to make a phone call about a committee meeting, help the youngest child build a blockhouse, spend fifteen minutes skimming the newspapers so I can be well-informed, then scamper down to the washing machines where my thrice-weekly laundry includes enough clothes to keep a primitive village going for an entire year. By noon I'm ready for a padded cell.*[2]

This wasn't always so. We only have to go back to prehistoric times to discover that the 'hunter-gatherer' society lived largely off the food women could gather, supplemented by the occasional animal the male hunting party could bring down. Women had position and place in these matriarchal societies. This was no feminist dream or male nightmare: God *was* a woman. 'The last queen of the Ashanti, according to the outraged reports of British colonial administrators of the Gold Coast, regularly had several dozen 'husbands' liquidated, as she liked to wipe out the royal harem...and start again. Even when kingship was established, African queens had the power to condemn the king to death...and the right to determine the moment of execution.'[3(i)]

It's hard not to feel that time has spun backwards. For 4,000 years, women held power through the female line, most notably in Egypt; regiments of women fought as men; women had '…physical and sexual freedom, access to power, education, full citizenship, the right to own money and property, the right to divorce, custody of children and financial maintenance'. [3(ii)]

Sadly, it wasn't to last, and we all know how it ended; with serfdom, then suffragettes, and now the freedom our post-feminist daughters take for granted, one component of which seems to be the right to go about wearing next to nothing but remain inviolate.

Having fought for the right for equality in the workplace, we now have a society in which not only do women have to work to keep the family going because two incomes is what it takes these days, but that women are expected to be good at everything; bringing in money, cooking, cleaning, and childcare. As Jerry Hall apparently said: 'My mother told me it was simple to keep a man. You have to be a chef in the kitchen, a maid in the living room and a whore in the bedroom. I said I'd hire the other two and take care of the bedroom bit.'

But even she tired of it in the end, divorced Mick and started an Open University degree. She was quoted in the newspapers as saying: 'I haven't got a man, so no wonder I get so much done.'

At the end of the nineteenth century, in her story *An Extinct Angel*, Charlotte Gillman describes the woman's lot: 'It was the business of the angel to assuage, to soothe, to comfort, to delight. No matter how unruly were the passions of the owner, sometimes even to the extent of legally beating his angel with a stick… By an unfortunate limitation of humanity the angel was required, in addition to such celestial duties as smiling and soothing, to do kitchen service, cleaning, sewing, nursing and other mundane tasks. But these things must be accomplished without the slightest diminution of angelic virtues.'[4]

Sadly, these attitudes still prevail. And there still is a serious issue about our relative freedoms. Claire Tomalin records in her biography of Jane Austen, the words of Eliza Chute, a contemporary of Jane's: 'Mr Chute … seems to think it strange that I should absent myself from him for four and twenty hours when he is at home, tho' it appears in the natural order of things that he should quit me for business or pleasure, such is the difference between husbands and wives. The latter are sort of tame animals whom the men always expect to find at home ready to receive them: the former are lords of the creation, free to go where they please.'[5]

How much has changed in the last two hundred years? Not much, it seems. It is also a hard fact of life that men are often restless. In Hanif Kureishi's novel *Intimacy*, the heroine is a 'well organised woman'. Initially, her husband is attracted by this: 'Mostly I liked her humdrum dexterity and ability to cope. I envy her capability. She is an effective, organised woman. Our fridges and freezers are full of soup, vegetables, wine, cheese and ice-cream: the children's clothes are washed, ironed and folded.'[6]But ultimately he doesn't like the fact that she reads cookbooks in bed and leaves her for a younger woman.

Many women will find in the story of another literary wife – Penelope Betjeman – an echo of their own. According to Bevis Hillier, Betjeman's biographer: 'In later life [Betjeman's daughter] realised that John had avoided household chores and the discipline side of bringing up children; these were left to Penelope. Paul and Candida connected John with treats and presents, Penelope with disagreeable work and crossness.'[7] Hugo Williams can't contemplate a child with a new girlfriend in his poem *Her News* because: '…no I couldn't go through all that again/not without my own wife being there/not without her getting cross about everything'.[8]

Vacuum cleaners were invented in 1901. It is debatable whether this has led to less housework or simply higher standards of cleanliness; it's certainly led to more neurosis. As Alan Bennett has said:

> *My mother fought a war against dirt all her life. The campaign against this dirt produced its own elaborate weaponry, an armoury of Ewbanks, Hoovers, wringers, possers and mops in daily and wearisome use. Besides these implements my mother maintained an elaborate hierarchy of cloths, buckets and dusters, to the Byzantine differences of which she alone was privy.*[9]

Labour saving devices do not save labour in the way they were intended, releasing women for more relaxation, creativity and leisure. They simply raise expectations of domestic order and cleanliness to God-like levels.

A 95-year-old woman of Janice's acquaintance had a notice on her kitchen wall that she immediately adopted: *A tidy house is the sign of a wasted life*: 'And yet… it tends to be quoted against us by our teenage children when we want order in *their* bedrooms.'

Yet another survey proves 'the average woman between 18 and 80 spent nine years, two months and twenty-five days of her waking life cleaning and tidying'. The majority of women apparently said it made them feel in control of their lives and was mentally therapeutic. For mental therapy, we'd suggest reading Kierkegaard and leaving the vacuum cleaner under the stairs.

'One of the things my now ex-husband held against me,' says Julia, 'was the fact that I didn't pull out the kitchen appliances and clean behind them enough (Wanted: tart in the bedroom/removal woman in the kitchen?) Deborah Ross, in *The Independent*, has promised 'never to go right to the bottom of the laundry basket because from what I've glimpsed it is a really, really scary place' So's mine. And like Deborah I keep 'the following items at the back of at least one kitchen cupboard: a tin of golden syrup with the lid half-cocked, revoltingly sticky and covered in fluff and lentils; a pot of hundreds and thousands; several bottles of food colouring (all green)'.

Whatever our circumstances, we almost by definition struggle as mothers. Who can forget Kate, distressing bought mince-pies to make them look home-made in the first scene of Allison Pearson's *I Don't Know How She Does It*? You don't have to be something in the City to identify with this. Janice has certainly been down the same road; you really have to be desperate *to pretend you grew your own carrots for the school's Harvest Festival.*

Rachel Cusk, in her book *A Life's Work*, a long essay on motherhood, is troubled by the difficulties of young working mothers:

> *Those of my friends who had children seemed to labour under the stress of lean, contingent arrangements which added to rather than relieved their enslavement: racing out of the house to drop them at a child minder, racing back from work to collect them, frantically bargaining over minutes with au pairs or nannies: panicked negotiations conducted against the threat of some certain expiry, as if at six o'clock the nanny would vanish in a puff of smoke, or the childminder put the baby outside in the rain.*[10]

And as ever, there is the perennial problem of women and creativity. Helen Dunmore, first winner of the women-only Orange Prize for Fiction, defended it by saying that while men were writing novels, women were often pouring their creativity into their children, thereby losing a couple of decades of writing time. This extract from Finuala Dowling's *Found* poem describes what she means:

When asked by concerned parties
whether I've submitted
any creative writing lately, you know, rhymes
I want to scream & scream,
Where Do You Think I Would Find the Time?
Every moment I have is mortgaged
off another moment.
If I go for a walk I fall behind,
I fall behind and I mind falling behind
with the marking. Or at two in the afternoon,
poised on the brink
poised on the brink of a thought
a child interrupts

And to add to the recent debate about the virtual absence of female inventors, Helen Goddard writes in a letter to *The Independent*: 'It all hinges on time. In the past, and still in many households today, men can sit and think while waiting for their supper. Women have no time to think because they are doing the cooking.' The physicist Freeman Dyson, describing creativity in Mihaly Csikszentmihalyi's eponymous book, says: 'I am fooling around not doing anything, which probably means that this is a creative period, although of course you don't know until afterwards. I think it is very important to be idle; people who keep themselves busy all of the time are generally not creative.'[11]

It's no surprise, then, that female inventors are few and far between; if women sit down, they are considered to be lazing about.

It is true that TV and conversations block out thought. We find like many people that we have some of our best ideas when out walking (or in Janice's case riding), and particularly driving somewhere alone; keeping a notebook in the car is essential. Playing music in the car can help creative thought and the mental meandering so essential for ideas. The designer Margaret Howell, now aged 60, said in an interview for *The Sunday Telegraph* how refreshing it is to be able to hand over to younger designers and escape from the general hurly burly: 'It's nice to free up time, because ideas can come when you are walking or sitting in the bath, when you let your mind drift a bit.'

The playwright Simon Gray, in his memoir *Fat Chance*, has written a good description of the tension involved in the creative process: 'There was always the knot of anxiety in my stomach every morning that never completely unloosened itself during the course of the day and tightened again when I sat in my study at night and into the early morning, contemplating the work done, the work to be done.'[12] No wonder creativity is seldom compatible with any kind of domestic routine. Last summer, Julia had a distraught fax from a painter friend trying to mount an exhibition:

> *A thousand apologies for not having been in touch for so long, the past four weeks have just been a haze of activity, panic, anxiety, exhaustion and frustration. I managed to get the 'open studio' thing off the ground okay but it did need me to clear the space in a friend's studio, paint it and somehow turn it into a presentable gallery before I could even begin to display anything. I managed to start ticking things off my 'to do' list but I'm sure that there must be a devilish sort of list fairy that comes along when one's back is turned and adds hundreds of things previously unseen. Of course as you are well aware life is not put on hold whilst I am otherwise occupied: still need to do the Waitrose shop, the washing up, the laundry, not to mention the interminable bloody meals! Despite the fact that there are two perfectly capable grown men in the house, I still come home after a gruelling day being charming, trying to sell my work to find that Matt and Jamie had*

done nothing towards supper and I had to turn-to and do it. I was just too
tired to protest, and couldn't face the prospect of a row. Jamie even had the
gall to say that he thought it would be so much better if I didn't get so het
up. AGH!!!

It's always exhausting to come home to chaos, but for most women, going to work is far easier than working from home. 'My office was like a craft workshop in the holidays, with children, glue and paint everywhere,' says Janice. 'I did more than one interview with my toddler standing behind me on my chair, earnestly plaiting my hair. I just had to hope she wouldn't pull it at the wrong moment.'

Many women do not even have the time for relationships. As Barbara in Somerset Maugham's *The Constant Wife* says, 'I have my business. When you work hard eight hours a day you don't much want to be bothered by love'.[13] Although written in 1927, this can be just as true for women today. More accurately it might be 'can't find love', or 'too tired for love' or a recognition that energies can rarely be stretched to encompass both.

Men often try to take the high moral ground when it comes to who works the hardest. In Pearson's *I Don't Know…* Judith does not demur when 'her husband Nigel said that, as he was under such pressure at the bank, he would need to take a skiing holiday while Judith got on with the relaxing business of being at home with three children under four'.[14(i)]

A few years ago Janice was struggling up her snowy, icy road in her MGB GT to get to a shift at the *Daily Mail*. 'The postman stopped and gave me a push but after he left the car began slithering all over the road once more. In my rear view mirror I noticed a neighbour had stopped his car. "How sweet," I thought and hopped out of the car, ready to thank him. "GET OUT OF MY WAY! DON'T YOU REALISE I HAVE A TRAIN TO CATCH???" he roared. Did I shout back? Did I tell him I wasn't off for a leg wax (at 6am!!) but I too, had a train to catch? No. I didn't say anything. I got back in the car, backed into the nearest driveway and waited until he had gone. I don't need to tell you this is wrong on so many levels. Leaving aside his overwhelming assumption that I couldn't have had anywhere important to get to, no woman would have left another in that predicament.'

Christmas epitomises the disparity between the sexes and highlights what women are still expected to do. On Christmas Day, we would love to take a leaf out of Mrs Beeton's book and commandeer the help of a tweeny maid to clear out the fireplaces and pick up the orange peel. If we were proper mistresses of our houses, we would, 'after an early breakfast, make a round of the kitchen and other offices to see that they are all in order', not slop about doing all the chores ourselves in slippers and pyjamas. Teenagers do not rise till lunchtime and then only to eat chocolate for breakfast and watch re-runs of *Friends*. Whatever the ages of one's children at Christmas there is a lot of sulking, pinching and shrieking and Granny will observe that in the modern family there is a lot of bad behaviour and not enough discipline. As Deborah Ross points out in *The Independent*: 'What amuses one family member does not necessarily amuse another.'

Allison Pearson describes the festive season in her novel:

> *Like any other family, the Shattocks have their Christmas traditions. One tradition is that I buy all the presents for my side of the family and I buy all the presents for our children and our two godchildren and I buy Richard's presents and presents for Richard's parents and his brother Peter and Peter's wife Cheryl and their three kids and Richard's Uncle Alf who drives across from Matlock every Boxing Day and is keen on rugby league and can only manage soft centres. If Richard remembers and depending on late opening hours he buys a present for me.* [14(ii)]

This is echoed in a reader's letter to *The Daily Telegraph*:

> *Huh! So Andrew Marr is boycotting Christmas shopping because the shops are festooned too early. Retailers will be pleased to know his one-man boycott will not dent their profits much. For this is a man who loathes shopping – early, late or right on time.*

Indeed, the biggest annual row in the Marr household happens each December, when the long-suffering Mrs Marr complains that, as usual, she has bought every single present for the numerous children, nieces, nephews, aunts, uncles, grannies and granddads that the Marrs are blessed with.

I'm afraid this latest excuse is one of the limpest I have yet heard. He will be sent out this weekend with four large shopping bags and not allowed back into the house until they are full.

Jackie Ashley (Mrs Andrew Marr), London

Jane Giddins' letter to *The Independent* shows these habits can start early: 'My four year old son attends a school that has 75% boys. I have noticed that every one of his Christmas cards is from a girl (none of whom he claims to know). Does this mean that he is a big hit with the opposite sex? Or could it be, as I suspect, that women are programmed at birth to be the mugs that do everything at Christmas?'

Mrs Beeton did a lot of corresponding; once she had cast her eye over the house and checked that all tasks had been accomplished, 'she would simply retire to her parlour after breakfast and write letters'. No need for Mrs Beeton to scribble 'write soon' in last-minute cards and then fail to do it. We can't believe she would have sullied her pen by writing round robin letters like the following:

Lexie settled into school from Day One, has made crowds of friends, and is more than surviving. Academically I caught her reading her Latin textbook the first weekend as she wanted to know more about it ... her grades have been brilliant. Poppy has just been a King in the school nativity play which was the most brilliant nativity play I have ever seen.[15]

These usually arrive when you have just lost the corkscrew, the Sellotape and any number of plots in the frenzied run up to Christmas. This is the point at which we begin to dream of escape. Perhaps the solution to a stress-free festival is to go away? Sophie Hannah soon knocks this idea on the head:

Seasonal Dilemma

Another Christmas compromise. Let's drink another toast.
Once more we failed to dodge the things that put us out the most.
To solve this timeless riddle I would crawl from coast to coast:
Which is worse at Christmas, to visit or to host?

To spend a week with relatives and listen to them boast,
Try not to look too outraged when they make you eat nut roast
Or have them drive their pram wheels over each new morning's post?

Which is worse at Christmas, to visit or to host?

Dickens, you let me down. You should have made Scrooge ask the ghost

Which is worse at Christmas, to visit or to host?

Sophie Hannah

Ian Flintoff, in a letter to *The Independent,* is concerned that women in the workplace only create another kind of 'servant class' in the home:

> *For every liberated diva there is another woman forced to do her dirty*
> *work. How can this possibly be liberating for women as a whole? A new*
> *class of paid skivvy is being created ... and you can bet your ironed shirt it'll*
> *be a class of females.*

He rather misses the point. Who, after all, is likely to be wearing the ironed shirt? Why, it's the man of the house, of course. Janice once pointed out the obvious to her husband as she felt he might not have quite grasped it – that the nanny and cleaning lady enabled them both to work, rather than just her. A prospective employer remarked that she seemed to work very hard and yet had two young children. 'I smiled brilliantly and said I had "an absolutely *wonderful* nanny". I might have added, "who does for me everything that your wives do for you" (except the obvious) …but I wanted the job, so I didn't.'

And in any case, as Janice says, 'There is another way to look at what women do. As a woman, I haven't been trapped in a single career all my life. I've had the pure joy of motherhood along with its pains. I've had the pleasure of women's friendship and the relief of not having to take the commuter train every day for 25 years (though I did it for many years). I have actively liked the contrast between giggling with a baby in the morning and attending a business meeting in the afternoon; between holding a candlelight vigil for the local maternity unit and flying to Boston for a management conference. I *like* being more than one person.

'In many ways I feel sorry for men, many of whom are trapped in high-earning jobs, which may give them power – but doesn't give them much freedom. I've seen them on the six-thirty to Cannon Street and they have the glazed look of pit-ponies.'

One of the difficulties of motherhood is that it is a job with built-in redundancy. Mothers can be left high and dry when they are no longer needed. And yet the way we are needed and depended upon can draw on our life-blood. As Susie Orbach says in *Fat is a Feminist Issue*:

> *Since women are not accepted as equal human beings but are nevertheless expected to devote enormous energy to the lives of others, the distinction between their own lives and the lives of those close to them may become blurred. Merging with others, feeding others, not knowing how to make space for themselves are frequent themes for women.*[16]

At least the modern woman can think about these issues and discuss them in the hope of adjusting their lives one way or another; our generation does have it better. There was a poignant letter in *The Independent* from Kevin Curley, describing the sacrifices his own mother had made:

> *My beloved mother who died last year at a great age was widowed at 37 with two young boys. She froze her emotions and devoted herself to bringing us up in rural poverty and got us both to university in the 1960s. From 1952 when my father died, to 2005 she had no other partner – not even a boyfriend.*

Many women remain trapped in the catch-all trap of 'care'. First they care for their children, then their elderly parents, then their ailing husbands. But this is not some kind of insurance policy that they will be cared for in their turn. Women who have spent years at home caring for their families are the least likely to qualify for the state pension – only 16% of newly retired women do – and they are even less likely to have contributed to a personal pension. Therefore, is it a cynical or a wise woman who keeps these 'what ifs' in her head?

• •

What if my husband came home tonight and said he wanted a divorce?

What if I discovered he's remortgaged the house without consulting me?

What if he hid any money he had – or moved it abroad – and claimed to have no income?

I'm 54 and haven't 'worked' (except for the unpaid job of child-raising) for twenty years... what would I live on? Where would I live?

• •

If you think this sounds unlikely, it's almost certainly happened to someone near you. (It happened to someone near us.) So it's worth thinking the unthinkable when deciding, for example, about whether to continue working after having a child. It's all too easy to downscale your ambitions and lose momentum in your career; ground that can be very hard to regain.

This woman, in Andrea Levy's *Small Island* for example, is possibly both cynical *and* wise – keeping her options open without alerting her husband to the fact: 'In front of my sober father my mother insisted her cake-baking was just a hobby. She told him, "No problem I just fix up a cake in the kitchen, earn me a little 'for extras' ". Behind his drunken back my mother and Auntie May ran a serious business, with orders, deliveries, overheads, shortages, labour disputes and taxable income carefully assessed.'[17]

Even when things are going right, it is essential as we age to know when we have done enough, to strike the right note between equilibrium and overload; this seems more important in mid-life than at any other time. Even when we attempt to look at our circumstances and try to change them for the better, we so often find ourselves restricted and emotionally exhausted by the constraints of marriage, money and children. In addition, there is the dilemma of bringing up our daughters to withstand these things in their turn. And it requires effort to make life simpler: rather like putting make-up on for the no-make up look, it is actually no less demanding.

Our advice to our own daughters would be: 'Don't give up the day job', for the following reason, put most succinctly by Julie Harrison in a letter to *The Independent*:

> *I am now 63 and stayed at home with my children when they were young. I think that the value of being brought up with an interested parent at home is incalculable. However, I eventually came to realise that an independent income is the only guarantee of equality and autonomy for women, both here and throughout the world. Regardless of the family's financial situation, therefore, women are wise to seek paid work.*

As Betty Friedan has said, 'It is the economic imbalance which matters most in the end', or in the more memorable words of Holly Golightly, 'diamonds are a girl's best friend'.

We intend to break the cycle of wanting our daughters to suffer as we have done. Sophie Hannah speaks her mind and speaks for us:

Now and Then

'Now that I'm fifty-seven,'
My mother used to say,
'Why should I waste a minute?
Why should I waste a day

Doing the things I ought to
Simply because I should?
Now that I'm fifty-seven
I'm done with that for good.'

But now and then I'd catch her
Trapped in some thankless chore
Just as she might have been at
Fifty-three or fifty-four

And I would want to say to her
(And have to bite my tongue)
That if you mean to learn a skill
It's well worth starting young

And so, to make sure I'm in time
For fifty, I've begun
To do exactly as I please
Now that I'm thirty-one.

Sophie Hannah

Enough

There are people for whom
Nothing is enough.
You could cut yourself in half
And serve yourself up.

They would say, The flavour's not quite right.
They would say, The sauce needs truffles.
You should have studied cordon bleu
And learned the soft-shoe shuffle

Janice Warman

The good girl

It's a phrase we are all familiar with: and if we have daughters, it's a phrase, God help us, we have in all probability used ourselves. Good girl. We would have heard it as children; being good was, after all, the ultimate goal. Pleasing others: our teachers, our parents, our friends, our siblings; the world at large. It's well documented that while boys at primary school are more adventurous and rebellious in the playground and less interested in classroom work, most girls do better academically simply because they are eager to please. They live for that approving word.

Out of school, at home, we were also expected to help, and out of the home, to be careful; not to climb that tree or run too fast or swim out too deep. At work, we were expected to keep our heads down, make the coffee, stay late and not to expect any glory.

Why is this? Because good girls are functional. Good girls marry, breed – and stay married. Good girls give up their careers to look after their children and their husbands. Good girls do charitable works. Good girls underpin the fabric of society. They hold it all together for everyone else. And if they're successful, they're not too successful; as Fay Weldon has it, they 'reflect glory'.

The question remains: after the rise of seventies feminism, following the lead of Betty Friedan, who exploded the myth of the happy fifties housewife in *The Feminine Mystique*; after Shulamith Firestone, who wanted to do away with men entirely; why do we do it? Why do women still put themselves last? Was our childhood conditioning that effective? Certainly, we do not have to look too far in literature or history to find images of women sacrificing themselves for others – usually their men and their children.

An article said to be from a 1950s magazine that does the rounds on email (it's particularly popular with men) illustrates the context in which Friedan wrote – the time directly after the Second World War when Rosie the Riveter was shooed straight back into the kitchen to make way for the men: 'Have dinner ready. Plan ahead…Touch up your make-up, put a ribbon in your hair…Be a little gay…Let him talk first – remember, his topics of conversation are more important than yours…Don't greet him with complaints and problems…Don't complain if he is late home for dinner….Remember he is the master of the house.'[1]

It seemed things had scarcely changed from the century before. 'Freud's letters to Martha, his future wife, written during the four years of their engagement (1882-6) have the fond, patronising sound of Torvald, in *A Doll's House*, scolding Nora for her pretences at being human. Freud was beginning to probe the secrets of the human brain in the laboratory at Vienna; Martha was to wait, his "sweet child", in her mother's custody for four years, until he could come and fetch her. From these letters one can see that to him her identity was defined as child-housewife, even when she was no longer a child and not yet a housewife.

> *I know, after all, how sweet you are, how you can turn a house into a paradise, how you will share in my interests, how gay yet painstaking you will be. I will let you rule the house as much as you wish, and you will reward me with your sweet love and by rising above all those weaknesses for*

which women are so often despised. As far as my activities allow, we shall read together what we want to learn, and I will initiate you into things which could not interest a girl as long as she is unfamiliar with her future companion and his occupation...'[2]

Good girls abound elsewhere in literature and history; Hardy's *Tess of the d'Urbervilles*, the second Mrs de Winter in Daphne du Maurier's *Rebecca*, MPs' wives who pose for photo-calls with children and Labrador after revelations of their husband's affairs. Many of them are our Hey Nonny heroines. They abound in film too: think of Celia Johnson in *Brief Encounter*, giving up her chance of happiness. 'I want to die. If only I could die.'

In theatre, there is almost any heroine in Chekhov (think of *Uncle Vanya*'s Sonya) while Ibsen's heroines tend to surprise: Nora in *A Doll's House*, playing the little squirrel, the plaything, while nursing a secret.

She had taken out a large loan to pay for her husband to recuperate in Italy after a spell of severe illness and had spent the intervening decade secretly working to earn money to pay off the interest on the loan, and squirrelling away money from her housekeeping and dress allowance, while pretending to still be the perfect wife and mother. The tensions are evident from the first scene of the play and by its end she has rejected a stifling marriage for freedom – a shocking message for the audience of 1879, making Nora a Good Girl who became, in society's terms, a Bad Girl: 'I have been your doll wife, just as at home I was Papa's doll child; and here the children have been my dolls. I thought it great fun when you played with me, just as they thought it great fun when I played with them. That is what our marriage has been, Torvald.'[3(i)]

And with these words, she becomes a proto-feminist and a flag-carrier for those who reject the good girl tag: 'I must stand quite alone if I am to understand myself and everything about me. It is for that reason that I cannot remain with you any longer.'[3(i)] She points out that she has other duties just as sacred as her duties to her husband and children: 'Duties to myself...I believe that before all else I am a reasonable human being just as you are – or, at all events, that I must try and become one.'[3(ii)]

Like the actor Billie Piper, divorcing millionaire DJ husband Chris Evans two-and-a-bit centuries later, she says she will take nothing with her but what is hers.

'For intellectual women of the 1880s, *A Doll's House* was not about the New Woman walking out on the Old Man, but rather a revolutionary call for the redefinition of marriage,' Elaine Showalter points out. 'From the beginning of the play, where the Helmers have what most would see has a happy marriage, with its three children, servants, and nannies, to the shattering end, Ibsen forced his audience to rethink the meaning of marriage as a relationship between equals.'[4]

These changes were on the agenda: the terms New Woman and feminist, says Showalter, were being used among women intellectuals of the 1890s. But a scant century later, Ira Levin wrote his satire *The Stepford Wives*, whose smooth surface – affluent suburbia and perfect housewives – hid a horrifying, murderous underworld, a perfect counterpoint to the rise of feminism in the 1970s. Here's Kit:

> *"These things came out nice and white, didn't they?" She put the folded T-shirt into the laundry basket, smiling.*
>
> *Like an actress in a commercial.*
>
> *That's what she was, Joanna, felt suddenly. That's what they all were, all the Stepford wives: actresses in commercials, pleased with detergents and floor wax, with cleansers, shampoos, and deodorants. Pretty actresses, big in the bosom but small in the talent, playing suburban housewives unconvincingly, too nicey-nice to be real.*[5]

Many of the women we spoke to immediately recognised that the role of the good girl had a powerful pull in their lives: 'Being a good girl means being a chameleon,' says Jay after a lifetime of good behaviour. 'Changing colours, mirroring back what everyone else wants from you. Doing this successfully, and over a long period, means you become no-one. You are only valid as long as the other person is happy. It is exhausting, destructive and dishonest for both participants. I am now 54 years old and still don't know who I am. What I *do* know is what is wrong with me. You learn that when you are trained to be a good girl.'

What she knows is, of course, not what is wrong with her, but rather what she has been told in order to keep her in her place. Like Lynne, her good behaviour is rooted in her childhood: 'It's only really when it's too late that you realise you have a responsibility to yourself as well. You've spent too much time *being responsible*. Being a good daughter. Being a good wife. Being a good mother. Because you feel *guilty* if you do something that is just for yourself. That's why you never relax. That's why you don't sleep well. That's why you have an all-pervading sense of guilt. It's because there is *always something you haven't done*. Always. It's because you feel utterly responsible for everyone and everything.'

Some women had been rebellious as teenagers but later found that marriage (but more especially children, with the consequent lower income and dependence on a partner) pulled them back into the role.

Many had done time as a good girl and then (like Ibsen's Nora) had a revelation that changed their lives. Sometimes it takes a real shock to stop you being a good girl – sometimes it's emotional (a husband's affair, no real surprise for one friend, but somehow just the final straw on top of the abusive behaviour); sometimes it's physical, as in the kind of illness that comes after working too hard, for too long; and sometimes it's mental, as in a nervous breakdown after bullying in the workplace comes on top of bullying at home – in medical terms, an acute situation on top of a chronic one. And sometimes, of course, it's a toxic combination of all three.

Rebecca is an American singer who grew up in the South: 'I spent my entire life being the "good girl" before I started getting angry inside, realising that I had followed rigid, ridiculous rules and guidelines set for me by my parents, church and society without ever doubting what I was being told. On top of this, I thought that if I was the "good girl" I would surely find true love, respect and a Cinderella life waiting around the corner.

'I was the perfect example of someone trying to stay within the lines, don't upset anyone, make everyone feel good about themselves – and never, ever put yourself before others. I had become invisible.

Still I Rise

You may write me down in history
With your bitter, twisted lies,
You may trod me in the very dirt
But still, like dust, I'll rise.

Does my sassiness upset you?
Why are you beset with gloom?
'Cause I walk like I've got oil wells
Pumping in my living room.

Just like moons and like suns,
With the certainty of tides,
Just like hopes springing high,
Still I'll rise.

Did you want to see me broken?
Bowed head and lowered eyes?
Shoulders falling down like teardrops.
Weakened by my soulful cries.

Does my haughtiness offend you?
Don't you take it awful hard
'Cause I laugh like I've got gold mines
Diggin' in my own back yard.

You may shoot me with your words,

You may cut me with your eyes,
You may kill me with your hatefulness,
But still, like air, I'll rise.

Does my sexiness upset you?
Does it come as a surprise
That I dance like I've got diamonds
At the meeting of my thighs?

Out of the huts of history's shame
I rise
Up from a past that's rooted in pain
I rise
I'm a black ocean, leaping and wide,
Welling and swelling I bear in the tide.

Leaving behind nights of terror and fear
I rise
Into a daybreak that's wondrously clear
I rise
Bringing the gifts that my ancestors gave,
I am the dream and the hope of the slave.
I rise

I rise
I rise.

Maya Angelou

'Then my husband took a job in England and my world changed. Family and friends were thousands of miles away. It took this change for me to see myself with different eyes.'

Even the feminist writer Jill Tweedie was subject to (though resisted) the same kind of conditioning: 'Mother, in between mourning my general unsatisfactoriness as a daughter – "Why don't you ever want to come shopping with me? Why won't you wear that pretty dress I bought you?" – and nagging me to be tidier, cleaner, quieter, more thoughtful and altogether nicer than she had any reason to hope for, tried to lighten things with a rosy picture of what lay ahead if I would only be patient. "When you're grown up you'll meet a man and you'll marry him and have your own house, perhaps quite near me, and then, later, you'll have some beautiful children and be very happy. I know you will." '[6(i)]

Her father used a different method to keep her in the same place. He told her after she'd won an essay prize: ' "You think you're clever? Let me tell you, you haven't half my brains, never will have so don't give yourself airs…it's a whole lot better to be wise like your mother and your brother. It's she who ought to be your example. Look at the way she sacrifices herself, sewing away at your dratted ballet frocks. Work on your character, that's my advice, and never mind the scribbling. I'm telling you this for your own good, so you can take that look off your face and listen for once." '[6(ii)]

Janet Street-Porter, another journalist with trenchant views, clearly didn't swallow the good girl myth: 'My mother and I heartily loathed each other – and I accept that wasn't the norm. But at least it gave me the space to develop my own style, and my own voice. And to find friends she disapproved of.'[7]

There are those of us who are born rebels: but many of us are well trained from birth, adapting for our survival to the family we are born into, and as Alice Miller explains in *The Drama of the Gifted Child*, learning to hide our own feelings, needs and memories in order to meet our parents' expectations and win their 'love'. Only in therapy, says Miller, does the patient come 'to the emotional insight that all the love she has captured with so much effort and self-denial was not meant for her as she really was, that the admiration for her beauty and achievements was aimed at this beauty and these achievements and not at the child herself. In therapy, the small and lonely child that is hidden behind her achievements wakes up and asks: "What would have happened if I had appeared before you sad, needy, angry, furious? Where would your love have been then?" And I was all these things as well. Does this mean that it was not really me you loved, but only what I pretended to be? The well-behaved, reliable, empathetic, understanding, and convenient child, who in fact was never a child at all?'[8(i)]

We are trained, says Miller, in the art of hiding our own feelings even from ourselves. 'Even as an older child, she was not allowed to say, or even to think: "I can be sad or happy whenever anything makes me sad or happy; I don't have to look cheerful for someone else, and I don't have to suppress my distress or anxiety to fit other people's needs. I can be angry and no one will die or get a headache because of it. I can rage when you hurt me, without losing you." '[8(ii)] And we can see that *not* being able to say this could result in a lifetime of behaving well, without proper reference to (or even knowledge of) what we really feel.

In *The Dance of Anger*, Harriet Lerner explains how women's anger, so often seen as unnatural and unladylike, is bottled up – or surfaces as self-criticism, denial or guilt: 'Sugar and spice are the ingredients from which we are made. We are the nurturers, the soothers, the peacemakers, and the steadiers of rocked boats. It is our job to please, protect, and placate the world. We may hold relationships in place as if our lives depended on it...Why are angry women so threatening to others? If we are guilty, depressed, or self-doubting, we stay in place. We do not take action except against our own selves and we are unlikely to be agents of personal and social change...thus we too learn to fear our own anger, not only because it brings about the disapproval of others, but also because it signals the necessity for change.'[9]

'I think for myself and my sisters, and for many females being invoked to be good also meant *not being angry*,' says another friend, Pauline. 'I was often told to "take that horrible face off to your room", thus any signs of my not being a good girl promptly meant banishment. The impact of that on my growing and adult life meant discounting a lot of authentic feelings and pretending to have ones I did not, so as not to be rejected.

It took a lot of personal development and therapy work, to acknowledge that the whole range of feelings I have are perfectly acceptable as a rounded human being.'

And let's face it, bad girls have more fun. We're happy to report that a couple of our interviewees felt they were bad girls. There's Jeanne, who says: 'I have always been a "bad girl". I have never felt that I am defined by the wishes and expectations of others.'

And Gill, a sculptor with three grown-up children, who says: 'No, I'm not a "good girl". I don't think I ever quite made it into that category. I don't feel any pressure to be good now – too bloody late, thank God! To me, good girl means "nice" but that's also boring. I frequently rebelled especially if people thought I was nice. I do feel that it's our role in society to keep the peace because until we genetically modify men there's very little chance of peace. When you've finished, let's have *lunch*..."

Kate Figes' *The Big Fat Bitch Book* suggests reclaiming the term 'bitch' (just as the terms 'gay' and 'nigger' have been reclaimed by those thus pilloried). As the actor Bette Davis once said: 'When a man gives his opinion, he's a man; when a woman gives her opinion, she's a bitch.'

> *Many of us are still so constrained by conventional stereotypes of how women should be – selfless, kind, enabling of others, calm and supportive – the good girl essentially, that the real girl inside gets denied. We take insults on the chin and say nothing. We find it hard to compete or ask for that pay rise because we are not sure we deserve it. We are not supposed to shout or get angry about all the inequities we face as women. We become the bitch, the bad girl, when we want more, when we are not prepared to make do with what we have and when being heard is more important than being liked. That is a liberating feeling. If we fear being labelled as a bitch, we still seek validation from men on their terms rather than ours.[10]*

We have tried not to be too deadly serious in this book. It's a sad fact, though, that the climate we live in urges women to be 'good' but then doesn't reward them for it. A country in which women are paid less, routinely abused and beaten, exposed topless on Page Three of daily newspapers (did you know you can download these images to your mobile phone?) is a climate in which women are not necessarily going to thrive.

It's tempting to think that we have left these restrictions behind. We have grown up with images of the actresses Bette Davis, Tallulah Bankhead ('It's the good girls who keep diaries; the bad girls never have the time.'); Mae West ('There are no good girls gone wrong, just bad girls found out.') We are fed images of hard-drinking, opinionated ladette culture; the more glamorous end occupied in the nineties by the actor Denise van Outen, the Radio 1 DJs Sarah Cox and Zoë Ball, among others, and the lower end by drunken girls vomiting in a city centre gutter (though this is hardly aspirational). We live with daughters who stand back for nobody; we have nieces who earn far more than we do; it would be all too easy to get the impression that the good girl is a thing of the past.

And it has certainly been women who were not good girls who have advanced the cause of women. Like Gloria Steinem, whose campaigning (and campaigning journalism) gave us examples of how to behave. Like the Cambridge graduate and suffragette Dame Margery Corbett Ashby (interviewed by Janice shortly before her death at the age of 99) whose father taught her to drive a coach and four, and who insisted that his daughters were taught Algebra, Greek and Latin and not just how to embroider.

Like Virginia Woolf, whose absorbing and inspiring exploration of women's creativity, *A Room of One's Own*, introduced us to the hypothetical Shakespeare's Sister, just as talented as her brother, but with so few opportunities to exercise her skill for writing that eventually she despaired and '...killed herself one winter's night and lies buried at some cross-roads where the omnibuses now stop outside the Elephant and Castle.'[11]

This is a good girl struggling under the weight of talent, thwarted in her ambition, much like the following: 'When...one reads of a witch being ducked, of a woman possessed by devils, of a wise woman selling herbs, or even or a very remarkable man who had a mother, then I think we are on the track of a lost novelist, a suppressed poet, of some mute and inglorious Jane Austen, some Emily Brontë who dashed her brains out on the moor or mopped and mowed about the highways crazed with the torture that her gift had put her to.'[11]

From Virginia Woolf to Linda Lovelace, the abused, terrified star of the world's most notorious porn movie, *Deep Throat*. Gloria Steinem's article questions the public's sceptical approach to her life with Chuck Traynor: 'If you accept the truth of Linda's story, the questions are enraging, like saying, "What in your background led you to a concentration camp?" ' And 'Inside the patience with which she answers these questions – the result of childhood training to be a "good girl" that may make victims of us all – there is some core of strength and stubbornness that is itself the answer. She will make people understand. She will not give up. In the microcosm of this one woman, there is a familiar miracle: the way in which women survive – and fight back.'[12]

Some have been less fortunate; Traynor soon had a new victim, porn star Marilyn Chambers. Nicole Brown, wife of OJ Simpson, famously did not survive being a battered wife, though no one has ever been convicted of her murder. Any daughter who sees a mother beaten or bullied absorbs that message with the air that she breathes. (And importantly, a son who sees this happening may feel protective towards his mother – or he may simply accept that this is how women can be treated.)

In writing this book, we have had to struggle against our own perceptions of being a good girl, or a good daughter, or a good mother, or a good wife (how often our descriptions of ourselves are predicated on our relationships with others and therefore what we should be doing for them, rather than for ourselves!) Ginny, one of the three daughters in Jane Smiley's Midwest treatment of King Lear, *A Thousand Acres*, is also a good girl. As she says: 'Of course, it was silly for me to talk about "my point of view". When my father asserted his point of view, mine vanished.'[13(i)] Her sister adds: 'When we are good girls and accept our circumstances, we're glad about it... When we are bad girls, it drives us crazy.'[13(ii)]

It is extraordinary how much strength this image holds for many of us in the most appalling of circumstances. Alice Sebold, in her memoir *Lucky*, is waiting to be picked up from college by her mother the day after she was raped. She recalls how she and her sister had been dressed as teenagers by her mother: 'Our hair was neat and pulled back over the ears. We were not allowed to wear jeans more than once a week....no heels except pumps from Pappagallo...the heels did not exceed 1.5 inches. I was told whores and waitresses chewed gum…' Most shocking, however, is this: 'I knew, now that I had been raped, I should try to look good for my parents…I was trying to prove to them and to myself that I was still who I had always been. I was beautiful, if fat. I was smart, if loud. I was good, if ruined.'[14]

'When sexual reputation means so much more to a girl than it does to a boy, preserving the "Good Girl" façade is crucial,' says Kate Figes. 'Girls soon learn how to pretend to be what's expected of them, suppressing anything that appears to be too overtly unfeminine. 'Good' girls are thin and keep their mouths shut, mask their emotions, are self-effacing and nice to everyone and they don't swear or sleep around. But any girl with more than an ounce of intelligence can see that she needs a great many other skills which appear to contradict the 'good girl' image if she also wants to succeed. The real girl loves food, feels sexy, has opinions and ambitions. She needs to compete, strive, show her strengths, be outspoken and persistent.'[15]

For Janice, being a good girl kicked in with a vengeance after she had her first baby. 'Even in the (relatively) liberated world of the late-eighties *Guardian* city office, I was told just before departing on maternity leave that along with my baby, I would be giving birth to something else, something rather less welcome, which would become my constant companion: guilt.

"Complete strangers will feel free to come up to you in the street and tell you that you are not looking after your baby properly," said a colleague. "My neighbour rang and told me I should not have put my baby out in his pram because it was far too cold. A woman came up to me in the street and shouted at me because my baby didn't have a sunhat on."

'However, nobody was more dangerous than your own family, I discovered. Back in South Africa with three-month-old Dominic, I came up hard against my mother-in-law's expectations. Holding him close, she said: "But Janice, how *could* you leave him with a stranger?"

'I bit my tongue – I was, after all, a good girl. But that trip showed me that giving birth to a baby had introduced something else into my life as well as guilt: fear. I had written a couple of pieces for *The Guardian* while I was there. Did I want to take on the correspondent's job while he was away?

'This was an opportunity the Janice of three months before would have killed for. And do you know what? I said no. The minute he said it, I felt a stomach-clamping, totally illogical fear flooding me: If I took this opportunity, because I wanted it, *something awful would happen to Dominic*. I had to be good, I had to keep my head down, I had to not want anything for myself. *Or something would happen to Dominic*.

'I didn't understand what was happening to me. I was a feminist; always had been. Yet here I was, throwing away opportunities I had spent a decade working to create: late nights and long hours at the *Financial Times*, the BBC; a further degree: and now, just when I could reap the rewards, I was turning into a feeble creature, just the kind of mother that old-fashioned male bosses denigrate. The kind you can't rely on.

'Then we discovered Dom had a heart murmur and we were told he had a hole in his heart. I left *The Guardian* immediately, against all advice. "Don't go," said the city editor, Ben Laurance. "Speaking as your boss and as a friend – just take a couple of weeks and sort it out."

'But I still resigned. It was another example of my fucked-up thinking. I had to give up my job and concentrate on Dominic. Thank God, the whole thing turned out to be a monstrous false alarm.

'For some inexplicable reason, having a baby had, instead of making me more adult, thrown me back into my own childhood. I felt more anxious, less powerful, more fearful and constantly guilty. I had scorned the idea of being anything less than a strong, dynamic mother: now I felt I had to be a good girl again.

'This sense of helplessness was one that I had imagined I'd left behind. As a child, I'd thought that if I was good, and pleased my parents, and my teachers, and remembered to vacuum the pool and clean the filter and make my bed and do my homework, everything would be all right. It was, I suppose, a kind of arrogance. How on earth could it make any difference? But I wasn't to know that then; the only surprise is that

I managed to sustain that illusion into adulthood.

'I truly thought that if I was good – no, *perfect* – that my husband would love me, that my bosses would appreciate me, that my path through life would be smooth and easy. Every time I was told I wasn't perfect, I would simply try harder, run faster, work later, earn more. It didn't work, of course – or it only appeared to work, for a while; and eventually, I simply ran into the sand.

'So for me, being a good girl ended around five years ago: Post 9/11, I leaped from a sinking London dot.com to another publishing company nearer home, and within six months, was made redundant. Shortly afterwards I began having panic attacks and then sank into a depression I had managed to fend off – just – for years.

'The irony was that the loss of a job and subsequent collapse had unexpected benefits. The financial disaster that loomed large, never actually happened. Help came, and not always from expected quarters.

'In short, the world that I had imagined I held up on my increasingly weary shoulders did not come to an end when I, an exhausted Atlas, could no longer carry it.

'And I began to realise that the whole imaginary construct had been one created by my pride. It was all down to me, I had thought. Well, of course it wasn't.

'A similar experience is typical of women whose husbands gamble, as I had found years earlier in interviews for *The Guardian* women's page (but which naturally enough I had not applied to my own life…) These women, above all, feel that everything depends on them. That they must keep going so their children won't starve, that they must make up the huge shortfall caused by partners who will gamble everything and anything that comes to hand – even, in the case of one of my interviewees, a loan taken out to clear previous gambling debts: "I felt such a fool," she said. "The money was secondary. It was the deceit and the lies which I hated – that he could watch me work and still go out and gamble."

'When I began therapy, my counsellor told me that I didn't have to be the perfect parent – but just a "good-enough" parent. Every fibre of my being rebelled. He told me I ought to have the same sense of self-worth if I had spent the day chilling out on a sofa ("the slob test") or if I had spent it working. That my sense of worth ought to come from within, not from somebody else, or from some external title or role. *No!* I thought. That can't be right. I knew I only ever felt OK if someone told me I was OK – and then only for a short while. The effect wore off; and then I needed another hit. I was an approval addict.

'How, then, do women get out of this way of thinking? I have learned, through cognitive behaviour therapy, that although you cannot change the past, and in particular your childhood, you can change the future. You *can* change the way you think. And you do this by a process of, first, understanding *why* you felt the way you did, and then *learning* how to unlearn what may be the habits of a lifetime. It's not easy to do – but once you have begun to make some progress, you look back in astonishment at the old you.

'At one of the papers I worked on, there was a section editor who was talented, rather loud, opinionated, who swore, smoked, and occasionally slammed the phone down on someone annoying.

'Who was, in other words, a typical journalist. Except for the fact that she was a woman.

'This unfortunate fact meant that people thought her behaviour shocking. Now, remember that she didn't drink or (so far as I knew) do drugs. She simply expressed her opinions forcefully. She was also extremely able, kind to her staff (of whom I was one) and ran a good, tight section.

'But she was criticised heavily. Not to her face; people were frankly rather nervous of her. But everyone (mainly her male colleagues) thought she was simply too much. Too aggressive, too opinionated, too strident, too loud. Everything that in her male equivalent would have been valued and admired as a sign that he really knew his stuff; characteristics that would have marked him out as confident, able, powerful.'

Like this woman, we need to break free of the cycle. This was recommended two decades ago by the redoubtable Shirley Conran, whose *Superwoman* was instrumental in freeing many women from the need to dust under the rug (or, as we reminded readers earlier in this book, to stuff a mushroom!) – but unfortunately she gets it very slightly wrong by putting the emphasis on care for others: 'Be constructively selfish. Think of yourself first. If you're not healthy and functioning efficiently, you can't look after your family or do your job.'[16] Right thought; wrong reason.

Like many of the women in this chapter, we have tired of being good girls. In fact it's our premise that being a good girl impacts on all the problems women face – many of which we have examined in this book – and in particular their physical and mental health.

We have shied away from being too prescriptive, but feel emboldened to suggest advice offered by a cognitive therapist: 'Me first, with due consideration for others.' Now, be honest. That shocked you, didn't it? Your first reaction was: 'But that's so *selfish*!' It was ours, too – we admit it.

We'd say that proves our point...that we (but please, please, not our own daughters) have been raised to be quiet, and good, and supportive, and not to ask for too much. That this leads to highly intelligent and creative women who are frustrated at a deep level; to battered wives who go back for more; to the whole wretched cycle of co-dependency; and to powerless women who've learned to manipulate the system – getting their way by *appearing* to be good girls.

Have things changed? For some women, yes. And where they haven't, it's down to us to make sure they do. Hence this poem:

Advice to a Daughter

Whatever you do,
Don't try to please us;
Please yourself instead.
Be wild. Be kind. Be happy.
Try to keep your head.

Janice Warman

And we would wish you, in the words of Derek Walcott:

Love after Love

The time will come
when, with elation,
you will greet yourself arriving
at your own door, in your own mirror,
and each will smile at the other's welcome

and say, sit here. Eat.
You will love again the stranger who was yourself.
Give wine. Give bread. Give back your heart
to itself, to the stranger who has loved you

all your life, whom you ignored
for another, who knows you by heart.
Take down the love letters from the bookshelf,

the photographs, the desperate notes,
peel your own image from the mirror.
Sit. Feast on your life.

Derek Walcott

My smiles, my tears, my words were fake.
Cut me in half; the core was bad
And when you made your big mistake
I can't deny that I was glad

From *Equals* by Sophie Hannah

Plus ça change, plus c'est la même chose

We wanted to end *Hey Nonny* on a positive note and could think of no better way than a chapter devoted to Sally Ann Lasson, whose acerbic *As If* cartoon strips delight an enthusiastic following in *The Independent*. We begged her to let us borrow them and were overjoyed when she agreed.

Her subjects are male dissembling, female manipulation, sex and dogs, not necessarily in that order. She quite rightly puts dogs above men; having met her dog, we understand.

Janice is more of a cat person but Julia, who started off as a cat person, 'cats no less liquid than their shadows', has come round to the opposite way of thinking and now thinks dogs are the only way to get true adoration. 'Dogs, unlike cats and husbands, don't dance about wanting feeding as soon as you put your foot in the door; they are pleased to see you for your own sake. They also have sensitivities that your partner may not understand.'

Sally Ann draws a veil over what A.N. Wilson has described as their similarities – 'the over-excitement of males and the irresponsibility of dogs' – but makes a great deal of the innate superiority of dogs over chaps.

She reminds us of the things we already know:

Tell a man you love him if you want to drive him away.

There will always be a percentage of husbands who run off with the au pair. 'That fellow seems to me to possess but one idea, and that is a wrong one.' (Samuel Johnson)

Men send e-mails to end a relationship. (Or a post-it note – remember Sex and the City?) 'I am feeling a bit anxious re a few of my emails. There are one or two I might rather were not scrutinised,' says Martin Lukes in *Who Moved My Blackberry?*[1]

Divorce; for years it can't be contemplated, then, as Fay Weldon says, 'Think it and it's done'.

Men hate it when women behave well, unless they need them for a photo opportunity (like David Mellor).

It's not just men who like making love.

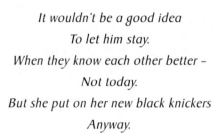

It wouldn't be a good idea
To let him stay.
When they know each other better –
Not today.
But she put on her new black knickers
Anyway.

From *Prelude*, Wendy Cope

It was Mary Wollstonecraft who said 'While [women] are absolutely dependent on their husbands they will be cunning, mean and selfish'; Ibsen's *Hedda Gabler* confirms it. Janet Street Porter's review describes Hedda as 'a mixture of boredom and malice, frustrated with her surroundings, her lack of skills and her enclosed world'. Sounds familiar? It is.

It's true we can be really nasty, and not just before our period. As Judith Holden says: 'The rest of the world see you as a boring old bag. If only they knew how remarkable, how fantastic, how funny, how sexy we all really are.'[2]

Clothes are fundamental to a woman's existence. As Katherine Hamnett said in *The Sunday Telegraph*: 'You've got to be able to put clothes on and then just forget about them and be the best person you can be. Clothes empower you – but they can work the other way and take your strength away.'

And so on to male dissembling. If only our husbands, in particular, could remember this when they are working late at the office. Here is an extract from Rachel Cusk's novel, *The Temporary*:

> One night she stayed late, offering to help him with his work, until it grew dark outside and they were alone in the office. They had talked, and Francine had cleverly steered the conversation towards the personal. David had revealed that his wife ran a local advertising agency and often didn't get home until late herself. In answer to Francine's questions, he admitted that he did often have to make his own dinner and occasionally even iron his shirts, and she gave him her utmost sympathy. The next day, she had made sure to meet his eye frequently and they had shared several intimate glances. Eventually, after more than a week, he became flustered and tried to grab her behind a filing cabinet.[3]

Fay Weldon has observed that 'It is not necessarily the ravishing beauty who runs off with other women's men. Beware most of all the spare woman at the dinner party with lowered lids, quiet and sweet, dressed like a country mouse'. Or the woman 'who bribes her way into a man's affection with little gifts'.[4] We are all these women in their many disguises. No wonder men fear us so. However, there is such a national shortage of attractive men that perhaps they have to be shared. Look how evenly Boris Johnson has been distributed, for example. *The Saudi Gazette* even helpfully suggests that polygamy could solve the spinsterhood problem: 'Women, help your husbands for the sake of society. A second wife is a must in order to eradicate spinsterhood.'

We rarely even get our same-sex friendships right. Like Fay in Anita Brookner's novel *Brief Lives*, we can find our 'friends' intimidating: 'Basically I found her alarming and she found me boring, yet in our heyday it was natural for us to telephone each other two or three times a week'.[5]

We all do this. Why? In fact do we actually want our friends to tell the truth? A neighbour writes: 'We are off to spend a long weekend with friends at Sandbanks, I adore them and a big plus the beach!! I've been on that cabbage soup diet for 10 days and according to "friends" stink of onions and cabbage but have lost 7lbs.'

Even women who don't obsess about their own body image are always pleased to see their friends putting on weight. As Deborah Ross says in *The Independent*: 'Some of my best friends are women so long as they stay heavier than me.'

And India Knight hits the nail on the head: 'What happens is that women who should stick together are divided into two camps and reserve their most toxic venom for each other. Working mothers despise stay-at-home mothers who they think are sad and women who stay at home despise working mothers as the devil.'[6]

Is this why women are not running the world already? It must be time, if Martin Amis says so. One thing's for sure, men won't be nagged into doing things better. This tale of a railway journey, described by Joseph Conrad's wife, Jessie, will sound familiar to many:

He [Joseph] had taken our tickets and intended travelling in the same carriage but on no account were we to give any indication that he belonged to our party. He seated himself in a far corner, ostentatiously concealing himself behind his newspaper and completely ignoring his family. All my efforts to soothe the infant proved unavailing and the whole carriage re-echoed with his lusty howls. From all sides came murmurs of consternation and sympathy for him, the only man, the stranger in the carriage…Then the whole carriage was convulsed with suppressed merriment when my young sister turned to him and demanded that he should reach down the baby's bottle.[7]

The maestro of this type of passive resistance is the character Simon Hench in Simon Gray's play *Otherwise Engaged*, who manages to remain apart from and oblivious to everyone else; his friend, his lodger, his brother, even his wife. Next to infidelity, what women most resent (but also envy) about men is their ability to switch off or simply go missing when required. No surprise, then, that Asperger's, so much more common among men, is said to be simply an extreme form of male behaviour.

Perhaps this is neither denial nor pedantry. Is the male mind simply more literal, as in Ogden Nash's poem, *The Purist*?

The Purist

I give you now Professor Twist,
A conscientious scientist,
Trustees exclaimed, 'He never bungles!'
And sent him off to distant jungles.
Camped on a tropic riverside,
One day he missed his loving bride.
She had, the guide informed him later,
Been eaten by an alligator.
Professor Twist could not but smile.
'You mean,' he said, 'a crocodile.'

Ogden Nash

Would it be better, perhaps, to turn to cats?

Horses, dogs and men

Horses, dogs and men
All thrive on attention:
Cats don't give a damn.

Horses, dogs and men
All need a lot of food:
A cat will catch its own.

Horses, dogs and men,
Like you to be home:
Cats will leave you alone.

Horses, dogs and men
All like to be groomed:
Cats will do it for themselves

Horses, dogs and men
All need exercise:
A cat will purr and sigh.

In short: if you need to be needed,
You know who to choose:

But if you're independent of mind
It's the felines fit the shoes.

Janice Warman

On the other hand...

Fireworks Poem II

Write it in fire across the night:
Some men are more or less all right.

Wendy Cope

Epilogue

So, this is the book that we wrote. We hope the Hey Nonny philosophy is simple and sustainable, provides an alternative to instant fixes, diets and treatments, and helps women to examine the pressures they are put under by both family and society.

In our search for truth we may well have mixed abstract intellectual values with complete trivia, but this is the way of things; the mish-mash called life. 'I noticed myself having to be constantly alert to the possibility that someone was taking me for a ride,' said Atul Gawande while examining new gizmos at a medical conference. It's the same for women.

We often have occasion to revise our opinions, even to come full-circle. Before Julia had children, she used to think that selfish mothers who still managed to lead interesting lives were the best, 'but the act of giving birth changed my mind. Once I'd had children, they so directed how I felt and acted that selfishness became an impossibility'.

Janice, on the other hand, never quite understood what women who were at home full time were going on about, until she had to do it herself. 'I would come back from New York and go on about how busy I'd been and how there weren't enough hours in the day. Julia would say, *Yes, it's been a bit like that around here*. I would think, *No it hasn't*. But when I had to do it, I understood. There's just as much to do – or more, as women who work tend to delegate! – but it's more frustrating and often less satisfying.'

How often we need to eat our own words. As Fay Weldon had said in her memoir, *Auto Da Fay*: 'It was a lesson that was to repeat itself at intervals through life. You could be going along calmly and cheerfully, and suddenly the ground beneath you would erupt and a whole spew of nastiness and corruption would toss itself out like lava from a volcano.'[1]

The American writer Terry Martin Hekker championed the virtues of marriage and motherhood until her husband dispensed with her services on their fortieth wedding anniversary (handing her divorce papers with a 16-page list of her faults) and she was thrust abruptly into poverty. Her first book was called *Ever Since Adam and Eve*; her new book, not surprisingly, is to be called *Disregard First Book*. There are no long service awards for marriage, no thanks for motherhood and we will always love our children far more than they will ever love us. Of course, they will love their children far more, too – it's in the natural order of things.

The most difficult thing for women, especially married women, and especially married women with children, is focus. Here are a few of the unsolicited opinions Julia received about this book.

Daughter: *It is rubbish, no one will ever read it.*

Mother: *You won't have to be very good to be better than some of the stuff I get from the library.*

Mother-in-law: *What IS this book?*

There is only one way to achieve and be creative, as Louise Doughty explains in her *Times* column, 'How to Write a Novel': 'What is your core time? Where is the space in your life when nothing short of nuclear disaster stops you from sitting down to your keyboard? Work out exactly when your core time is. Then surround it with barbed wire.'

Anyway, with or without core time, we have reached the end. What was the brief we gave each other before we started? Well, no funny religions and no funny diets was one rule, and we have managed to stick to this at least.

We tried to keep sex out of the picture but given the current obsession with it, this was difficult. In fact, sex was one of the knottiest problems of the book, because there is so much attention given to it these days. You can't even have your hair cut without someone thrusting a magazine in front of you describing ten supposedly 'new' sexual positions; haven't magazine editors heard of tantric sex or read the Kama Sutra? Apparently, there is now an *animated* online Kama Sutra. Now don't pretend you aren't going to look it up…

What most women would like from a partner is commitment and understanding. Unfortunately, for most men, this expectation is set too high; yet women who have love and romance encoded in their DNA ('…'tis women's whole existence') somehow cannot bear to give up on this hope. Virginia Nicholson, in *Among the Bohemians*, observes that while the Bohemian movement in the early twentieth century was the precursor to the 'swinging sixties', it didn't necessarily benefit women; 'free love' can mean sex with neither love nor responsibility and was often for the convenience of the man. It is her belief that 'some things have been lost; graciousness and sobriety perhaps, and the measured graduation from formality to intimacy in human relationships'.[2] As Joan Smith says in her review in *The Independent* of *Tête-à-Tête*, a biography of Jean Paul Sartre and Simone de Beauvoir by Hazel Rowley: 'Sartre's entire world was built on lies. He argued for complete freedom in sexual relationships, disregarding the asymmetrical positions of men and women, and did not even follow his own principle of "transparency" with his lovers. De Beauvoir's willingness to go along with all this self-serving nonsense undermined her morally and emotionally.'

As for an extreme lack of graciousness, the post-feminist generation hasn't worked out what it feels about lads' magazines like *Nuts* and *Zoo*. Do we ignore them, sanction them, or tutt at them? Or are we simply to raise our eyes to heaven, a female gesture that probably predates history? Does this soft porn denigrate us, celebrate us or does it not matter much either way?

Julie Myerson, in a recent *Harper's Bazaar* article, gave the intelligent woman's view of sex; it's one we agree with. 'Sex should be dark, exciting, quiet, loving, terrifying, glorious, disappointing, exhilarating, lovely – and an intensely private matter between two people. Sometimes it's frequent and sometimes it isn't.' Perhaps men who find their sex lives temporarily in decline during or after pregnancy should take note, and be a bit more grown up about it.

It seems to us that the problem is not sex *per se*, but the fact that we live in a society with fewer and fewer taboos. As Terence Blacker has observed in *The Independent*: 'Activities which would not so long ago have been a source of private shame are, thanks to the glories of the cyber age, openly and proudly acknowledged.' Do we really want a state of total sexual fluidity, with our moral compass not just set aside, but hurled out of the window at speed?

Even today, women in all strata of society feel threatened. Young men still classify women as prudes or tarts, yet no woman wants to be either. Men still call us lesbians or say we are frigid if they can't get us into bed. And Elodie Harper, in a letter to *The Independent*, describes what a great many young women feel about sexual coercion:

> *Like many people I was saddened to read about the levels of violent abuse teenage girls suffer at the hands of their boyfriends ("One in five girls hit by boyfriend", 21 March) but perhaps unlike other readers I was not surprised.*

> *Most of the media attention has focused on the correlation between girls who witness or suffer abuse at home and go on to suffer abuse from boyfriends. While this obviously needs to be addressed, I am surprised that nobody has focused on the more startling fact that the majority of teenage girls who accept being hit by their partners (over two-thirds) have never had experience of abuse before.*

> *As a young woman in my early twenties I have been concerned since my teenage years by my peer group's distressing lack of self-esteem. On all sides in film, commercials and magazines we are fed the message that finding and keeping a man is the ultimate goal and the ultimate status of cool. You cannot open a girls' or women's magazine without finding myriad surveys on what clothes men find attractive, how to get a date, what sex tips to use etc. The implied message is that to take part in mainstream culture you have to have a man.*

> *The result is that girls find their self-image depends on sexual*

relationships and they become increasingly prepared to take a man at any price, violence being the extreme end of the scale. I cannot name one girl of my acquaintance (myself included) who has not at some point put up with bullying behaviour or given into sexual demands they secretly didn't want rather than lose a man. Sometimes this is not even a case of girls acting on misguided love but because they believe this is what they should be doing. As one friend who was sexually coerced told me, "Maybe I'm just uptight; isn't this what everyone else is doing?"

Until we address the way our culture presents sex and relationships to young girls, I'm afraid we will continue to see figures like these.

There is a relevant passage in Peter Bradshaw's novel *Dr Sweet and His Daughter* when Hattie is presented with an unexpected dilemma on her wedding night.

Arlen disconcerted his young bride with the ardour, and indeed the volume, with which he demanded one specific sexual practice. It was something in which he had never before shown any interest, in the course of what Hattie considered their respectably bold and adventurous lovemaking.

When Hattie hesitated, Arlen said nothing, but reached into his travel bag, from which he extracted a sheaf of images downloaded from the Internet, putting his interest and connoisseurship of this practice beyond question. Hattie was not a prude, but there was something less than loveable in the furtive way Arlen had hidden it all from her until now, and his evident assumption that the married state made this a conjugal right.[3]

Adam Phillips has written in *Going Sane*: 'It is dehumanising to treat people sexually in ways they have not consented to'.[4] As parents, this is a topic we shy away from, but it is one of the most important lessons to teach our children. How do we give our daughters the confidence not to submit to these pressures? Do they need to invent their own kind of feminism in response to the mores of the day?

We agree with FJM McKenna, who wrote in a letter to *The Sunday Telegraph*: 'Surely the true feminist is the confident woman who resists pressure to conform to a fashionable ideal?' And yet how do women set standards of behaviour without being regarded as priggish?

The picture is further complicated by the way men themselves lack confidence in the new social order. As Anthony Clare has said, 'Men were in command. Men today are in shock. Boys and grown men have always taken for granted that what they were doing was more important than what girls and women were doing. The very traits which once marked out women as weak and inferior – emotional, spontaneous, intuitive, expressive, compassionate, empathic – are increasingly being seen as the markers of maturity and health'.[5]

Marriage is changing too. Men do not want high-powered women as they are too demanding on the one hand and too inattentive on the other (although research in the journal *Labour Economics* shows the pay gap between husband and wife is narrowing – so alpha males are also apparently discarding trophy wives for equal earners. Each truth has its opposite truth, it seems.) Older couples are filing for divorce in increasing numbers. The personals are full of 70+ men who find themselves without a woman. According to the ads at least, there are plenty of active (and optimistic?) gents, 'still firing on all cylinders'. Love and its attendant jealousies can flourish at any age. In January 2007, according to The Times, 'a pensioner is to be jailed for shooting a love rival at his allotment, after the pair became involved with the warden of their sheltered housing complex'.

In our local free magazine, attractive Thai ladies are described seeking 'sincere western gentleman'. Mature western gentlemen, judging by the picture. And we wonder who could possibly fall for the following advert: 'My secretary said don't mention the fine restaurants, hotels and distant travel. Just say you're kind, mature, successful and seeking a lady, below 40.' Or does the fact that it seems to be permanently running indicate that no one has?

Sophie Hannah's poem comes to mind:

Person Specification

The ideal candidate for the position
of soul mate to the all-important you
should say she loves you, of her own volition,
every five minutes, and it should be true.

She must be motivated and ambitious
but feminine. She will be good at art,
at homely things. Her meals should be nutritious.
The ideal candidate will win your heart

with her prowess in bed. She will look stunning
in public, turn at least ten heads per day.
She should do most of (if not all) the running
and be prepared for marriage straight away.

Points will be lost for boring occupations,
excessive mood swings, drugs and other men.
To those who fail, your deep commiserations.
This post will not be advertised again.

Sophie Hannah

Women may read the above and decide to remain single.

The Post-Dictator Plan

Do you have a post-dictator plan?
Are you planning to replace him with just another man?
Better, surely, to declare a dictator-free zone,
Live alone; be a democracy,
Run up the flag, go for a hike,
Live free as a fish – one that doesn't need a bike.

Janice Warman

Women are more likely to come out of divorce feeling liberated and spend more time with friends and family. Men, in contrast, are likely to have casual sex, call up old flames and go online.

Many women do prefer to live alone, especially now the stigma of failure has been removed. After a certain age we become wary. As Wendy Cope has said in her poem

Rondeau Redouble (which we quoted earlier): 'And so the gambler was at least unwed/And didn't preach or sneer or wield a pen/Or hoard his wealth or take the scotch to bed/ She'd lived and learned...'

Population statistics can be contradictory. While more people are living alone, family homes are filling up once more: young people who cannot afford to rent or buy are staying at home or returning after university. More students are attending their local university on grounds of cost, so the natural break that occurred when children left home to study is lost. Older people are moving back in with their children because of the high costs or poor standards of social care. There are no prizes for guessing who bears the burden of work for the three-generation household – and whose freedom is most curtailed. In any case, as Julia's 85-year-old mother says: 'Women *never* retire!'

Does this sound suspiciously like 'Down with Men, Up with Prozac'? We have tried to check ourselves, examine our motives, and beware of generalisations, although we did undeniably go off at tangents. This was a book that grew organically; things we thought unimportant at the beginning became vital at the end. We tried to be objective, but as Alan Bennett has said: 'You do not put yourself into what you write, you find yourself there.'[6]

We owe an enormous debt to mightier women who have gone before us. It was Yasmin Alibhai-Brown who dared to champion publicly the late Angela Dworkin, who was often reviled for her extreme antagonism towards the male sex: 'She was an absolute heroine for exposing and damning the nasty evil traders of hard core pornography and sexual sadism.'

And it was Donatella Versace who has said, 'We can achieve so many different things that men cannot. I think women are stronger. Our strength is not really well seen by everybody.'

We hope we have not neglected the male point of view. Jonathan Coe, in his novel *The Rotters' Club*, describes the wife-versus-mistress dilemma: 'He thought about Irene and found himself aching for her company: not for anything in particular she might say or do: just for her wordless kindly presence. He thought about his son, about how he would feel if he could see his father in this ridiculous situation. And then he watched Miriam as she went to the bar for more drinks, and his body was galvanised yet again, with the knowledge that he had somehow won the affection of this beautiful woman – this beautiful young woman, more to the point.'[7]

Anne Sexton gives us the mistress's viewpoint:

For My Lover, Returning to His Wife

She has always been there, my darling.
She is, in fact, exquisite.
Fireworks in the dull middle of February
and as real as a cast-iron pot.

Let's face it, I have been momentary.
A luxury. A bright red sloop in the harbor.
My hair rising like smoke from the car window.
Littleneck clams out of season.

She is more than that. She is your have to have,
has grown you your practical, your tropical growth.
This is not an experiment. She is all harmony.
She sees to oars and oarlocks for the dinghy,

I give you back your heart.
I give you permission—

She is so naked and singular.
She is the sum of yourself and your dream.
Climb her like a monument, step after step.
She is solid.

As for me, I am a watercolor.
I wash off.

Anne Sexton

We like to think that we have given men a voice too, not least among them that self-appointed curmudgeon, Kingsley Amis, who has a starring role. And some of the best insights have come from men. Howard Jacobson deals convincingly with male insecurity in his novel *The Making of Henry*: 'But it wasn't only because he lacked certainty in all matters pertaining to the heart that Henry needed a pre-existing second opinion about women. It was also because he doubted his capacity to look after anybody, to "be there for her", in contemporary parlance, to bear the burden of making her happy until death did them… Death being the hardest part. Though even in the matter of helping out should she cut her finger or get something in her eye Henry knew himself to be unreliable.'[8]

As Fay Weldon has said about her late husband, 'Like so many men of his generation he found death embarrassing. He sometimes did not know where to put himself in a crisis except somewhere else.'[9]

Alan Bennett, in *Untold Stories*, describes the feelings men have about some women, in this case his mother: 'Of course the only way she is killing me is, in the way of women with men, not letting me have my own way, nor allowing me to lead the relatively liberated life I've lately discovered in London.'[10] These sentiments are echoed in his play, *The Lady in the Van*: 'One of the functions of women is to bring an element of trouble into the otherwise tranquil lives of men.'[11]

Kingsley Amis was debating whether women were worth all the bother as long ago as the seventies, when he wrote *Jake's Thing*. By the end of the book, Jake discovers that his impotence may not be psychological after all and could be easily treated with simple medication:

> *"You mean it may be physical after all? And cured just by taking something?"*
>
> *"Yes. As I said, we'll have to run tests."*
>
> *Jake did a quick run-through of women in his mind, not of the ones he had known or dealt with in the past few months or years so much as all of them; their concern with the surface of things, with objects and appearances, with their surroundings and how they looked and sounded in them, with seeming to be better and to be right while getting everything wrong, their automatic assumption of the role of injured party in any clash of wills, their certainty that a view is the more credible and useful for the fact that they hold it, their use of misunderstanding and misrepresentation as weapons of debate, their selective sensitivity to tones of voice, their unawareness of the difference in themselves between sincerity and insincerity, their interest in importance (together with noticeable inability to discriminate in that sphere), their fondness for general conversation and directionless discussion, their pre-emption of the major share of feeling, their exaggerated estimate of their own plausibility, their never listening and lots of other things like that, all according to him.*
>
> *So it was quite easy. "No thanks," he said.*[12]

This passage illustrates in no uncertain terms why middle-aged men get fed up with us.

Another male writer, Justin Cartwright, feels all this is so much indisputable fact that it is a waste of time even bothering to debate it:

What happens between men and women, how they see each other and apportion blame, and how they believe that the other is diminishing them deliberately, and how they feel jealousy and hide behind big statements of principle, and how they make accommodations with life and with failure and with disillusionment, can be seen from a certain perspective as being preordained. Like ants, like bees, people have allotted roles. What you are saying about the conflicting pulls of maternity, the insecurity of being a single mother, the unreliability of men, the cruelty of human beings to each other, none of this is news. In fact the reverse would be news: the constancy of men, the selflessness of human beings, the joy of marriage, et cetera, et cetera.[13]

One annoyance that women feel about men is that they still seem to share the seemingly infuriating point of view that all females are unpredictable and irrational due to their 'natural' hormone balance. In Saudi Arabia one of the reasons that women are still not allowed to drive is that they are thought to be unreliable at certain times of the month. Girls are also discouraged from taking part in sports, according to *The Saudi Gazette*, for 'medical reasons' (i.e. periods) and because their hymen could be broken. Although running away from home is a crime, it is hardly surprising that 'the cases of Saudi females eloping or fleeing are on the rise'.

Another dilemma to remain unsolved is the problem of the chap wanting his dinner on the table. Julia's teenage son, although competent to self-feed during the day (though not self-clear-up), draws the line at cooking his own evening meal. Janice's can produce a fine breakfast for friends who've stayed overnight and has been known to throw a steak in the pan when she is still on the train home; she has a daughter who's a whiz at cakes and a husband who cooks. But she's not smug!

Kathryn Hughes writes in *The Guardian* about women throughout history who 'worked anonymously to keep their households fed, watered and comfortable with as little fuss and drama as possible. No one threw saucepans or stamped their foot because the master of the house had gobbled down his supper without remembering to sigh with pleasure or send his compliments to the kitchen.' This situation still applies today... men do cook but whether it is as a chef in a restaurant or at home, it is generally the showy-off kind of cooking that prevails. Many men also require a whole string orchestra to serenade them if they have stacked the dishwasher.

The male of the species still seems able to organise life to suit himself. The journalist Piers Morgan describes his 'perfect weekend' in *The Daily Telegraph*: 'On Friday night I would have dinner at a restaurant I can really relax in. On Saturday I would wake to the thud of a massive pile of newspapers being dropped outside my door.' Later he would play cricket for the village First Eleven (after picking up his sons and presumably leaving them with his family?) 'My perfect Sunday lunch would be with my parents, prepared by mum or dad, then I would drive back to London in the evening, drop the boys off and head for the Lots Road pub for a little relaxer.'

A friend, Sarah, says: 'Sounds idyllic. Mum and Dad to cook the lunch. Granny to play with the children. Brothers and wives to do the washing up. No washing, school runs or chores and no wife to nag him. No wonder he's laughing.'

When women are brave enough to take a break from their responsibilities it is disliked by almost everybody. Pamela Stephenson, psychotherapist (and former star of *Not the Nine O'Clock News*) wrote *Treasure Islands* while sailing the Pacific for 10 months. In an interview with *The Daily Telegraph* she revealed that she decided going away from her family was necessary because she was so stressed 'that she became quiet and overwhelmed and sort of disappeared inside myself. There's an underlying frustration that you can't achieve everything for everybody'. Pamela has five children and is married to the comedian Billy Connolly, who, she says, 'is away a lot and needy himself'. She was well aware of the seriousness of the decision she took in taking time off: 'It's risky to go against your husband, it's risky to leave your children.' Pamela was inspired by the ghost of Fanny Stevenson, the wife of the author Robert Louis, who sailed the Pacific with him.

'This has been a voyage of discovery for me in every way,' she said. 'It has made me a better therapist, a better wife, a better mother, better in every way. I'm healthier, stronger, much less spoiled and much more resilient. You have to face yourself on the ocean. I've never felt so alive, so humbled, so moved or so terrified as I have in the past year. Honestly, I can't wait to head off again.'

Julia's experience was rather different: 'When I left my own family for a short break in Greece where I could write uninterrupted, I'd hoped to be more appreciated on my return, but found they had all simply been made furious by my absence. Not at all the effect I'd intended.'

On a more superficial level (and one of the criticisms of this book will be the way it lurches from the profound to the trivial, practically in mid-sentence), the modern man must beware of becoming too demanding and unreasonable. There is the baked bean precedent. In 2005, a husband who assaulted his wife after she bought the wrong brand of baked beans was found guilty of common assault. As Janice says, *There are so many angry men*:

⌒∾⌒

There are so many angry men

There are so many angry men,
The reasons multifold.

The crimes against them endless
If only they could be told.

You can see them out at dinner
With their silent wives.
Chewing steak with grim demeanour;
Clashing knives.

You can see them slamming car doors
You can see them in the dock.
You can see their women standing by them,
Pale faced in flowery frocks.

They are angry when you're home
And angry when you're not.
They are angry if you're cold with them;
And if you're hot.

There are so many angry men.
They are angry in the morning and in the evening too.
Is it something in the water?
I wish I knew.

Janice Warman

These days, men (however reluctantly) now see the need to do some of the household chores. As Emma Parkinson wrote in *The Sunday Telegraph*: 'Sir – I may not undertake such arduous housework as my grandmother, but at least I have the pleasure of seeing my boyfriend attempt some.'

And where men may previously have tried to impress women with tales of derring-do, there is new research to suggest that women favour cautious males over thrill-seeking ones. So it seems it's only men themselves who are impressed by driving too fast or dangerous stunts. You only have to read about all the bodies scattered on Everest to see that men need to find new ways to be heroic.

Neither is risk-taking at work such a great idea. More cautious female fund managers are doing better than their male counterparts. According to *The Sunday Telegraph* in August 2004, 'In the year to July 31 women boosted the value of their investments by an average of 10%. This compared with an increase of just 6% by the average man.' It was Gloria Steinem who said: 'Women's total instinct for gambling is satisfied by marriage.'

The sexes also have greatly differing ideas about the way they spend money. It is not unusual for a man to query the amount of petrol his wife is using, whilst deciding a thousand pound satellite navigation system is essential expenditure.

Will it be the end of infidelity, now there are navigation systems that can check the whereabouts of your partner at all times? Or once you feel the need to start snooping, is the relationship almost certainly doomed anyway? No prizes for guessing that most of these gadgets are sold to men, who set higher store in fidelity than one might imagine. Personally, if we found ourselves globally positioned, we would say it was all over bar the shouting; women are already subject to too much routine surveillance.

One of the ways men are resisting the feminisation of society is by developing increasingly complex technology. Women often fear the word interactive yet it can be argued that it is the female sex that does most of the interacting – even from a young age. According to an Ofcom report, girls aged 12-15 are more likely than boys to have a mobile phone, listen to the radio and read newspapers and magazines. Surely this is yet another phenomenon that didn't need a survey to prove its existence?

Paradoxically, it is on the subject of technology that some of the best advice we have come across came from a man:

Sir, Nina Brink gets up at 6am and answers 123 emails by 7.30 ("The woman with the world at her feet", 8 March). By 8am, she's dressed and usually flies "somewhere". She works a 16-hour day, was only at her luxury villa in Antwerp for 50 days in the last year. On holidays, she works at least four hours a day. Her first marriage failed, she is on her second but her husband was not mentioned in the article.

OK, so lots of men live that kind of life. But – hey, kid, chill out! Lie back on that beach, drink the wine, eat the grapes, and soak up those rays! You are a long time looking at the lid![14]

Or in other words, when you stand ready for presentation at the pearly gates, you won't wish you'd picked up that last bit of dry-cleaning.

Younger women are least likely to accept that life is unequal, but this could be because, as Germaine Greer says, 'they have yet to come across the barriers'. The issue of personal security is a good example; it is older women who can no longer run who are most vulnerable on buses and trains and out at night. Younger women may be more preyed upon, but it is older women who fear crime, vandalism and drunks.

Younger women are also better received by men. A tribunal in 2003 ruled that two careers of women in their forties had been blocked by a leading city law firm. During the tribunal, evidence was produced that one of the firm's partners had said: 'The firm should sack you all and get in better looking recruits than you old bags.' (We couldn't help wondering if this man was himself an Adonis...)

Melanie Phillips, in *The Ascent of Woman*, her study of the suffragette movement, which we quoted earlier, points out that the vote was not the fundamental issue: 'It was rather a means to an end; a society and above all, a male sex – transfigured by a woman's apparently distinctive values of spirituality, self-restraint and sensibility.'[15] Women wanted to challenge the prevailing double standards of men who insisted on marital rights and insisted on wifely loyalty whilst they themselves behaved just as they pleased.

Fay Weldon, in her memoir *Auto da Fay*, describes her father's position on unfaithfulness; her mother, 'to demonstrate to him just how upsetting she found his persistent adultery, had spent a night with a passing stranger, and told him that she had. But instead of showing remorse for his own behaviour he had been outraged by hers, and had started divorce proceedings within the hour'.[16]

There was a particularly poignant story in *The Daily Telegraph* in 2005. A woman called Carol Jewell, who had been married for 33 years, donated a kidney to her husband, after which he left her for another woman despite the fact that she was now suffering from breast cancer. Well, clearly if women have been trying to improve men for a hundred years, as Melanie Phillips suggests, we are all flogging a dead horse.

Hey Nonny is not in fact about improvement, although that would be nice; it's more about crisis management and coping with the fallout of our lives. We are some way off the kind of feminism that Bridget Jones's friend Sharon imagines in the future: 'There won't be any men trying to have sex with women without any niceness or commitment, because the young mistresses and women will just turn round and tell them to sod off and men won't get any sex or any women unless they learn how to behave properly.'[17]

Feminism has led, however, to a great deal more honesty and understanding in society in general. Women who remain unmarried are no longer social failures, unless perhaps Bridget Jones herself could be considered a new sub-section. We do believe that marriage and motherhood remain vital roles; we wouldn't have written this book without being part of this particular club.

Perhaps the most important part of feminism is not to band together against men, but to concentrate on helping each other. Frances Power Cobbe was the Suffragette forerunner for Hey Nonny: 'Women should use their superior moral qualities outside the home in any cause of humanity, but above all in the cause of their own sex and the relief of the misery of their own sisters.'[18(i)]

There remains so many issues that women should redress. There is still the issue of domestic abuse. John Stuart Mill in 1851 was brave enough to state that 'unbridled power over women had corrupted the psyche of man', 'rendering him domineering, exacting, self-worshipping, when not capriciously or brutally tyrannical'. [18(ii)] Yet 'Even that great feminist performed only one domestic chore: he made tea when he returned home in the evening.' [18(iii)] It is still a tragic fact that many women who are economically dependent on men, or wish to keep the family together, still endure abusive behaviour.

One in four women are assaulted by a partner at some time in their lives, while there are two murders and up to ten suicides a week caused by domestic violence. For British women under 44, it is the most common cause of death – above cancer and road accidents. In many American states, pregnant women are more likely to die violently than from natural causes or accidents. In Britain, the police are now piloting a new head-camera worn by police attending 'domestics' so they can gather evidence at the scene. This will also counter the abuser's habit of bullying his victim into dropping charges.

Associated with domestic violence, there is the question of rape. As Deborah Orr has written in The Independent: 'Complete strangers raping in the street are as uncommon as in the past. But men hanging around bars and clubs, scraping acquaintance with women, then raping them, are on the increase.' The fact that rape convictions in the UK have hit a record low is a national scandal. Only 14% of cases make it to the courts; and only 5.6% result in convictions, according to figures from the police and the Crown Prosecution Service. As women we need to lobby for change, for who will do it for us? An even greater scandal is the fact that rape is still used as a weapon of war by armies. During the recent Balkan war, thousands of women (mainly Bosnian Muslims) were raped by Serbs as part of a systematic strategy of humiliation.

There are so many other areas where women's rights are still in question; the fastest increase in HIV infections in Africa, for example, is among women and girls. Women are twice as likely to become infected during sex and more prone to be forced into unprotected sex because of their lack of social power. The newfound 'freedom' of Eastern European women has led to an increase in their human trafficking as sex workers. Surely, as many (not only female) commentators have said, the focus should shift from the women who sell sex to the men who buy it? After all, it's a crime they cannot, by definition, commit alone.

Many women become prostitutes in order to survive, yet it's the most dangerous of professions: the play *Unprotected*, created by a writing collective, contains the words of Anne Marie Foy, a murdered prostitute: 'You're never safe, it's like every car you get into, you don't know whether you're going to get out.'

So, all in all, we hope we have done no harm and some good. We certainly raised more questions than we had answers for and in fact this may be the only handbook to date that offers few actual suggestions. We may have offered 'every assistance short of actual help', but as we said in the Prologue, we sought debate and illumination, not certainties. We have found what we discovered transforming in the way snow changes a landscape; outlines clearer and pathways redefined. We understood more fully that there is no right time for getting married, having a child, crossing the world or leaving a lover.

This book may be foolish in part, quirky, anecdotal, rambling, illogical, and contradictory; we are all too aware of the dangers of overstatement, but we hope we have achieved a gathering of wisdom that has identified so many of the difficulties with which women grapple.

Some awkward facts were thrown up along the way. For instance, there is some credible scientific evidence that post-menopausal women are not only less intelligent but talk more. And we were appalled to read that the once talented and beautiful Rosamond Lehmann apparently feigned blindness in old age to gain sympathy and attention.

We also discovered that women were not always supportive of each other; they were often insecure, jealous of other women's perceived beauty, talent or sex appeal and often put each other down in the same way that they sometimes treated men. We found this an unpalatable truth, not one we'd particularly looked for or wished to find. We've also discovered that we are not in fact the superior sex; that we are also vulnerable to the folly of our own desires and aspirations.

What we have written may have left us exposed but we considered it a small price to pay if we could be of use to others. Adversity is often a catalyst for achievement and so it was with us. We have written this book because it seemed the blindingly obvious thing to do, even if we did not exactly understand why, except that there were a lot of unspoken things about and for women that needed to be said; we were certain that others would share and identify with us. In the end the format and the content declared itself and everything fell into place.

Words, we found, can actually cure. It is because words matter that the dying Ruth Picardie wrote her column 'Before I Say Goodbye' for *The Observer*. In his poem, *Reading the Elephant*, about the early coma and death of his mother after a riding accident, Andrew Motion refers to a book as a parachute. This seems to us what reading and writing do: both offer a lifeline and soften the landing.

Women's lives rarely reflect their aspirations; struggle still dominates; we need support and encouragement to lighten the load. Here is a final word on the subject of creativity and age. David Mamet prompted a discussion in *The Guardian* by stating: 'Playwriting is a young man's game. It requires the courage of youth still inspired by rejection and as yet unperverted by success.' Not surprisingly, we agree instead with David Jones, who responded with: 'The purpose of theatre is to illuminate people's lives, to bring a mirror to our own experience, our society and our reaction to that society. And that self-examination should never stop. It is as necessary at 80 as it is at 20.'

As we look back on this book and the years it has taken to write it, not to mention the years of experience put into it, it seems to us the most useful personal warnings that we have come across are those of Nelson Algren: 'Never sleep with anyone whose troubles are worse than your own', and Wendy Wasserstein's observation, 'The worse the boyfriend, the more stunning the American Express bill!' We would also avoid any man who had a personalised number plate. Or, as Dorothy Parker says:

Social Note

Lady, lady, should you meet
One whose ways are all discreet,
One who murmurs that his wife
Is the lodestar of his life,
One who keeps assuring you
That he never was untrue,
Never loved another one …
Lady, lady, better run!

Dorothy Parker

Above all, this book is a testament to the courage of the women who have gone before us and have brought every chapter to life. Throughout history, society has been glued together by women. All women are teachers who are responsible for education, nurture and care. The role is unsung, silent and unending. May we honour them and keep their flags flying.

Prospect

Though loves languish and sour
Fruit puts the teeth on edge,
Though the ragged nests are empty of song
In the barbed and blistered hedge,

Though old men's lives and children's bricks
Spell out a Machiavellian creed,
Though the evil Past us ever present
And the happy Present is past indeed,

Though the stone grows and grows
That we roll up the hill
And the hill grows and grows
And gravity conquers still,

Though Nature's laws exploit
And defeat anarchic men,
Though every sandcastle concept
Being ad hoc must crumble again,

And though to-day is arid,
We know – and knowing bless –
That rooted in futurity
There is a plant of tenderness.

Louis MacNeice

Detailed references

Please see the Bibliography for full details of the books.

Prologue

1. *Something in Disguise* by Elizabeth Jane Howard, p111

2. *She May Not Leave* by Fay Weldon, p84. Reprinted by permission of HarperCollins Publishers Ltd. © Fay Weldon, 2005.

3. *The Short Life and Long Times of Mrs Beeton*, by Kathryn Hughes, p164. Reprinted by permission of HarperCollins Publishers Ltd. © Kathryn Hughes, 2005.

4. Mildred Levius, Obituary, *The Independent*

5. *Giving up the Ghost* by Hilary Mantel, (i) p154, (ii) p70. Reprinted by permission of HarperCollins Publishers Ltd. © Hilary Mantel, 2004.

6. From *Experience* by Martin Amis (p6), published by Jonathan Cape. Reprinted by permission of The Random House Group Ltd.

7. *Betjeman: The Bonus of Laughter* by Bevis Hillier, p118-9

8. Extract from *Jig* from *Complete Verse*, C. Day Lewis (copyright the Estate of C. Day Lewis 1970) is reprinted by kind permission of PFD on behalf of the Estate.

9. *The Girl from the Fiction Department*, Hilary Spurling (p91). Reproduced with the permission of David Higham Associates Limited.

10. *Two Lives*, Vikram Seth, p461-2. Reproduced with the permission of Little, Brown Book Group Limited.

11. *Walking in the Shade* by Doris Lessing, p123. Reprinted by permission of HarperCollins Publishers Ltd. © Doris Lessing, 1998.

12. *A Vicious Circle* by Amanda Craig, p255. Copyright © Amanda Craig.

13. *The Promise of Happiness* by Justin Cartwright, p89

14. *Among the Bohemians: Experiments in Living 1900-1939* by Virginia Nicholson, p91 (Viking, 2002, Penguin Books, 2003). Copyright © Virginia Nicholson, 2002. Reproduced by permission of Penguin Books Ltd.

15. From *Take a Girl Like Me* by Diana Melly (p7), published by Chatto & Windus. Reprinted by permission of The Random House Group Ltd.

16. *Untold Stories* by Alan Bennett (p58). Reproduced with the permission of Faber and Faber Ltd.

17. *Berlin: The Downfall 1945* by Anthony Beevor, p410 (Viking 2002, Penguin Books 2003). Copyright © Anthony Beevor, 2005. Reproduced by permission of Penguin Books Ltd.

18. *Self-Help for Your Nerves* by Dr Claire Weekes, p86

19. *The Importance of Being Earnest* by Oscar Wilde, Act II, p52

General Review of the Sex Situation by Dorothy Parker. Copyright © Dorothy Parker.

Lenten Thoughts of a High Anglican by John Betjeman. Copyright © John Betjeman.

Fox by Janice Warman. Copyright © Janice Warman.

If People Disapprove of You by Sophie Hannah. Copyright © Sophie Hannah.

Ballet by Janice Warman. Copyright © Janice Warman.

Procrastination by Janice Warman. Copyright © Janice Warman.

Hey Nonny heroines

1. *Much Ado About Nothing* by William Shakespeare

2. *Frightening People* by Jill Tweedie, p303. Reproduced by permission of Penguin Books Ltd.

3. *The Observer*, 10th September 2006

4. *Mantrapped* by Fay Weldon, p146. Reprinted by permission of HarperCollins Publishers Ltd. © Fay Weldon, 2005.

5. *Rosamond Lehmann: A Life* by Selena Hastings, p281

6. *She May Not Leave* by Fay Weldon, p149. Reprinted by permission of HarperCollins Publishers Ltd. © Fay Weldon, 2005.

7. *Painted Shadow: A Life of Vivienne Eliot* by Carole Seymour-Jones, p562

8. *Giving Up the Ghost* by Hilary Mantel, (i) p171, (ii) p179, (iii) p205. Reprinted by permission of HarperCollins Publishers Ltd. © Hilary Mantel, 2004.

9. *The Week*, Simon Callow on Orson Welles

10. *George Orwell* by Gordon Bowker, p431. Reproduced with the permission of David Higham Associates Limited.

11. *George Orwell: A Life* by Bernard Crick, p473

12. *The Girl from the Fiction Department* by Hilary Spurling, (i) p95, (ii) p16, (iii) p174. Reproduced with the permission of David Higham Associates Limited.

13. *The Letters of Kingsley Amis* by Zachary Leader (editor), (i) p624, (ii) p876. Reprinted by permission of HarperCollins Publishers Ltd. © Zachary Leader (editor), 2001.

14. From *Experience* by Martin Amis (p217), published by Jonathan Cape. Reprinted by permission of The Random House Group Ltd.

15. The later Alan Clarke Diaries document the same kind of aggression and despair and are informative not just for their scurrilous allegations and self-aggrandisement, but for women who have ill and/or ageing husbands; read these diaries and you will realise you are not alone with your own particular curmudgeon.

16. *The Letters of Kingsley Amis* by Zachary Leader (editor), p757. Reprinted by permission of HarperCollins Publishers Ltd. © Zachary Leader (editor), 2001.

17. From *Gwen John, A Life* by Sue Roe (p37), published by Chatto & Windus. Reprinted by permission of The Random House Group Ltd.

18. *Among the Bohemians* by Virginia Nicholson, p68 (Viking, 2002, Penguin Books, 2003). Copyright © Virginia Nicholson, 2002. Reproduced by permission of Penguin Books Ltd.

19. From *Gwen John, A Life* by Sue Roe (p90), published by Chatto & Windus. Reprinted by permission of The Random House Group Ltd.

20. *Married to Genius* by Jeffrey Meyers, p245. Reprinted with permission of Southbank Publishing.

21. *The Charlotte Perkins Gilman Reader: The Yellow Wallpaper & Other Fiction* by Charlotte Perkins Gilman, p20

22. From *On Men: Masculinity in Crisis* by Anthony Clare (p69, p207), published by Chatto & Windus. Reprinted by permission of The Random House Group Ltd.

23. *No Ordinary Man* by Dominic Carman, p285, p288, p293

24. *The Scotsman*, 24th January 2002

25. *The Sunday Telegraph*, 22nd January, 2006

26. *Spike Milligan: The Biography* by Humphrey Carpenter, p342

27. *The Week*

28. *Anthony Blunt: His Lives* by Miranda Carter, p371-2

29. Obituary, *The Independent*, 6th July 2006

30. *The Two of Us* by Sheila Hancock, p143

31. *The Independent*, 25th April 2003

32. *Untold Stories* by Alan Bennett, p51. Reproduced with the permission of Faber and Faber Ltd.

33. *The Girls of Slender Means* by Muriel Spark, p7. Reproduced with the permission of David Higham Associates Limited.

Autobiography by Louis MacNeice, reproduced with the permission of David Higham Associates Limited.

Talking in Bed by Philip Larkin. Copyright © Philip Larkin.

A Slice of Wedding Cake by Robert Graves. Copyright © Robert Graves.

Eunice by John Betjeman, reproduced with the permission of Aitken Alexander Associates Ltd.

The Baize Door by Janice Warman. Copyright © Janice Warman.

Enquire within

1. *Bridget Jones's Diary* by Helen Fielding, p254

2. *Diary of a Breast* by Elisa Segrave, p120. Reproduced with the permission of Faber and Faber Ltd.

3. *The Hungry Years: Confessions of a Food Addict* by William Leith, p125

4. From *Misconceptions* by Naomi Wolf (p19, p244), published by Chatto & Windus. Reprinted by permission of The Random House Group Ltd.

5. *A Life's Work: On Becoming a Mother* by Rachel Cusk, p29. Reprinted by permission of HarperCollins Publishers Ltd. © Rachel Cusk, 2002.

6. *Tell Me Doctor* by Roderick Wimpole, p32

7. *Superwoman* by Shirley Conran, p5. Reproduced by permission of Penguin Books Ltd.

8. *Falling for Therapy: Psychotherapy from a client's point of view* by Anna Sands, p76

9. *Complications*, Atul Gawande, (i) p223-224, (ii) p94. Reproduced with the permission of Profile Books.

10. From *Fat is a Feminist Issue* by Susie Orbach (pvii), published by Arrow Books. Reprinted by permission of The Random House Group Ltd and Susie Orbach.

11. *The Hungry Years: Confessions of a Food Addict* by William Leith, (i) p244, (ii) p240

    William Leith's book has many uses; it's informative on men, sex and alcohol quite as much as food and should be given to all teenage girls as a health warning!

12. From *The Integrated Health Bible* by Dr Mosaraf Ali (p55), published by Vermilion. Reprinted by permission of The Random House Group.

13. *Fathers and Sons* by Alexander Waugh, (i) p353, (ii) p279-80

14. *A Short History of Tractors in Ukrainian* by Marina Lewycka, p76 (Viking Press 2005). Copyright © Monica Lewycka, 2005. Reproduced by permission of Penguin Books Ltd.

15. *The Waiting Game* by Bernice Rubens, (i) p52, (ii) p28. Reproduced with the permission of Little, Brown Book Group Limited.

16. *The Old Wives' Tale* by Arnold Bennett, (i) p32, (ii) p314, p588, p591

17. *Rosamond Lehmann* by Selina Hastings, p377

18. *Slipstream* by Elizabeth Jane Howard, (i) p94, (ii) p172, p180, p202, (iii) p320, (iv) p477

Comment by Dorothy Parker, by permission of Gerald Duckworth & Co. Ltd.

Rondeau Redouble by Wendy Cope, reproduced with the permission of Faber and Faber Ltd.

Advice by Janice Warman Copyright © Janice Warman.

Metamorphosis

1. *She May Not Leave* by Fay Weldon, p13. Reprinted by permission of HarperCollins Publishers Ltd. © Fay Weldon, 2005.

2. Dr John Stevenson, Chairman of Women's Health Concern, quoted in *The Lady*, 17th April 2006

3. *Tell Me Doctor* by Roderick Wimpole, p34

4. *The Ascent of Woman* by Melanie Phillips, p64. Reproduced with the permission of David Higham Associates Limited.

5. *A Passionate Sisterhood* by Kathleen Jones, (i) p189, (ii) p209. Reprinted by permission of A M Heath & Co.

6. *Eating Children* by Jill Tweedie, (i) p8, (ii) p7

7. *Giving up the Ghost* by Hilary Mantel, p22. Reprinted by permission of HarperCollins Publishers Ltd. © Hilary Mantel, 2004.

8. *The Guardian*, (i) 5th May, 2006, (ii) 25th October, 2006

9. *She May Not Leave* by Fay Weldon, p256. Reprinted by permission of HarperCollins Publishers Ltd. © Fay Weldon, 2005.

10. *In the Name of Love* by Jill Tweedie, p192. Copyright © Jill Tweedie.

11. *The Cat that could open the Fridge: A Curmudgeon's Guide to Christmas Round Robin Letters* by Simon Hoggart, p55

Sleep

1. *A Better Woman* by Susan Johnson, p91

2. *Bridget Jones's Diary* by Helen Fielding, p275

3. *She May Not Leave* by Fay Weldon, p226. Reprinted by permission of HarperCollins Publishers Ltd. © Fay Weldon, 2005.

4. From *Grumpy Old Women*, BBC Books, published by BBC Books (p65). Reprinted by permission of The Random House Group Ltd.

5. *Intimacy*, Hanif Kureishi, p37. Reproduced with the permission of Faber and Faber Ltd.

6. *Tale of the Flopsy Bunnies*, Beatrix Potter, p199

7. *The Independent*, 3rd February 2005

8. *Alan Clark: The Last Diaries 1993-1999*, Alan Clark, (i) p204, (ii) p300. Reprinted with permission of The Orion Publishing Group Ltd.

9. *White Lightning*, Justin Cartwright, p165

10. *Time out of Mind*, Jane Lapotaire, p111. Reproduced with the permission of Little, Brown Book Group Limited.

11. *A Grief Observed*, C. S. Lewis, p39. Reproduced with the permission of Faber and Faber Ltd.

12. *The Strings are False*, Louis MacNeice, p153. Reproduced with the permission of David Higham Associates Limited.

13. *Marie Antoinette: The Journey*, Antonia Fraser, p78. Reprinted with the permission of The Orion Publishing Group Ltd.

14. From *The Bedroom Farce* from *Three Plays* by Alan Ayckbourn, p220 published by Chatto & Windus. Reprinted by permission of The Random House Group Ltd.

15. From *Free at Last*! *Diaries 1991-2001* by Tony Benn, (i) p325, (ii) p403, published by Hutchinson. Reprinted by permission of The Random House Group Ltd.

16. From *The Bedroom Farce* from *Three Plays* by Alan Ayckbourn, p220 published by Chatto & Windus. Reprinted by permission of The Random House Group Ltd.

Things by Fleur Adcock, reproduced with the permission of Bloodaxe Books.

6 a.m. Thoughts by Dick Davis, reproduced with the permission of Anvil Press Poetry.

Mother and Child: 5am Feed by Sheila Pollock. Copyright © Sheila Pollock.

At 3 a.m. by Wendy Cope, reproduced with the permission of Faber and Faber Ltd.

Not to Sleep by Robert Graves, reproduced with the permission of Carcanet Press Limited.

Song of the Master and Boatswain by W.H. Auden, reproduced with the permission of Faber and Faber Ltd.

Autumn Journal by Louis MacNeice, reproduced with the permission of David Higham Associates Limited.

Health and safety

1. Our bodies sometimes let us down before middle-age. As Matt Seaton reports after the death of his wife, Ruth Picardie, 'Ruth's arduous experience of pregnancy taught her to mistrust her body; pregnancy was an ordeal for her in every sense'. For many women pregnancy and childbirth is both the best of times and the worst of times.

2. From *Clementine Churchill* by Mary Soames, p482, published by Doubleday. Reprinted by permission of The Random House Group Ltd.

3. *Time Out of Mind* by Jane Lapotaire, (i) p251, (ii) p6, (iii) p100. Reproduced with the permission of Little, Brown Book Group Limited.

4. *The Two of Us* by Sheila Hancock, p210

5. From *I Don't Know How She Does It* by Allison Pearson, p223, published by Chatto & Windus. Reprinted by permission of The Random House Group Ltd.

6. From *Fifty Years of Hancock's Half Hour* by Richard Webber, p66, published by Century. Reprinted by permission of The Random House Group Ltd.

7. *Dr Sweet and His Daughter* by Peter Bradshaw, p12

8. *The Lucky Ones* by Rachel Cusk, p132. Reprinted by permission of HarperCollins Publishers Ltd. © Rachel Cusk, 2004.

9. *Harper's Bazaar*, Anna Purslove, February 2004

10. *The Independent*, 23rd March, 2005

11. *The Cat that Could open the Fridge* by Simon Hoggart, p88

12. *The Independent*, Thomas Sutcliffe, July 2004

13. *A Vicious Circle* by Amanda Craig, p142. Copyright © Amanda Craig.

14. From *Fat is a Feminist Issue* by Susie Orbach, p39, published by Arrow Books. Reprinted by permission of The Random House Group Ltd and Susie Orbach.

15. *Complications* by Atul Gawande, (i) p169, (ii) p163. Reproduced with the permission of Profile Books.

16. *Madam Secretary* by Madeleine K. Albright, p345

17. *The Distance Between Us* by Maggie O'Farrell, p103

18. *Living with Mother: Right to the very end* by Michele Hanson, p252

19. Extract by A. N. Wilson from *Iris Murdoch As I Knew Her*, p58 (Copyright © A. N. Wilson 2003) is reproduced by permission of PFD () on behalf of A. N. Wilson

20. *Rosamond Lehmann, A Life* by Selina Hastings, p404

21. *Slipstream* by Elizabeth Jane Howard, p246

22. *Giving up the Ghost* by Hilary Mantel, p54. Reprinted by permission of HarperCollins Publishers Ltd. © Hilary Mantel, 2004.

23. *Toast* by Nigel Slater, p154. Reprinted by permission of HarperCollins Publishers Ltd. © Nigel Slater, 2004.

24. *Untold Stories* by Alan Bennett, p614. Reproduced with the permission of Faber and Faber Ltd.

25. *Martin Lukes: Who Moved My Blackberry?* by Lucy Kellaway, p98. Reproduced by permission of Penguin Books Ltd.

26. From *Case Histories* by Kate Atkinson, p29, published by Doubleday. Reprinted by permission of The Random House Group Ltd.

27. From *Take a Girl Like Me* by Diana Melly, published by Chatto & Windus. Reprinted by permission of The Random House Group Ltd.

28. From *Grumpy Old Women* by Judith Holder, p23, published by BBC Books. Reprinted by permission of The Random House Group Ltd.

29. *Bridget Jones's Diary* by Helen Fielding, p203

30. *The Lucky Ones* by Rachel Cusk, p162. Reprinted by permission of HarperCollins Publishers Ltd. © Rachel Cusk, 2004.

31. From *Take a Girl Like Me* by Diana Melly, published by Chatto & Windus. Reprinted by permission of The Random House Group Ltd.

32. *Wodehouse: A Life* by Robert McCrum, p128 (Viking, 2004). Copyright © Robert McCrum, 2004. Reproduced by permission of Penguin Books Ltd.

33. *John Betjeman: New Fame, New Love* by Bevis Hillier, p591

34. Alan Bennett refused to be what he called a celebrity cancer sufferer but in *Untold Stories* describes his own chemotherapy (which was successful in curing his cancer) 'As if every fortnight I have to fly to Australia'. p604. Reproduced with the permission of Faber and Faber Ltd.

35. *Before I Say Goodbye* by Ruth Picardie with Matt Seaton and Justine Picardie, (i) p30, (ii) p99, (iii) p78, (iv) p79 (Penguin Books, 1998). Copyright © Ruth Picardie, 1997.

36. *Diary of a Breast* by Elisa Segrave, (i) p102, (ii) p260. Reproduced with the permission of Faber and Faber Ltd.

37. *A Better Woman* by Susan Johnson, p236

38. *Diary of a Breast* by Elisa Segrave, p138. Reproduced with the permission of Faber and Faber Ltd.

39. *The Independent*

40. *The Hungry Years* by William Leith, p256

41. *The Independent*, 2nd December, 2004

42. *Virginia Woolf: An Inner Life* by Julia Briggs, p166 (Penguin Books 2005). Copyright © Julia Briggs, 2005. Reproduced by permission of Penguin Books Ltd.

43. 'We've become a nation of whingers and spongers', *Independent on Sunday*, 10th April, 2005

44. *The New Spend Less Revolution* by Rebecca Ash, p46. Reproduced by permission of Harriman House Ltd.

45. *Time out of Mind* by Jane Lapotaire, p271. Reproduced with the permission of Little, Brown Book Group Limited.

46. *The Ascent of Woman* by Melanie Phillips, p38. Reproduced with the permission of David Higham Associates Limited.

47. *Something in Disguise* by Elizabeth Jane Howard, p260

48. *Princess Alice: Queen Victoria's Forgotten Daughter* by Gerard Noel, p243

The Ted Williams Villanelle by Wendy Cope, reproduced with the permission of Faber and Faber Ltd.

What it says on the tin by Janice Warman Copyright © Janice Warman.

Healing Powers by Sophie Hannah, reproduced with the permission of Carcanet Press Limited.

Weighing In by Seamus Heaney, reproduced with the permission of Faber and Faber Ltd.

The crack-up

1. *The Stories of Scott Fitzgerald* by F. Scott Fitzgerald, (i) p391-400, (ii) p41. Reproduced with the permission of David Higham Associates Limited.

2. *Virgina Woolf: An Inner Life* by Julia Briggs, p46 (Penguin Books, 2005). Copyright © Julia Briggs, 2005. Reproduced by permission of Penguin Books Ltd.

3. *Intimacy* by Hanif Kureishi, p59. Reproduced with the permission of Faber and Faber Ltd.

4. *The Old Wives' Tale* by Arnold Bennett, p599-600

5. *The Grasmere Journal* by Dorothy Wordsworth, as quoted in a review

6. From *Take a Girl Like Me* by Diana Melly, published by Chatto & Windus. Reprinted by permission of The Random House Group Ltd.

7. From *Open Secret: The Autobiography Of The Former Director-General of MI5* by Stella Rimington, p48, published by Hutchinson. Reprinted by permission of The Random House Group Ltd.

8. *The Sunday Telegraph*, Adam Nicholson, 1999

9. *Malignant Sadness* by Lewis Wolpert, p49. Reproduced with the permission of Faber and Faber Ltd.

10. *A Vicious Circle* by Amanda Craig, p103. Copyright © Amanda Craig.

11. *The Letters of Kingsley Amis* by Zachary Leader (editor), p981-2. Reprinted by permission of HarperCollins Publishers Ltd. © Zachary Leader (editor), 2001.

12. *Heartburn* by Nora Ephron, p ix-x

13. *A Passionate Sisterhood* by Kathleen Jones, (i) p237, (ii) p247. Reprinted by permission of A M Heath & Co.

14. Obituary, Nicholas Tucker, *The Independent*

15. *Walking in the Shade* by Doris Lessing, p243. Reprinted by permission of HarperCollins Publishers Ltd. © Doris Lessing, 1998.

16. From *The Noonday Demon* by Andrew Solomon, p79, published by Chatto & Windus. Reprinted by permission of The Random House Group Ltd.

17. One Life, www.bbc.co.uk

18. *A Vicious Circle* by Amanda Craig, p126. Copyright © Amanda Craig.

19. *Asylum Piece* by Anna Kavan, (i) p129, (ii) 44. Reproduced with the permission of Peter Owen Ltd, London.

20. *Marrying the Mistress* by Joanna Trollope, p88

21. From *The Life of Kingsley Amis* by Zachary Leader, published by Jonathan Cape. Reprinted by permission of The Random House Group Ltd.

22. *Vera* by Elizabeth von Arnim, (i) pxiii, (ii) pxiv. Reproduced by permission of Penguin Books Ltd.

23. From *The Lost Life of Eva Braun* by Angela Lambert, published by Century. Reprinted by permission of The Random House Group Ltd.

24. *They F*** You Up* by Oliver James, p196-7

25. *Memoir* by John McGahern, p38, p151, p159. Reproduced with the permission of Faber and Faber Ltd.

26. *The Centre of the Bed* by Joan Bakewell, p18

27. *Janey and Me* by Virginia Ironside, (i) p232-3, p252, (ii) p233. Copyright © Virginia Ironside.

28. *Living with Mother* by Michele Hanson, p213

29. *A Passionate Sisterhood* by Kathleen Jones, pxvi. Reprinted by permission of A M Heath & Co.

30. *The Ghost Road*, Pat Barker, p91 (Viking, 1995, Penguin Books, 1996). Copyright © Pat Barker, 1995. Reproduced by permission of Penguin Books Ltd.

31. *Slipstream* by Elizabeth Jane Howard, p438

32. *Self-Help for Your Nerves* by Claire Weekes, p79

33. *Bridget Jones's Diary* by Helen Fielding, p187

34. *Who Moved My Blackberry?* by Lucy Kellaway with Martin Lukes, p140 (Viking 2005). Copyright © Lucy Kellaway, 2005. Reproduced by permission of Penguin Books Ltd.

35. *Falling for Therapy* by Anna Sands, p202

36. *Malignant Sadness* by Lewis Wolpert, (i) p154, (ii) px, pxi. Reproduced with the permission of Faber and Faber Ltd.

37. *Martin Lukes: Who Moved My Blackberry?* by Lucy Kellaway, p323. Reproduced by permission of Penguin Books Ltd.

What women do

8. *Billy's Rain* by Hugo Williams, p53. Reproduced with the permission of Faber and Faber Ltd.

9. *Untold Stories* by Alan Benett, p35. Reproduced with the permission of Faber and Faber Ltd.

10. *A Life's Work* by Rachel Cusk, p144

11. *Creativity* by Mihaly Csikszentmihalyi, p98. Copyright © Mihaly Csikszentmihalyi.

12. *Fat Chance* by Simon Gray, p45. Reproduced with the permission of Faber and Faber Ltd.

13. *The Constant Wife* by Somerset Maugham, p9. Reproduced with the permission of A & C Black Publishers Limited.

14. From *I Don't Know How She Does It* by Allison Pearson, (i) p101, (ii) p46, published by Chatto & Windus. Reprinted by permission of The Random House Group Ltd.

15. *The Cat That Could Open the Fridge*, Simon Hoggart, p16

16. From *Fat is a Feminist Issue* by Susie Orbach, p27, published by Arrow Books. Reprinted by permission of The Random House Group Ltd and Susie Orbach.

17. *Small Island* by Andrea Levy, p144

A Woman's Work by Dorothy Nimmo. Copyright © Dorothy Nimmo.

Twelve Things I Don't Want to Hear by Connie Bensley. Copyright © Connie Bensley.

Found by Finuala Dowling reproduced with the permission of Finuala Dowling.

Seasonal Dilemma by Sophie Hannah, reproduced with the permission of Carcanet Press Limited.

Now and Then by Sophie Hannah, reproduced with the permission of Carcanet Press Limited.

The good girl

1. It's arguable whether this is from '*Housekeeping Monthly*, 13th May, 1955', from a 1950s home economics textbook, or is a fake – the photo appears to have been taken from the cover of *John Bull* magazine. Whatever the truth, the views were of the time.

2. *The Feminine Mystique* by Betty Friedan, p97-8. Reprinted with the permission of The Orion Publishing Group Ltd.

3. *A Doll's House* by Henrik Ibsen, (i) p67, (ii) p68

4. *Inventing Herself* by Elaine Showalter, p66

5. *The Stepford Wives* by Ira Levin, p59

6. *Eating Children* by Jill Tweedie, (i) p100, (ii) p89

7. *The Independent*, Janet Street-Porter, 25th June, 2006

8. *The Drama of the Gifted Child* by Alice Miller, (i) p14, (ii) p15. Reprinted by permission of Suhrkamp Verlag GmbH & Co.

9. *The Dance of Anger* by Harriet Lerner, p1-3. Copyright © Harriet Lerner.

10. *The Guardian*, 26th January, 2007

11. *A Room of One's Own* by Virginia Woolf, p50. Reprinted by permission of The Society of Authors as the Literary Representative of the Estate of Virginia Woolf.

12. *Outrageous Acts and Everyday Rebellions* by Gloria Steinem, p250-1

13. *A Thousand Acres* by Jane Smiley, (i) p176, (ii) p99. Reprinted by permission of HarperCollins Publishers Ltd. © Jane Smiley, 2004.

14. *Lucky* by Alice Sebold, p37

15. *The Big Fat Bitch Book* by Kate Figes, p48

16. *Superwoman* by Shirley Conran, p168-9

Enough by Janice Warman. Copyright © Janice Warman.

Advice to a Daughter by Janice Warman. Copyright © Janice Warman.

Still I Rise by Maya Angelou, reproduced by permission of Little, Brown Book Group Limited.

Love after Love by Derek Walcott. Copyright © Derek Walcott. Reproduced by permission of Farrar, Straus and Giroux, LLC.

Plus ça change, plus c'est la même chose

1. *Martin Lukes: Who Moved My Blackberry?* by Lucy Kellaway, p202. Reproduced by permission of Penguin Books Ltd.

2. From *Grumpy Old Women*, Judith Holden, p68, published by BBC Books. Reprinted by permission of The Random House Group Ltd.

3. *The Temporary* by Rachel Cusk, p92

4. *She May Not Leave* by Fay Weldon, p148. Reprinted by permission of HarperCollins Publishers Ltd. © Fay Weldon, 2005.

5. *Brief Lives* by Anita Brookner, p3

6. From *Grumpy Old Women*, Judith Holden, p47, published by BBC Books. Reprinted by permission of The Random House Group Ltd.

7. *Married to a Genius*, Jeffrey Meyers, p80-1. Reprinted with permission of Southbank Publishing.

Equals by Sophie Hannah, reproduced with the permission of Carcanet Press Limited.

Prelude by Wendy Cope, reproduced with the permission of Faber and Faber Ltd.

The Purist, by Ogden Nash, Copyright © 1935 by Ogden Nash. Reprinted by permission of Curtis Brown, Ltd.

Horses, dogs and men by Janice Warman. Copyright © Janice Warman.

Epilogue

1. *Auto Da Fay* by Fay Weldon, p134. Reprinted by permission of HarperCollins Publishers Ltd. © Fay Weldon, 2003.

2. *Among the Bohemians* by Virginia Nicholson, p280 (Viking, 2002, Penguin Books, 2003). Copyright © Virginia Nicholson, 2002. Reproduced by permission of Penguin Books Ltd.

3. *Dr Sweet and His Daughter* by Peter Bradshaw, p166

4. *Going Sane* by Adam Phillips, p123 (Hamish Hamilton 2005). Copyright © Adam Phillips, 2005. Reprinted by permission of Penguin Books Ltd.

5. From *On Men: Masculinity in Crisis* by Anthony Clare, published by Chatto & Windus. Reprinted by permission of The Random House Group Ltd.

6. *Untold Stories* by Alan Bennett, p345. Reproduced with the permission of Faber and Faber Ltd.

7. *The Rotters' Club* by Jonathan Coe, p80 (Viking, 2001). Copyright © Jonathan Coe, 2001. Reproduced by permission of Penguin Books Ltd.

8. From *The Making of Henry* by Howard Jacobson, p100, published by Vintage. Reprinted by permission of The Random House Group Ltd.

9. *Mantrapped* by Fay Weldon, p188. Reprinted by permission of HarperCollins Publishers Ltd. © Fay Weldon, 2005.

10. *Untold Stories* by Alan Bennett, p104. Reproduced with the permission of Faber and Faber Ltd.

11. *The Lady in the Van* by Alan Bennett, p292. Reprinted by permission of Profile Books.

12. From *Jake's Thing* by Kingsley Amis, published by Hutchinson. Reprinted by permission of The Random House Group Ltd.

13. *White Lightning* by Justin Cartwright, p202

14. *The Independent*, Letters, John Richards

15. *The Ascent of Woman* by Melanie Phillips, p xi. Reproduced with the permission of David Higham Associates Limited.

16. *Auto da Fay* by Fay Weldon, p48. Reprinted by permission of HarperCollins Publishers Ltd. © Fay Weldon, 2003.

17. *Bridget Jones's Diary* by Helen Fielding, p126

18. *The Ascent of Woman*, Melanie Phillips, (i) p117, (ii) p47, (iii) p21. Reproduced with the permission of David Higham Associates Limited.

Fireworks Poem II by Wendy Cope, reproduced with the permission of Faber and Faber Ltd.

Person Specification by Sophie Hannah, reproduced with the permission of Carcanet Press Limited.

The Post-Dictator Plan by Janice Warman. Copyright © Janice Warman.

For My Lover, Returning to His Wife by Anne Sexton. Copyright © Anne Sexton.

There are so many angry men by Janice Warman Copyright © Janice Warman.

Social Note by Dorothy Parker. Copyright © Dorothy Parker.

Prospect by Louis MacNeice, reproduced with the permission of David Higham Associates Limited.

Bibliography

Poetry

Jig [part] by C. Day Lewis taken from *Complete Verse* by C. Day Lewis

General Review of the Sex Situation by Dorothy Parker taken from *A Question of Sex* by John Nicholson, p159, Fontana Paperbacks, 1979

Lenten Thoughts of a High Anglican by John Betjeman taken from *The Best Loved Poems of John Betjeman*, by John Betjeman, p93, John Murray, 2003

Easter returns [part], p458/9, *Autumn Journal* [part], p104, *Autobiography* [part], p183 all by Louis MacNeice taken from *The Collected Poems of Louis MacNeice* by Louis MacNeice, Faber & Faber, 1966

Talking in Bed by Philip Larkin taken from *101 Poems To Help You Understand Men (and Women)* Edited by Daisy Godwin, p101, Harper Collins, 2002

A Slice of Wedding Cake [part] by Robert Graves taken from *Poems selected by himself*, p208, Penguin Books, 1968

Eunice [part] by John Betjeman taken from *John Betjeman, Poems Selected by Hugo Williams*, p.66. Published by Faber & Faber, 2006.

Comment by Dorothy Parker taken from *The Best of Dorothy Parker* by Dorothy Parker, Gerald Duckworth & Co Ltd, 1996

Rondeau Redouble [part] by Wendy Cope taken from *Making Cocoa for Kingsley Amis* by Wendy Cope, p29, Faber & Faber, 1997

The Future by Jill Tweedie taken from *In the Name of Love* by Jill Tweedie, Granada, 1980

Burial by Dorothy Molloy taken from *Hare Soup* by Dorothy Molloy, p45 Faber & Faber, 2004

Before Sherratt & Hughes Became Waterstone's [part] by Sophie Hannah taken from *The Hero and the Girl Next Door* by Sophie Hannah, p14, Carcanet Press, 1995

Things by Fleur Adcock taken from *101 Poems that could Save Your Life*, Edited by Daisy Goodwin, p56, Harper Collins, 1999

6 a.m. Thoughts is taken from *Devices and Desires: New and Selected Poems 1967-1987* by Dick Davis. Published by Anvil Press Poetry in 1989.

At 3 a.m. by Wendy Cope taken from *Making Cocoa for Kingsley Amis* by Wendy Cope, p20, Faber & Faber, 1997

Not to Sleep by Robert Graves taken from *Complete Poems in One Volume* by Robert Graves, Carcanet Press, 2000

Song of the Master and Boatswain [part] by W.H. Auden taken from *As I Walked Out One Evening* by W.H. Auden, p94, Faber & Faber, 1969

The Ted Williams Villanelle by Wendy Cope taken from *If I Don't Know* by Wendy Cope, p35, Faber & Faber, 2001

Equals [part], p58, *Healing Powers*, p38, *Seasonal Dilemma*, p15, *Now and Then*, p37, all by Sophie Hannah, taken from *First of the Last Chances* by Sophie Hannah, Carcanet Press, 2003

Weighing In [part] by Seamus Heaney taken from *The Spirit Level* by Seamus Heaney, p17, Faber & Faber, 1996

In Memoriam by Alfred Lord Tennyson taken from *The Concise Oxford Dictionary of Quotations*, p325, Oxford University Press, 2001

A Bookshop Idyll [part] by Kingsley Amis taken from *Penguin Modern Poets 2* by Kingsley Amis, Dom Moraes, & Peter Porter, p26, Penguin Books, 1963

Book Club by Gus Ferguson taken from *Arse Poetica* by Gus Ferguson, p16-17. Published by Kwela, 2003

Her News [part] by Hugo Williams taken from *Billy's Rain* by Hugo Williams, p53, Faber & Faber, 1999

A Woman's Work by Dorothy Nimmo, p31, *Social Note* by Dorothy Parker, p43, *If People Disapprove of You* by Sophie Hannah, p33, taken from *101 Poems that could Save Your Life* Edited by Daisy Goodwin, Harper Collins, 1999

Twelve Things I Don't Want to Hear by Connie Bensley, taken from *101 Poems to Keep You Sane*, Edited by Daisy Goodwin, p16, Harper Collins, 2001

Found [part] by Finuala Dowling taken from *I Flying* by Finuala Dowling, Carapace, 2002

Still I Rise by Maya Angelou, taken from *And Still I Rise* by Maya Angelou, Little, Brown, 1986

Love after Love by Walcott, Derek taken from *Sea Grapes* by Derek Walcott, Farrar Straus & Giroux, 1976

From June to December, 1 Prelude [part] by Wendy Cope taken from *Making Cocoa for Kingsley Amis* by Wendy Cope, p21, Faber & Faber, 1997

The Purist by Ogden Nash taken from *The Quentin Blake Book of Nonsense Verse*, p94, Viking, 1994

Fireworks Poems [part] by Wendy Cope taken from *If I Don't Know* by Wendy Cope, p10, Faber & Faber, 2001

Person Specification by Sophie Hannah taken from *Hotels Like Houses* by Sophie Hannah, p32, Carcanet Press, 1996

For My Lover, Returning to his Wife by Anne Sexton taken from *Poem For The Day – One* by Nicholas Albery, p290, Chatto & Windus, 2001

Prospect by Louis MacNeice taken from *Collected Poems* by Louis MacNeice, Faber & Faber, 2007

Books

ADCOCK Fleur: *Selected Poems*, Oxford University Press, 1983

ALBRIGHT, Madeleine K.: *Madam Secretary: A Memoir*, Macmillan, 2003

ALI Dr Mosaraf: *The Integrated Health Bible*, Vermillion, 2001

AMIS Kingsley: *Jake's Thing*, Hutchinson, 2004

AMIS Kingsley, MORAES Dom and PORTER Peter: *Penguin Modern Poets 2*, Penguin Books, 1962

AMIS Martin: *Experience*, Jonathan Cape, 2000

ASH Rebecca: *The New Spend Less Revolution*, Harriman House, 2006

ATKINSON Kate: *Case Histories: A Novel*, Doubleday, 2004

AUDEN W.H.: *Selected Poems*. Edited by Edward Mendelson, Faber & Faber 1979

AUDEN W.H.: *As I Walked Out One Evening: Songs, ballads, lullabies, limericks and other light verse*, Edited by Edward Mendelson, Faber & Faber, 1995

AYCKBOURN Alan: *Three Plays*, Chatto & Windus

BAKEWELL Joan: *The Centre of the Bed*, Hodder & Stoughton, 2003

BARKER Pat: *The Ghost Road*, Viking, 1995, Penguin Books, 1996

BEEVOR Antony: *Berlin: The Downfall 1945*, Viking, 2002, Penguin Books, 2003

BENN Tony: *Free At Last! Diaries 1991-2001*, Edited by Ruth Winstone, Arrow Books, 2003

BENNETT Arnold: *The Lady in the Van*, Profile Books, 1999

BENNETT Arnold: *The Old Wives' Tale*, Penguin Books, 1990

BENNETT Alan: *Untold Stories*, Faber and Faber/Profile Books, 2005

BETJEMAN John: *The best loved poems of John Betjeman*, John Murray Publisher 2003

BETJEMAN John: *Poems Selected by Hugo Williams*, Faber & Faber 2006

BLAKE Quentin: *The Book of Nonsense Verse*, Viking, 1994

BOWKER Gordon: *George Orwell*, Little, Brown & Co UK, 2003

BRADFORD Sarah: *America's Queen: The Life of Jacqueline Kennedy Onassis*, Viking, 2000

BRADSHAW Peter: *Dr Sweet and His Daughter*, Picador, 2003

BRIGGS Julia: *Virginia Woolf: An Inner Life*, Penguin Books, 2005

BROOKNER Anita: *Brief Lives*, Penguin Books, 1991

BROOKNER Anita: *Incidents in the Rue Laugier*, Penguin Books, 1996

BROOKNER Anita: *Look at Me*, Triad Grafton Books, 1982

CALLOW Simon: *Love is where it Falls*, BBC Radio 4 Books, 2001

CARMAN Dominic: *No Ordinary Man: A Life of George Carman, QC*, Hodder & Stoughton, 2000

CARPENTER Humphrey: *Spike Milligan: The Biography*, Hodder & Stoughton, 2003

CARTER Miranda: *Anthony Blunt: His Lives*, Macmillan, 2001

CARTWRIGHT Justin: *The Promise of Happiness*, Bloomsbury, 2005

CARTWRIGHT Justin: *White Lightning*, Sceptre, 2003

CLARE Anthony: *On Men: Masculinity in Crisis*, Chatto & Windus, 2001

CLARK Alan: *Diaries*, Phoenix, 1994

CLARK Alan: *The Last Diaries: 1992-1999*, Weidenfeld & Nicolson, 2003

CLARK Alan: *The Last Diaries: In and Out of the Wilderness*, Phoenix/Orion Books, 2003

CLINE Sally: *Zelda Fitzgerald: Her Voice in Paradise*, John Murray, 2002

COE Jonathan: *The Closed Circle*, Viking, 2004

COE Jonathan: *The Rotters' Club*, Viking, 2001

CONRAN Shirley: *Superwoman*, Penguin Books, 1977

COPE Wendy: *Poem for the Day – one*, Chatto & Windus, 2001

COPE Wendy: *If I Don't Know*, Faber & Faber, 2001

COPE Wendy: *Making Cocoa for Kingsley Amis*, Faber & Faber, 1986

CRAIG Amanda: *A Vicious Circle*, Fourth Estate, 1997

CRAIG Elizabeth: *Elizabeth Craig's Enquire Within*, Collins Press, 1948

CRICK Bernard: *George Orwell: A Life*, Penguin Books, 1982

CRICK Margaret: *Mary Archer: For Richer, For Poorer*, Simon & Schuster, 2005

CSIKSZENTMIHALYI Mihaly: *Creativity*, Harper Perennial, 1996

CUSK Rachel: *A Life's Work: On Becoming a Mother*, Fourth Estate, 2001

CUSK Rachel: *The Lucky Ones*, Fourth Estate, 2003

CUSK Rachel: *The Temporary*, Picador, 1996

DAY LEWIS, C.: *The Complete Poems*, Stanford University Press, 1992

DODDS, E.R.: *The Collected Poems of Louis MacNeice*, Faber & Faber, 1966

DOWLING Finuala: *I Flying*, Carapace, 2002

DRABBLE Margaret: *The Oxford Companion to English Literature*, Oxford University Press, 2000

EPHRON Nora: *Heartburn*, Virago, 1996

FEINSTEIN Elaine: *Ted Hughes: The Life of a Poet*, Weidenfeld & Nicolson, 2001

FIELDING Helen: *Bridget Jones's Diary*, Picador, 1996

FIGES Kate: *The Big Fat Bitch Book*, Virago, 2007

FINN, F.E.S.: *The Albermarle Book of Modern Verse*, John Murray, 1961

FITZGERALD, F. Scott: *The Crack-up with Other Pieces and Stories/The Stories of F Scott Fitzgerald*, Penguin Books, 1965

FITZGERALD Zelda: *Save Me The Waltz*, Penguin Books, 1971

FRASER Antonia: *Marie Antoinette: The Journey*, Weidenfeld & Nicolson, 2001

FRIEDAN Betty: *The Feminine Mystique*, Weidenfeld & Nicolson

GAWANDE Atul: *Complications*, Profile Books, 2003

GERARD Noel: *Princess Alice, Queen Victoria's Forgotten Daughter*, Michael Russell (Publishing) Ltd, 1992

GRAVES Robert: *Poems Selected by Himself*, Penguin Books, 1957

GRAY John: *Men are from Mars, Women are from Venus*, Thorsons/Harper Collins, 1993

GRAY Simon: *Fat Chance*, Granta Books, 2005

GREER Germaine: *The Female Eunuch*, Paladin, 1971

GREER Germaine: *The Whole Woman*, Anchor, 2000

GOODWIN Daisy: *101 Poems to Help You Understand Men (and Women)*, Harper Collins, 2002

GOODWIN Daisy: *101 Poems that could save your life: An Anthology of Emotional First Aid,* Harper Collins, 1999

GOODWIN Daisy: *101 Poems to keep you sane: Emergency rations for the seriously stressed.*

Harper Collins 2001

HANNAH Sophie: *First of the Last Chances*, Carcanet Press, 2003

HANNAH Sophie: *Hotels Like Houses*, Carcanet Press, 1996

HANNAH Sophie: *Leaving and Leaving You*, Carcanet Press, 1989

HANSON Michele: *Living With Mother: Right to the Very End*, Virago, 2006

HASTINGS Selina: *Rosamond Lehmann: A Life*, Chatto & Windus, 2002

HEANEY Seamus: *The Spirit Level*, Faber and Faber ,1996

HENRY, Professor John A.: *The British Medical Association: New Guide to Medicines & Drugs*, Dorling Kindersley, 2001

HILLIER Bevis: *Betjeman: The Bonus of Laughter*, John Murray, 2004

HILLIER Bevis: *John Betjeman: New Fame, New Love*, John Murray 2003

HOGGART Simon: *The Cat That Could Open The Fridge: A Curmudgeon's Guide to Christmas Round Robin Letters*, Atlantic Books, 2004

HOLDER Judith: *Grumpy Old Women*, BBC Books, 2006

HOWARD Elizabeth Jane: *Falling*, Pan Books, 2000

HOWARD Elizabeth Jane: *Slipstream: A Memoir*, Macmillan Ltd, 2002

HOWARD Elizabeth Jane: *Something in Disguise*, Pan Books Ltd, 1993

HUGHES Kathryn: *The Short Life & Long Times of Mrs Beeton*, Fourth Estate, 2005

IBSEN Henrik: *A Doll's House*, Dover Thrift Editions, 1992

IBSEN Henrik: *Hedda Gabler: The Pillars of the Community, The Wild Duck*, Penguin, 1973

IBSEN Henrik: *Hedda Gabler: A new version by Richard Eyre*, Nick Hern Books, 2005

IRONSIDE Virginia: *Janey and Me: growing up with my mother*, Fourth Estate, 2003

JACOBSON Howard: *The Making of Henry*, Vintage, 2004

JAMES Oliver: *They F*** You Up: How To Survive Family Life*, Bloomsbury Publishing plc, 2002

JOHNSON Susan: *A Better Woman: A Memoir of Motherhood*, Aurum Press, 2000

JONES Kathleen: *A Passionate Sisterhood. The Sisters, Wives and Daughters of the Lake Poets*, Constable, 1997

KAVAN Anna: *Asylum Piece*, Peter Owen Ltd, London, 2001

KELLAWAY Lucy: *Martin Lukes: Who Moved My Blackberry?*, Penguin Books, 2006

KUREISHI Hanif: *Intimacy*, Faber & Faber, 1998

LAMBERT Angela: *The Lost Life of Eva Braun*, Century, 2006

LANE Ann J (editor): *The Charlotte Perkins Gilman Reader: The Yellow Wallpaper & Other Fiction*, The Women's Press, 1981

LAPOTAIRE Jane: *Time out of Mind*, Virago Press, 2003

LEADER Zachary: *The Letters of Kingsley Amis*, Harper Collins, 2000

LEADER Zachary: *The Life of Kingsley Amis*, Jonathan Cape, 2006

LEE Hermione: *Virginia Woolf*, Chatto & Windus, 1996

LEITH William: *The Hungry Years: Confessions of a food addict*, Bloomsbury, 2005

LERNER Harriet: *The Dance of Anger*, Element/Harper Collins, 2004

LESSING Doris: *Under My Skin*, Harper Collins, 1994

LESSING Doris: *Walking in the Shade*, Harper Collins, 1997

LEVIN Ira: *The Stepford Wives*, Pan, 1972

LEVY Andrea: *Small Island*, Review, 2004

LEWIS C. S.: *A Grief Observed*, Faber & Faber, 1966

LEWYCKA Marina: *A Short History of Tractors in Ukrainian*, Viking Press, 2005

MacNEICE Louis: *The Strings are False*, Faber & Faber, 1965

MacGREGOR Dr. Anne: *Is HRT Right for You?*, Sheldon Press, 1993

MANTEL Hilary: *Giving up the Ghost: a memoir*, Fourth Estate, 2003

MAUGHAM Somerset: *The Constant Wife*, A & C Black Publishers Ltd

McCRUM Robert: *Wodehouse: A Life*, Viking, 2004

McGAHERN John: *Memoir*, Faber & Faber, 2005

MELLY Diana: *Take a Girl Like Me*, Chatto & Windus, 2005

MEYERS Jeffrey: *Married to Genius: A Fascinating Insight into the Lives of Nine Modern Writers*, Southbank Publishing 2005

MILES Rosalind: *The Women's History of the World*, HarperCollins, 1989

MILLER Alice: *The Drama of the Gifted Child*, Basic Books, 1997

MOLLOY Dorothy: *Hare Soup*, Faber & Faber 2004

MOTION Andrew: *Dangerous Plan: Poems 1974-1984*, Penguin Books

MOTION Andrew: *Philip Larkin: A Writer's Life*, Faber & Faber, 1993

MURRAY John: *The Best Loved Poems of John Betjeman*, John Murray, 2006

NICHOLSON Virginia: *Among the Bohemians: Experiments in Living 1900-1939*, Viking, 2002, Penguin Books, 2003

ODHAMS: *Odhams Enquire Within*, Odhams Press Ltd, 1951

O'FARRELL Maggie: *The Distance Between Us*, Review/Headline Book Publishing, 2004

ORBACH Susie: *Fat is a Feminist Issue*, Arrow Books, 1998

PARTINGTON Angela: *The Oxford Dictionary of Quotations*, Oxford University Press, 1996

PEARSON Allison: *I Don't Know How She Does It*, Chatto & Windus, 2002

PECK M. Scott: *The Road Less Travelled*, Arrow, 1990

PHILLIPS Adam: *Going Sane*, Penguin Books, 2006

PHILLIPS Melanie: *The Ascent of Woman*, Little, Brown, 2003

PICARDIE Ruth: *Before I say Goodbye*, with Matt Seaton and Justine Picardie, Penguin Books, 1998

POEM FOR THE DAY – ONE, Foreword by Wendy Cope, Chatto & Windus, 2001

POEM FOR THE DAY – TWO, Edited by Retta Bowen, Nick Temple, Stephanie Wienrich, Nicholas Albery, Chatto & Windus, 2003

POTTER Beatrix: *The Complete Tales of Beatrix Potter*, Frederick Warne & Co., 1989

PRITCHARD John: *The New Penguin Guide to the Law*, Penguin Books, 2001

RIMINGTON Stella: *Open Secret: The Autobiography of the Former Director-General of MI5*, Hutchinson, 2001

ROE Sue: *Gwen John: A life*, Chatto & Windus, 2001

ROWE Dorothy: *Beyond Fear*, Harper Collins Publishers, 2002

ROWE Dorothy: *The Successful Self*, Harper Collins Publishers, 1993

ROWE Dorothy: *Guide to Life*, Harper Collins Publishers, 1995

ROWE Dorothy: *Depressions: The way out of your prison*, Routledge & Kegan Paul plc, 1983

RUBENS Bernice: *The Waiting Game*, Abacus, 1998

RUSSELL Lorna: *The Best of Girl*, A Prion Book by IPC Media Ltd, 2006

SANDS Anna: *Falling for Therapy*, Macmillan Press Ltd, 2000

SEBOLD Alice: *Lucky*, Picador, 2002

SEGRAVE Elisa: *The Diary of a Breast*, Faber & Faber, 1995

SETH Vikram: *Two Lives*, Little, Brown, 2005

SEYMOUR-JONES Carole: *Painted Shadow*: *A Life of Vivienne Eliot*, Constable & Robinson, 2001

SHAKESPEARE William: *The Complete Works*, Bickers & Son, Ltd, 1929

SHEEHY Gail: *The Silent Passage – Menopause*, Harper Collins, 1994

SHOWALTER Elaine: *Inventing Herself*, Picador, 2002

SLATER Nigel: *Toast: The Story of a Boy's Hunger*, Fourth Estate, 2003

SMILEY Jane: *A Thousand Acres*, Flamingo Originals, 1992

SMITH Jane: *Rehabilitation following Surgery to the Low Back*, 1997

SMITH Dr. Tony: *The British Medical Association: Complete Family Health Guide*, Dorling Kindersley Ltd, 2000

SOAMES Mary: *Clementine Churchill*: *The revised and updated Biography*, Doubleday, 2003

SOLOMON Andrew: *The Noonday Demon: An Anatomy of Depression*, Vintage Books, 2002

SPARK Muriel: *The Girls of Slender Means*, Penguin Books, 1996

SPURLING Hilary: *The Girl from the Fiction Department: A Portrait of Sonia Orwell*, Penguin Books, 2003

ST. JOHN Madeleine: *The Essence of the Thing*, Fourth Estate Ltd, 1997

STADLEN Naomi: *What Mothers Do: Especially When It Looks Like Nothing*, Piatkus, 2004

STALLWORTHY Jon: *Louis MacNeice*, Faber & Faber, 1996

STEINEM Gloria: *Outrageous Acts and Everyday Rebellions*, Fontana Paperbacks, 1984

STREET-PORTER Janet: *Baggage: My Childhood*, Headline Book Publishing, 2004

STREET-PORTER Janet: *Fall Out: A Memoir of Friends Made and Friends Unmade*, Headline, 2006

TOMALIN Claire: *Jane Austen A Life*, Penguin, 2000

TOMALIN Claire: *Samuel Pepys: The Unequalled Self*, Viking, 2002

TROLLOPE Joanna: *Marrying the Mistress*, Bloomsbury, 2000

TWEEDIE Jill: *Eating Children*, Penguin Books, 1994

TWEEDIE Jill: *In the Name of Love*, Granada Publishing, 1980

VON ARNIM Elizabeth: *Vera*, Virago, 1983

WAUGH Alexander: *Fathers and Sons*: *The Autobiography of a Family*, Headline, 2004

WEBBER Richard: *Fifty Years of Hancock's Half Hour*, Century, 2004

WEEKES Dr Claire: *Self-Help for your Nerves*, Thorsons (London), 1995

WELDON Fay: *Affliction*, Flamingo, 1993

WELDON Fay: *Auto Da Fay: A Memoir*, Flamingo, 2002

WELDON Fay: *Godless in Eden: A book of essays*, Flamingo/Harper Collins, 1999

WELDON Fay: *Mantrapped*, Harper Perennial, 2005

WELDON Fay: *She May Not Leave*, Harper Perennial, 2006

WILDE Oscar: *The Importance of Being Earnest and Other Plays*, Edited by Richard Allen Cave, Penguin Books, 2000

WILLIAMS Hugo: *Billy's Rain*, Faber & Faber, 1999

WILSON A.N.: *After the Victorians*, Hutchinson, 2005

WILSON A.N.: *Betjeman*, Hutchinso,n 2006

WILSON A.N.: *Iris Murdoch As I Knew Her*, Hutchinson, 2003

WIMPOLE Roderick: *Tell Me Doctor*, C. Arthur Pearson Ltd, 1954

WOLF Naomi: *Misconceptions*, Chatto & Windus, 2001

WOLPERT Louis: *Malignant Sadness: The Anatomy of Depression*, Faber & Faber, 2001

WOODHEAD Lindy: *War Paint*: *Miss Elizabeth Arden and Madame Helena Rubinstein, their Lives, their Times, their Rivalry*, Virago Press, 2003

WOOLF Virginia: *A Room of One's Own*, Penguin Books, 1928

Newspapers & Magazines

The Independent on Sunday – 2005

The Sunday Telegraph –1980-2007

The Guardian – 2006

The Observer – 2006

The Times

The Independent – 2004

The Daily Telegraph

The Lady – 2006

Harper's Bazaar

The Week

Acknowledgements

Our special thanks go to Penelope Grist, Jan Moffitt, Susie Tanous, Sally Ann Lasson and our editor Suzanne Anderson, all of whom had *Hey Nonny* thrust upon them.

Julia would also like to thank her colleagues at FHS (1977-1989) and her friends at CHS (1994-2005); in particular Petra Grimm, Chrissie White, Jason and Sarah Light, John and Cornelia Dyball, Anthony and Thalia Brotherton-Ratcliffe and Anne Menzies. Also grateful thanks to Annie Hewett, Jane Bleasdale, Anna Johnson, Hilary Hooper, Clare Watters, Liz Lelliott, Kathy Hathaway, Tom King and Emma Tinker. And most importantly her husband Keith Doherty, who showed her how to turn the computer on.

Janice would like to thank: Fi Powrie, Liz Wildi, Jeanne and Phil Samuels, Susie and Ed Rotberg, Joy Rosendale, Pauline Alexander, Richard and Jackie Portsmouth, Janet Fuller, Sue Rowland, Tich, Kate, Hannah and Thom Walker, Jay and Guy Louw, Herm and Teri Roup, Jenny Hong and Rebecca Wright for helping to keep me sane through the writing of this book; my sister Gail for her constancy and wise counsel; my children, Dominic and Imogen, for making me lunch and making me laugh; my parents, as ever a fount of advice, encouragement and wisdom – I wouldn't be doing this without you! And finally my husband, Julian, for his unfailing support and delicious cooking. (And I'm really, really sorry I didn't write *Return to Eden*.)

And lastly we'd like to thank Myles Hunt and Stephen Eckett at Harriman House for their extraordinary perspicacity in taking us on in the first place!